for Julie Schexnaildre,

With admiration
for the job you do
in teaching philanthropy

Joel J. Orosz

6-23-03

For the Benefit of All

A History of Philanthropy in Michigan

An Engaging Look at the Philanthropic Traditions of the Great Lakes State and Its People

Writer
Sandy Fugate

Editor
Dr. Joel J. Orosz

Published by the
W.K. Kellogg Foundation
in cooperation with the
Council of Michigan
Foundations

Distributed by the Council of Michigan Foundations, Suite 3, One South Harbor Avenue,
P.O. Box 599, Grand Haven, Michigan 49417

Library of Congress Catalog Card Number: 97-61674

ISBN Number: 1-891445-00-6

Dedication

*In memory of Governor George Romney
(1907-1995),
Michigan's consummate donor
of time and talent,
who never waivered
in his commitment to youth,
the philanthropists
of the future.*

Table of Contents

Prologue: Michigan's Philanthropic Roots — Page 1

A look at Michigan before 1783, including Native American traditions and the arrival of French, British, and American settlers.

1 Religion and Abolition, 1783-1860 — Page 5

Philanthropic contradictions and accomplishments abound as Michigan becomes a popular new home for evangelical settlers from the northeastern United States.

2 War, Charity, and the Gospel of Wealth, 1861-the early 1890s — Page 29

Michigan charity workers help to relieve the bloodshed and horror of the Civil War, then address the challenges of a major depression and the growth of urban areas. Also, the lumber industry takes hold, as do the philanthropic ideals outlined by Andrew Carnegie in his article, "The Gospel of Wealth."

3 Decades of Transition: Depression, Progressivism, and the Great War, the 1890s-1918 — Page 49

The financial Panic of 1893 poses new philanthropic challenges for both Michigan and the United States. In the wake of the severe depression, the Progressive Movement takes hold and brings with it a new view of poverty. The state's economy grows dramatically, and charitable groups deal with the devastation of the Great War.

4 The Roaring '20s, the Hungry '30s, and the Birth of Modern Michigan Philanthropy, 1919-1939 — Page 71

For Michigan, the 1920s are a heady time of industrial growth, particularly in the auto industry, and the result is an overwhelming influx of cash across the state. Although the new capital results in an impressive spurt in philanthropic activities, it is not enough to save Michigan from the Great Depression. Aided largely by prosperity experienced in the 1920s, many of the state's earliest foundations are established in this period.

5 World War II, the Postwar Boom, and the Emergence of the Foundations, 1940-1959 — Page 93

Michigan volunteers and philanthropic organizations focus on World War II efforts, then see their causes bolstered by the state's soaring economy in the 1950s. As the growth brings nearly unprecedented amounts of money into the state, foundations begin popping up across Michigan.

6 Reform, Reaction, and the Turbulent Sixties, 1960-1979 — Page 113

Nonprofit charity, in general, and private foundations, in particular, come under attack in Congress, resulting in the Tax Reform Act of 1969. Philanthropic organizations contend with provisions of the tax act, and explore new grantmaking arenas.

Epilogue: The 1980s and Beyond — Page 137

Government cutbacks in social welfare programs pose new challenges for philanthropy across the country, even as a new spirit of volunteerism sweeps the nation.

Appendices — Page 147

Bibliography — Page 148
Index — Page 157

Notes

In writing *For the Benefit of All: A History of Philanthropy in Michigan*, we chose to follow the model established by Frederick Lewis Allen in his outstanding book, *Only Yesterday, An Informal History of the 1920s*. To present a history that was approachable to the lay reader, and more than a little entertaining, Allen consciously, we believe, chose not to adopt academia's rules for in-text citations and footnotes. Instead, he presented acknowledgments at the end of *Only Yesterday* to illustrate where he had obtained the information he so eloquently packaged. While we cannot claim to have produced a text as remarkable as Allen's, we do hope that *For the Benefit of All* displays some of *Only Yesterday's* finer attributes, such as attention to historical accuracy and a writing style that appeals to the general public without shocking the sensibilities of professional historians.

In the appendix that follows this acknowledgment, you will find a comprehensive bibliography listing the multitude of sources consulted in the preparation of *For the Benefit of All*. Unfortunately, however, a straightforward bibliography presents all sources with equal weight—suggesting, for instance, that a reference book consulted for one specific piece of data had as profound an effect on this book as other sources that were used much more prodigiously. We'd like to set the record straight, albeit with care; providing a list of "special" resources seems an invitation to oversight. Nonetheless, we shall throw caution to the wind and accept the challenge.

First and foremost, we owe a significant debt to the prolific historian Willis F. Dunbar. His book, *Michigan, A History of the Wolverine State,* served as a de facto Rosetta stone for this book. For example, in situations where reference materials provided contradictory information, we chose to rely on Dunbar. His attention to detail and the amount of work and care he so clearly put into his history books were both humbling and reassuring—humbling, because his dedication and talent were so remarkable; and reassuring, because when we relied upon historical facts that he had divined, our sleep was not nettled by anxieties over accuracy.

We also feel compelled to give special recognition to a number of people who went out of their way to help with this book, often on very short notice. Sandy Fugate served as principal author, creating a text that is readable and historically accurate. Dorothy Johnson, Rob Collier, and Gail Powers-Schaub, respectively president, vice president, and librarian of the Council of Michigan Foundations (CMF) in Grand Haven, all helped in researching the book and reviewing its early drafts. Others who were instrumental in the production of *For the Benefit of All* are W.K. Kellogg Foundation (WKKF) Chief Executive Officer Emeritus Russell G. Mawby; WKKF President Emeritus Dr. Norman A. Brown, whose 1993 Burton Lecture for the Historical Society of Michigan served as the germ for this book; Tom Jones, former director of the Historical Society of Michigan, who first suggested that Dr. Brown's lecture be expanded into a book; Barbara Wittbrodt, who did extensive research and wrote an early draft of the book; Karen Lake of WKKF, who provided editorial suggestions; Jennifer Snyder, who wrote most of the sidebar material and assisted in writing and editing certain portions of the book; Lynn Smith Houghton and Pamela Hall O'Connor, who provided comprehensive research assistance; Mike VanBuren of WKKF, who coordinated the writers, editors, and production staff for the project; Lou Ann Morgan, whose graphic design skills are exhibited throughout; Connie Morse, whose careful proofreading caught many inconsistencies; Diane Worden who brought the index to bear; and Ruth Ann Hoiles and Robin Leonard of WKKF, who kept information flowing smoothly among all parties.

Additionally, we feel a need to thank all members of the Council of Michigan Foundations. In using the CMF library, and by accessing historical data about philanthropy in Michigan, we were able to garner an overwhelming amount of information about CMF members. Much of that information is reflected in *For the Benefit of All*. In effect, we wish to thank CMF member institutions for their very existence. By stepping into the world of Michigan philanthropy, they created an historical legacy that reflects well on our state.

Similarly, the activities of thousands of nonprofit organizations and civic-minded individuals across the state and throughout its history made our job considerably easier. To scan historical records and find such high-minded and fascinating individuals as Roberta Griffith, Ralph Ely, Hazen Pingree, Mary McCoy, and James Couzens—to name a few— qualifies as something of a gift. We did not have to look far to find an abundance of philanthropic spirit and colorful tales. In fact, much of the difficulty in assembling this book was the challenge of keeping it to something fewer than, say, a dozen volumes. The state's philanthropic heritage is that profound.

On that note, finally, we'd like to thank anyone and everyone who has ever participated in Michigan philanthropy. Your dedication and spirit are present on every page of this book, even where your name is not mentioned. You've created a remarkable history, a remarkable state, and, we hope, an interesting book. For all of these things, we can say only, "Thank You."

Dr. Joel J. Orosz, Editor
Program Director, W.K. Kellogg Foundation

Salvation Army food drives, like this one in the 1930s, offered the most basic, and critical, assistance to hungry Michiganians. (Courtesy of Willard Library, Local History Collection)

The national United Way grew from Michigan roots. Here the torch of the United Fund (the predecessor organization to the United Way) is lit by Miss United Fund at the 1974 Kent County Campaign Kickoff. (Courtesy of Heart of West Michigan United Way)

Much Michigan-based philanthropy has national influence. In 1968, the Kellogg Foundation announced a major commitment to programs that would lead to more job opportunities for graduates of the country's traditionally African-American colleges. (Courtesy of W.K. Kellogg Foundation)

Many beneficial programs, like the Boy Scouts, have been supported by local philanthropists throughout Michigan. (Courtesy of Willard Library, Local History Collection)

Introduction

Michigan has been blessed with remarkable philanthropic leadership and achievement. A glance at the institutions that make up Michigan philanthropy bespeaks not only current leadership, but also a long and brilliant history: several of the premier corporate giving programs in the United States; one of the largest and most active networks of community foundations; the birthplace of the two largest grantmaking foundations in America, and home to three of its handful of billion dollar foundations; and the largest regional association of grantmakers in the nation.

All of this infrastructure, of course, did not appear overnight. The story of how it came to be is a tale of Native American traditions mixed with French customs, strengthened by pioneer values, all forged in the crucible of entrepreneurship. It is a story of women as much as men, European-Americans, Latinos and African-Americans, Native Americans and Asian-Americans. It is the story of a penniless people trading acts of kindness and also the story of immense wealth, created by successful businesspeople, who felt compelled to give back to the state that had been so good to them. It is, above all, the immensely important story of voluntary actions for the public good.

Despite the great significance of the subject, very little has appeared in print—whether in the popular media or in the scholarly literature—about the history of philanthropy in Michigan. This is certainly not for lack of fascinating or historically significant subjects. The colorful life of Father Gabriel Richard, which included tending his flock in a wilderness outpost, battling catastrophic fires and deadly epidemics, promoting education and eventually being elected to Congress, is the stuff of which epic bestsellers are made. The means by which captains of industry like Henry Ford, S.S. Kresge, C.S. Mott, and W.K. Kellogg turned their entrepreneurial vision toward philanthropic endeavors contains insights enough to attract scholars from many disciplines. Whether popular or academic, however, this story is too important to be left untold.

It seems fitting, therefore, in celebration of the silver anniversary of the Council of Michigan Foundations, the nation's largest regional association of grant-makers, that the W.K. Kellogg Foundation should support the publication of *For the Benefit of All,* the first monographical history of philanthropy in Michigan. Although this story is recounted in accessible prose, it has been meticulously documented. Scholars will find its bibliography to be a rich source of departure for future inquiries into this fruitful subject.

As Michigan stands on the brink of a new century, its philanthropic future is bright because its past has been so brilliant. Paraphrasing Isaac Newton, if we as phil-anthropic leaders can do more than others, it is because we stand on the shoulders of giants—giants whose stories, for the first time, are told within the pages of this book.

Dr. William C. Richardson
President and Chief Executive Officer, W.K. Kellogg Foundation

x

Michigan's Philanthropic Roots

The first act of philanthropy in the land now known as Michigan occurred long before historians were on the scene to chronicle the names of either the donor or the recipient. We do know that about 13,000 years ago, in the vicinity of what would later be called Flint, Native American tribes made their earliest-known appearance in the land between the Great Lakes. And we can be reasonably certain that among them, the first Michigan philanthropist made that initial gift to a needful recipient.

To be sure, it was not a philanthropic act as most would understand the term at the dawn of the 21st century. No money changed hands, and no hospital wing was named in grateful recognition of the giver. Yet, philanthropy it was, and the tradition thus begun would do much to define the quality of life in both Native American and American societies in the centuries to come.

Before embarking on an effort to retrace the course of that tradition, it would be wise to define just what philanthropy means. Over the years, distinctions have been drawn between gifts of time and gifts of money. Gifts of time have been labeled volunteerism, and gifts of money have been christened philanthropy. To categorize thus is to create a false dichotomy. The Greek roots of the word philanthropy clearly translate, in English, to "love of mankind." This definition makes no distinction between gifts of time and money. Both are examples of the love of mankind made manifest in the world of action.

This Algonquin village, c. 1500, was typical of the woodland settlements built by Michigan's native residents.
(Courtesy of State Archives of Michigan)

(Chapter overleaf photos courtesy of State Archives of Michigan and *A History of Michigan in Paintings,* Ameritech Michigan)

In recognition of this fact, scholar Robert Payton has created the following definition for philanthropy, one that is used throughout this book: Philanthropy is voluntary action for the public good. Thus, a gift of two hours is every bit as much philanthropy as a gift of $200. Philanthropy is ultimately defined by its uncoerced nature, and by the larger-than-private good it creates for society.

The pages that follow will chronicle the evolution of philanthropy across three centuries, two peninsulas, and any number of ethnic groups. The one constant is people voluntarily giving time or money to improve the lot of their neighbors and their nation.

It was in this spirit that the Native American inhabitants of what would become Michigan invented giving in their corner of the world. The state's native tribes held sharing as a fundamental value and principle of existence as far back as the 1600s—the oldest recorded history in Michigan. During these early days, the region was home to the Potawatomi, Wyandot, Chippewa, and Menominee tribes, to name a few. Journals of French explorers and Jesuit missionaries (who often were one and the same) indicate that the region's native residents were a relatively peace-loving and generous people. As the explorers, missionaries, priests, and fur traders ventured into northern Michigan in the 1600s, they

did not often wander into the wilderness alone. Instead, the voyageurs were guided by the area's Native Americans, who helped most of them emerge from the woods healthy and unscathed, and able to write the journals, charts, and maps that ultimately led even more explorers into the Native Americans' homeland.

A typical transaction at one of the many remote Michigan trading posts during the fur era. When the supply of pelts was heavy, the trading value dropped; in lean years, the value of each pelt rose. This equation was counterbalanced by fierce competition among the traders. (Courtesy of *A History of Michigan in Paintings*, Ameritech Michigan)

By the 1700s, fur trade in the Great Lakes region had become a well-established and lucrative business for the French. Although one couldn't call the state crowded, there were a few hundred fur traders, missionaries, explorers, and soldiers traversing the Michigan landscape, primarily in the northern Lower and Upper peninsulas, but also in the Detroit area. As certain small animal populations fell because of heavy trapping, fur traders ventured farther inland; so, too, did explorers seeking wealth and glory, and French missionaries intent upon saving Native American souls.

The Potawatomi and other tribes considered sharing to be a fundamental way of life. Mere existence at the time could be harsh—one never knew when food and shelter would be in short supply—so clan members helped one another all their lives. Among the Chippewa, for example, reciprocal giving—giving to others as much as one could when one was able—was woven into the culture at a basic level. As one history book notes, "If anyone in an Ojibwa (Chippewa) camp had food, everyone had food." The notion of sharing so that the entire group prospers was so strong among the Potawatomis that those who sought to accumulate wealth and goods for themselves were treated harshly and even disciplined.

Although some exceptions probably existed, the notion of sharing served the region's tribes well. In the early 1600s, Michigan is believed to have been the home of more than 100,000 Native Americans. By way of comparison, Detroit's mostly French population had soared to a lofty 200 or so in the 1720s. By 1760, the city still would have fewer than 3,000 residents.

On June 14, 1671, Simeon François, Sieur de St. Lusson claimed the interior of North America for France's King Louis XIV. (Courtesy of *A History of Michigan in Paintings*, Ameritech Michigan)

The French approach to colonial development was less hospitable than that of the Native Americans. France did not encourage people from other countries to settle in "New France," as the Michigan area was called before the mid-18th century; and non-Catholics were forbidden to settle in the region at all. Under the circumstances, the slow growth of the state's European population is less than startling.

By 1760, after France handed its U.S. possessions to Britain (ignoring, of course, the fact that the

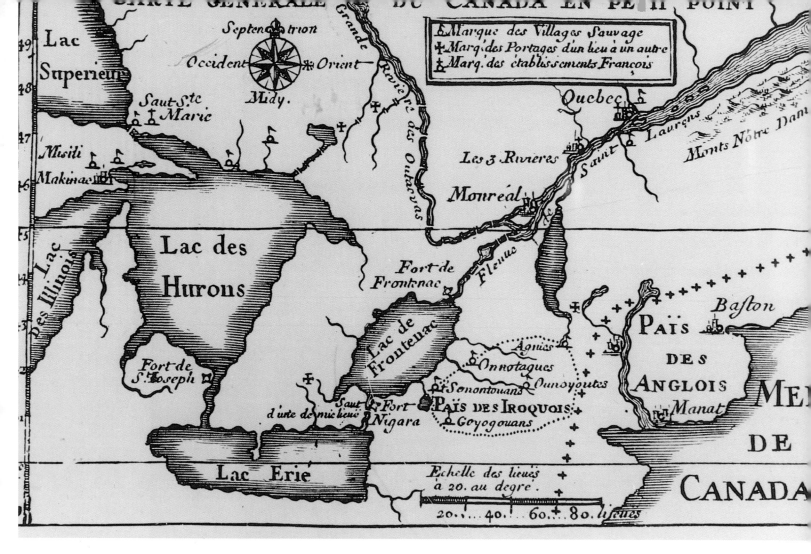

This early French map begins to define Michigan by its lakes. Dated 1703, it does not yet include representation of Detroit. (Courtesy of State Archives of Michigan)

land already belonged to someone else), the British flag was flying in Detroit. The French administration was gone, but French influence was more durable. Even 60 years after the British officers arrived to take over from the French, most of the state's non-Native American population would be of French descent.

Though their numbers were small, it did not take long for the British to begin mistreating the area's Native American population—by cheating them in business dealings and appropriating their land. But on the eastern seaboard, many U.S. residents had staked claims to Native American land tracts themselves. The notion that the British would take the land away with a mere wave of a scepter (doing what, essentially, the colonists themselves had done to the Native Americans) was the source of much outrage. When the British also refused to allow for democratic and civil government in the Michigan and Illinois regions in 1774—despite years of prodding from settlers—the colonies became sullen. Throw in a few problems with taxation and the quartering of soldiers, and the stage was set for revolution. The provinces, as ragged and discontented and imperfect as they might have been, were about to experience the convulsions of birth. When the upheaval was over, the United States of America would struggle to its feet and begin a new life. The history of American philanthropy in Michigan was about to begin.

1783-1860

Religion and Abolition

1

"Don't go to Michigan,

that land of ills;
the word means ague (influenza), fever, and chills."
—*a nineteenth-century ditty in eastern U.S. newspapers.*

*D*escribing Michigan philanthropy in the nineteenth century is a formidable task. As Charles Dickens might have said: "It was the best of times, it was the worst of times …."

How, for example, can you find any philanthropic fault with a state that was home to so many fierce and tenacious abolitionists in the 1800s—abolitionists like Laura Haviland, a woman who could stand down a trio of pistol-toting, runaway-slave-hunters and send them scurrying off a train to protect their hides?

On the other hand, how much philanthropic good is there to find in a time that saw Michigan offer its indigent citizens only the most meager medical services, and not out of sweeping concern for the poor, but because a sick poor person was a dreadful drain on the state coffers?

To paraphrase the state's motto: If you seek an interesting dichotomy, look about you. Look to the Michigan of the early- to mid-1800s, when state residents risked their lives to guarantee the safety of a single escaped slave, but also visited poor people in their humble homes not to deliver food or clothing, but to lecture them about personal improvement and

In 1805, fire leveled Detroit in a matter of hours. Said to have started when a stable hand knocked burning tobacco from his pipe into a pile of hay, the blaze claimed every wooden structure in the city and most of the townspeoples' possessions, but, miraculously, no lives.
(Courtesy of State Archives of Michigan and *A History of Michigan in Paintings,* Ameritech Michigan)

moral fortitude. Look also at some of the charitable associations in the 1800s that made it their policy not to spend a single cent on the poor people they felt God directed them to help, even as their reformist activities contributed to more across-the-board improvements in living conditions—for rich *and* poor—than at any other time in the state's history. (In considering that last statement, it is useful to keep in mind that the transition from filth, starvation, and disease to health, a full stomach, and a relatively clean place to sleep is more vital than the transition from a candlelit wooden shanty to a condo, a car, and a cellular phone. Progress is relative.)

Understandably, philanthropy as we know it today (with institutionalized giving through the United Way and foundations) did not exist at the turn of the nineteenth century. Granted, there were many instances of community-mindedness, such as Detroit's requirement that all citizens turn out to fight a fire (which didn't stop the town from burning down in 1805), but those cases tended to be situational and sporadic. U.S. residents were busy cleaning up after the Revolutionary War and going about the business of finding food, shelter, and creating a new country. Obviously, they lacked the concentrations of capital needed to undertake philanthropy at anything approaching today's scale.

Food and shelter were in particularly short supply in Detroit. The War of 1812 left much of the town filthy, dilapidated, and overcrowded, with low wages and unemployment a way of life for many. Most of its residents were either educated and relatively well-off on the one hand, or nomadic and poor on the other, and the poor population was growing.

For the first settlers, the journey to Michigan Territory was often a treacherous one. Here, the 156-foot steamship Michigan struggles through a storm to deliver emigrants from the northeast to our land of opportunity. (Nowlin, Bark Covered House. Courtesy of Dearborn Historical Museum)

It's fair to say that many residents had scarcely enough bread to keep their children fed, let alone a surplus to dole out to others. Furthermore, newcomers were not falling over one another on the trail to Michigan. For a variety of reasons, easterners didn't consider our fair state an attractive destination.

First, except in a few relatively small areas, a settler couldn't legally own land until a series of treaties ousted the area's Native American population to reservations between 1818 and 1837. Also, after the War of 1812, the Surveyor-General of the United States, Edward Tiffin, issued a dreary report about the prospects of cultivating and settling the Michigan Territory, telling President James Madison that Michigan was little more than swamps and bad soil.

"There would not be more than one acre out of a hundred, if there would be one out of a thousand that would, in any case, admit of cultivation," Tiffin wrote, a report that neatly fit the east coast's perception of Michigan as, essentially, the Land of Doom. For

*"When Uncle Sam did wean her,
'Twas but the other day,
And now she's quite a Lady,*

This Michigania."

—a poem published in a Detroit newspaper in 1831.

years, school maps out east would have the words "Interminable Swamp" written across Michigan's interior.

Neither did it help that, during the War of 1812, hundreds of soldiers died in Detroit of disease, mostly malaria, prompting this charming ditty in eastern newspapers: "Don't go to Michigan, that land of ills; the word means ague, fever, and chills."

In addition, getting to Michigan was just plain dangerous. Steamships didn't begin operating on the Great Lakes until 1818, and the Erie Canal wasn't opened until 1825. One can see how appealing the Michigan Territory, as it was known after 1805, must have been to easterners at the end of the War of 1812. The area wouldn't become a popular place to call home for a fair number of years.

Unpopular as Michigan was, its residents practiced philanthropy at a rudimentary level. In 1828, for example, Potawatomi chief Sag-e-maw helped Bazel Harrison and his party of settlers

A river trip, not unlike this example, brought foodstuffs to Alma during shortages in 1860.
(Courtesy of Clements Library University of Michigan)

Ralph Ely

If Ralph Ely is typical, the state's philanthropists of the nineteenth century were a feisty, dedicated lot. An early settler in the Alma area, Ely helped bring food and other supplies to the community in 1860, when too-rapid expansion made hunger and housing a problem there. Originally, he carried supplies in on one of three roads he had built to the city. It didn't take long, however, for Ely to realize that floating supplies in by boat, up the Saginaw River from Saginaw, would be easier.

Unfortunately, Ely's boatload of foodstuffs got only as far as the neighboring community of St. Louis before progress was impeded by a dam built there. The good (and irate) citizens of Alma promptly destroyed the dam and cleared the way for Ely's boat to dock in their community, where food was sold to those who could afford it and given away to those who couldn't.

Ely would go on to distinguished service in the Civil War. (He once tricked Confederate forces into retreating because they believed they were going to be attacked by an entire battalion of Union soldiers. The "battalion" was merely Ely and four other men putting on a show of bravado—bravado born of desperation, no doubt.) Ely later became a successful businessman and Gratiot County's first treasurer, and he was responsible for platting and helping to develop much of the community of Alma.

from Ohio become the first American settlers in Kalamazoo County. Despite a significant language barrier, the Potawatomi chief was able to lead Harrison and his band to the area's best land.

Settlers Instill Religion in Philanthropy

Other philanthropic roots for the state were growing in America's northeast, where many of Michigan's future residents still lived. Charitable traditions brought over by the Puritans just 200 years earlier grew from a religious creed that embraced education, a desire to better oneself, and kindness toward one's neighbor. This religious influence is important to remember, because once it became possible to own Michigan land, and once the steamships and Erie Canal made getting here more feasible, the Great Lakes became the Great Funnel, and northeasterners started pouring in. Suddenly, Michigan was, indeed, the place to be.

German immigrants typically settled in communities oriented around a religious (usually Catholic or Lutheran) denomination. The short-lived communitarian settlement of Ora et Labora in the Thumb was a notable exception; its founders were German Methodists.
(Courtesy of Clark Historical Library)

Usually landing in Detroit, settlers from the northeast fanned out across the state and started building towns and cities in short order. Even as late as 1860, about one-quarter of Michigan's residents were natives of New York State, where Puritan-born and -influenced religions flourished; a sizable number of the other three-quarters were born in New England states with a similar religious heritage.

As we will see, this theistic influence gave philanthropy in Michigan—and elsewhere—a largely religious bent. Then, as now, the deeply religious considered working hard, bettering oneself, and leading a clean and decent life to be ordered by God.

In 1800s Michigan, we would likely have had that very thought: Self-improvement is God's will; education is self-improvement; therefore, anything that contributes to education is divinely ordained. Small wonder, then, that so many of the first schools and colleges created in Michigan and elsewhere were of religious origin. Small wonder, too, that early philanthropists

French explorers and Jesuit missionaries were among the voyageurs who usually emerged from the Michigan wilderness unscathed, thanks to assistance from Native American guides.
(Courtesy of Frederic Remington Art Museum)

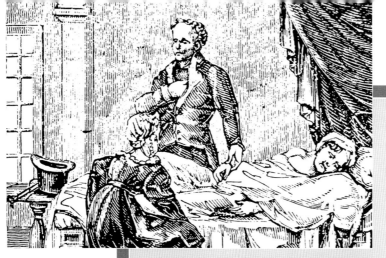

Diseases in Early Detroit

Early in Michigan's history, when epidemics routinely decimated cities, towns, and families in just a few days, charitable people and organizations spent much of their time on health-related causes. The era was one of few, if any, hospitals, bare-bones medical supplies, and a corresponding lack of medical knowledge.

For instance, in 1832 Detroit, a city with no hospitals, Asiatic cholera swept through the population, killing indiscriminately and quickly, sometimes within a few hours. Today, we know that enough intravenous fluids and minerals can save a person who contracts the disease; it typically runs its course in just a few days. But in the 1830s, physicians didn't understand the importance of compensating for the body fluids lost through violent bouts of vomiting and diarrhea. The astringents and counterirritants they prescribed often only made the condition worse.

In his diary, a local carpenter wrote, "Sunday [July] 8th. Morning, all hands called to make boxes for soldiers dead and dying of cholera." For it was on a troop ship that cholera came to town. On July 4, the steamer Henry Clay had docked in Detroit to deliver soldiers en route to what is now Wisconsin. The disease jumped ship and immediately spread to the townspeople. Fifty-eight cases and 28 deaths were reported by July 18.

The upper story of the Michigan Territory capitol (which was in Detroit at that time) was hastily made into a hospital. Father Gabriel Richard, priest at St. Anne de Detroit church, visited there to provide what spiritual comfort he could. Most often, it was in the form of last rites. Many Detroit residents tried to flee the city, but didn't get far. As word of the epidemic spread across the state, towns tore up bridges and set up guards to prevent travelers from Detroit from setting foot inside their borders.

In August 1834, cholera struck Detroit again, this time killing 7 percent of the city's residents in a single month. One account by the Michigan Pioneer and Historical Society paints the full horror of the time: "... old French carts could be seen in line ... stretching away to the old cemetery, a fearful line of festering corpses ..." In their wake, widows and orphans poured into the city poorhouse that had been established by Father Martin Kundig after the cholera outbreak two years earlier.

The 1832 scourge had not convinced the city it needed a permanent hospital, so when cholera struck again, Detroit was, again, unprepared. Kundig and Captain Alpheus White turned the old Holy Trinity Church into a hospital. With a wagon, Kundig gathered up the dying from the wharves and streets, brought them to the church, and carried them inside on his back. The priest also recruited a corps of young women to act as nurses. Many were members of the Catholic Female Benevolent Association. Several doctors also volunteered to provide care under what were horribly dangerous conditions.

Even the second cholera rampage didn't convince Detroit that it needed a community hospital. It wasn't until more than a decade later that four Sisters of Charity opened St. Vincent's, a 12-bed facility. Although it was obviously affiliated with the Roman Catholic Church, St. Vincent's did its best to live up to its motto: "We must take care of all."

focused so extensively on what many of us would consider religious issues today. Can you picture, for example, your local United Way paying a staff member to go out and lecture to the poor about their morals? (Although some might argue that they should; the ties among religion, philanthropy, and politics still bind.)

Nonetheless, moral guidance was the essence of more than a few charitable organizations in the 1800s. Most of these early nineteenth-century philanthropists accepted the existing order of society as God's will. In other words: The rich were rich and the poor were poor, and that's the way God wanted it. Furthermore, they felt the rich were rich so that they could guide the poor; the poor were poor so that they could be guided—a satisfying view of things as long as one was rich.

It follows, then, that poverty itself wasn't condemned as such a reprehensible thing. It had been commissioned by God, after all, and for that reason the poor were expected to demonstrate their appreciation by being industrious and docile. It was only during times of trial and distress—a bad winter, a crop failure, or an epidemic—that the wealthy thought it their duty to provide temporary assistance, in addition to moral direction, to the indigent. For example, leaders in Detroit agreed, in 1829, to fund a smallpox vaccination for those who couldn't afford it. Just five months later, the Territorial Legislature agreed to contract with a doctor to oversee medical concerns for the state's poor. (The governing body's primary concern appeared to be the financial strain caused by the indigent sick.)

Unfortunately, Detroit discontinued its smallpox vaccination service in 1830, just one year before this acute and often fatal disease broke out in the community. And no government could have foreseen the level of devastation that would be caused by cholera epidemics in Detroit shortly thereafter, in 1832 and 1834. (About 7 percent of the city's population died in the second outbreak.) In all fairness, though, the actions—meager as they were—of the city and territorial governing bodies were historic in addressing the issue of public health. By the time cholera struck again in 1849 and 1854, the city had improved its health care measures, and the death rate was much lower.

So we see that Detroit's charitable citizens believed that helping the poor when they were particularly down-and-out was an acceptably God-fearing thing to do because, after all, calamity-induced poverty could happen to anyone, even the morally upright. But "pauperism," or poverty and neediness as a way of life, was another matter entirely. According to the various benevolent societies that sprang up after the War of 1812, pauperism was the same as dependency—

The nation's first state fair was held in Detroit in 1849. Here, the secretary of the fair announces the awards for the best exhibits, which were quickly overshadowed by more entertaining attractions, seen through the window. The event almost certainly required generous donations of time and energy by a large group of organizers.
(Courtesy of Detroit Public Library Burton Historical Collection)

the inability to stand on one's own two feet—a notion that went against everything successful Americans believed about themselves and their nation. The country was rich with resources and opportunities, wasn't it? How could anyone, barring unforeseeable catastrophe, not succeed? Paupers had only themselves to blame.

Giving Advice, Not Alms

Because of this overwhelming belief that pauperism was a sign of moral deficiency, relief to the chronically poor was given not in the form of alms or jobs or housing, but in a moral regimen. Philanthropic associations created in the Territory at the beginning of the nineteenth century intended to prevent vice, promote virtue, and advance moral and religious education.

The Moral and Humane Society of Detroit, composed of prominent male merchants, professionals, and clergymen, was typical of such philanthropy. "The usual method of bestowing charities," the Society secretary wrote in a letter to the *Detroit Gazette* in January 1818, "without knowing the character to whom they are given, or the use to which they are applied, is generally a waste of property, and often increases the evil it is intended to remedy." The Society proclaimed in its constitution that "MONEY SHALL NOT BE PAID OUT." Instead, its members should give what the poor truly needed: advice, criticism, and encouragement to break free of idleness, drunkenness, impiety, and gambling—the vices the Society attributed to the "evil that is pauperism."

Members worked vigorously to eradicate that evil. To reach as many of the poor as possible, members swarmed across the city like an army of morality soldiers, dividing Detroit into wards and districts and placing a commissioner in charge of each. The Society's bylaws and constitution directed members to visit the poor in their homes and to "use constant vigilance in ascertaining the moral state as well as the temporal necessities of the inhabitants." Careful record of the character and financial condition of each resident was kept. The Society even investigated their church and school attendance. Unfortunately, no records exist of the reactions of the poor to these reconnaissance missions or beneficent lectures.

The members of the Moral and Humane Society were not alone in their beliefs, methods, or goals. The French Moral and Benevolent Society of Detroit and its Vicinity also sent members to hunt out and shut down "disorderly houses" within the city. Time and again, they attempted to suppress every species of vice, including "intemperance; gambling; profane language; the violation of the Lord's Day; quarreling and fighting; and cruel, tumultuous, rude, unmanly, and unbecoming conduct, sports, and amusements."

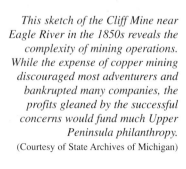

This sketch of the Cliff Mine near Eagle River in the 1850s reveals the complexity of mining operations. While the expense of copper mining discouraged most adventurers and bankrupted many companies, the profits gleaned by the successful concerns would fund much Upper Peninsula philanthropy.
(Courtesy of State Archives of Michigan)

When Father Gabriel Richard (1767-1832) was sent by church superiors to Detroit in 1798, the town was enclosed by a stockade and had only nine streets, and his congregation consisted of 80 families spread over a 100-mile tract of wilderness. Homesick, Richard (who had moved to Detroit from Indiana) hoped he soon would be called back to France.

His outlook changed dramatically on June 11, 1805, when a horrific fire burned all but two of 300 buildings in the fledgling city. After saving the sacred vessels from St. Anne's Church, which also burned, Richard sprang into action, sailing up and down the river to beg cornmeal and blankets from the farmers for the homeless in the city. Now desperately needed, he no longer considered leaving his flock. The priest's words of comfort and hope, "Speramus meliora; resurget cineribus" (We hope for better things; it will arise from its ashes), were eventually incorporated into the seal of the city.

Providing education for his parishioners and others in the city and surrounding region was one of Richard's most cherished pursuits. While private schools offered instruction for a fortunate few in Detroit, there was no general school system for poor children, let alone for children of the mostly friendly and increasingly Catholic Native Americans. Richard opened many schools between 1804 and 1818, some more successful than others. They included a boys' seminary, primary schools for both boys and girls, a classical academy, and a school for Native American children.

Father Gabriel Richard

To enlighten his townspeople about national and world events, Richard brought in the territory's only printing press in 1809. His goal was to produce a weekly newspaper, but the Richard Press turned out just a single issue of **The Michigan Essay; or Impartial Observer**. It did, however, print more than 50 different school texts and religious books, a rare commodity on the frontier.

Richard joined other influential men, including Judge Augustus Woodward, Governor Lewis Cass, Territorial Secretary William Woodbridge, and Reverend John Monteith (Michigan's first Protestant clergyman), to discuss plans for a university in the territory. Eventually, they pushed forward 1817 legislation that formed the Catholepistemiad or University of Michigania. Unfortunately, the valuable intent of the act, which would have established a comprehensive, state-funded education system, was lost in antiquated verbiage understood by almost no one but Woodward, its author. (The Catholepistemiad was eventually moved to Ann Arbor and began operating there as the University of Michigan in 1837, the year Michigan became a state.)

In 1823, and with 444 votes, Richard became the first Catholic priest elected to the Congress of the United States. In Washington, he promoted federal road building in Michigan and succeeded in gaining appropriations for what would ultimately become several major thoroughfares, including the roadway that would evolve into today's I-94, linking Detroit and Chicago.

Education, publishing, politics—all were pursuits in which Richard served Michigan admirably. Still, his "real" job was religion. He believed in the strictest Catholic doctrine, yet when large numbers of Protestants came to town in 1816, he loaned them use of a parish building for their services.

"The attitude of Richard was the first great exhibition of religious tolerance in America," wrote Michigan Governor Chase S. Osborn. "This might be the biggest single thing that Father Richard ever did." When the priest succumbed to cholera at age 65, his funeral was attended by 2,000 people (more than the population of the city), and they were Protestant and Catholic alike.

(Photo courtesy of State Archives of Michigan)

Apparently, the attitude that poverty was the result of individual failings was as prevalent as the list of potential failings was long.

However, even the benevolent societies recognized that children among the poor had not come to poverty through laziness or an inability to control their beastly passions. Some were orphans, some were simply unfortunate enough to be born to poor parents. While the male societies' members ventured into the midst of the city to render advice among poor men and women, their female counterparts worked to reach children in desperate straits. Their primary goal, like the men's, was to exert a moral influence.

One example is the Ladies Society of Detroit, which was formed in 1818 after its members daily encountered the neglected children who swarmed the streets, alleys, and waterfront. The disparity between the women's lifestyles and that of these children was acute; the ladies simply couldn't overlook the unfairness. As the Society took shape, its first priority was to rescue the children from the corruption of street life. After lengthy discussion and planning, members obtained the use of an abandoned soldiers' barracks and established a school in Detroit dedicated to saving children from a "downward path into degradation." They reached the poorest of the poor children in the city and took pride in their work, putting a great emphasis on teaching religious and moral values.

On the surface, the education of poor children seems impeccably right-minded. Consider, however, another slant: the women's emphasis upon a moral education stemmed from a desire to mold and control the poor by making them accept the model of industrious, deferential poverty.

In their own way, the women became—as their male counterparts were—protectors of the social and moral order, defenders of a particular status quo. Still, the school did help many children—by giving them food, clothing, and social skills, if nothing else—and the school had staying power: it ultimately moved to a new facility and remained as the only free public school in the city until after 1843, when state residents agreed to be taxed to pay for public education.

Awakening to Reform and "Improvement"

Benevolent societies such as those that formed the school are interesting not only because they illustrate what was happening philanthropically at a given time, but also because they portended the future. While the societies believed it was the duty of the rich to help the poor, and the duty of the poor to be grateful and accept the advice that was given, a new

spiritual movement would take those beliefs even further: It was every person's duty to help others improve themselves, and every person's duty to seek personal improvement. This new movement was called the Second Great Awakening, and it swept across the country like a fever, hitting Michigan just as the state was exploding with growth in the 1820s.

Michigan Territory was so popular that between 1820 and 1830 its population nearly quadrupled, from 8,765 to 31,640; by 1834, it nearly tripled, to 87,278. Public land sales grew at an equally outlandish rate, leaping from 147,062 acres to 498,423 acres between 1830 and 1834. Combine that disorderly growth with various state and U.S. economic difficulties (particularly the financial Panic of 1837) and you'll find a territory that was in drastic need of improvement.

Fortunately, the desire to improve not only oneself but other things—asylums, prisons, houses, businesses, schools, towns, sanitation systems, streets, health care, *people*—was part of the religious creed of those who were emigrating en masse from the northeast. The reformers, as one could accurately call them, arrived in Michigan fired by the zeal of the Second Great Awakening and armed with a formidable number of items on their checklist of "things that need improving." They weren't daunted in the least. In fact, the greater the challenge of making improvements and achieving divine perfection, the more stimulating the work.

The life of the Michigan pioneer woman was not an easy one. Typically, the home she kept was much like this 1829 log cabin near Bellevue. (Courtesy of Detroit Public Library Burton Historical Collection)

This early humanitarian zeal had two basic sources, one secular, the other religious. The secular wellspring was the belief in the inevitability of progress. By the second decade of the nineteenth century, the country was caught up in enthusiasm for growth and expansion. America was taking off, both geographically and figuratively, and the pioneers who headed west with the energy and optimism needed to create better lives for themselves were leading the way. This was truly the era of the "self-made man," a term coined at that time.

Headquarters for much of the philanthropic work of the time, numerous churches lined Detroit's Woodward Avenue in 1849. (Courtesy of Detroit Public Library Burton Historical Collection)

Madame Madeline Laframboise

Some of history's most interesting characters surprise you by what they were—and weren't. Madame Madeline Laframboise (1780-1846) was one such figure: fur trader and society hostess; an illiterate fluent in four languages; a devout Catholic who got rich by purveying liquor (among other essentials) to her Native American brothers. This tough businesswoman is also remembered for bestowing many gifts on her Mackinac Island community.

Laframboise's father was a French-Canadian fur trader who died soon after she was born. She was raised by her mother, the daughter of Chief Kewinaquot (Returning Cloud), in the Ottawa village at Grand Haven.

Nearby Jesuit missionaries hoped to counterbalance the little girl's Native American upbringing with religious training. By age 15, she was well-indoctrinated, beautiful, and married to Joseph Laframboise, a French-Canadian fur trader. She participated enthusiastically in the seasonal adventures of his work: summers in Mackinac, exchanging the previous winter's fur harvest for trade goods such as blankets, beads, muskets, and liquor; autumns aboard a bateau, bobbing down Lake Michigan to the mouth of the Grand River at Grand Haven; winters upriver at a trading post near today's Ada, trading with the Native American fur trappers.

Their life together lasted scarcely a decade. Joseph was murdered in 1806 by a brave mad for alcohol as they camped with friendly Potawatomi near Grand Haven. Months later, when a Potawatomi posse brought her husband's assassin to Laframboise's trading post, she revealed an amazingly generous soul and turned down the men's offer to execute the offender: "The Good Book," she said, "bids us forgive seventy times seven.... I will, therefore, forgive this captive and leave him to the Great Spirit. My desire is that you do likewise and give him his life."

Laframboise carried on the family business alone and made a great deal of money as a licensed agent of John Jacob Astor's American Fur Company. As her wealth grew, she forged friendships with government agents, missionaries, Fort Mackinac military leaders, and the newest island residents—American businessmen. Her success in business and place in island society grew from a remarkable ability to adapt to the times.

The Laframboise mansion was a showplace that drew guests from many circles—chiefs from the surrounding Native American settlements, travelers from the eastern United States and Europe, wealthy individuals from the island's highest social echelon. Their hostess conversed with them in fluent English, French, Ottawa, and Chippewa, and always wore Ottawa dress.

In the early 1820s, Laframboise retired from the fur trade to devote her time to charity. At 41, she learned to read and write in order to teach the catechism to groups of girls in her home. She also gave money to the island's poor residents, helped establish a school for Catholic children, supported the resident priests, and donated land for St. Anne's Church, erected beside her home. Madame Laframboise is buried in the churchyard there. Historical markers at the church and at her trading post in Ada commemorate the life of one of Mackinac Island's most colorful benefactors.

(Photo courtesy of Public Museum of Grand Rapids)

The second source stemmed from religious enthusiasm and activism, Bibles, tracts, and missionaries. It was an era when Michigan pioneers happily traveled 60 miles with an ox team just to hear a sermon. It was a generation in which missionary and millennial zeal colored virtually every aspect of American life—including philanthropy.

In New York State, large audiences sat spellbound by revivalists who preached that the proper test of God's love lay in overcoming one's self-interest and acting in a benevolent manner toward all humankind. The converts, preached one revivalist, began a new life in which "they have no separate interests.... They should set out with a determination to aim at being useful in the highest degree possible." Any conduct resulting in human misery was morally reprehensible. It was the duty of ALL to actively labor to make the world a better place. Anything less than a complete commitment to these ideals was more than misguided, IT WAS SIN!

Reformers believed in the righteousness of their motives and were united in their deep commitment to their idealistic mission: to wipe sin, evil, and misery from the world. In other words, they had their work cut out for them.

Ansel Bridgman was among those who decided to tackle the job. Arriving in Detroit on October 1, 1830, as a volunteer for the American Home Missionary Society, 26-year-old Bridgman was prepared "to encourage and strengthen Christianity" (as he wrote to friends) among impious frontier men and women. Such work, he felt certain, expressed sincere compassion to those in most need.

Bridgman's first call was to Eurotas P. Hastings, president of the Bank of Michigan and the unofficial leader of the Presbyterian missionary effort in Michigan. Hastings responded by writing a letter to Bridgman, directing the young minister to locate in the rural Farmington-Plymouth area, where "there is much—irreligion, false doctrine, Sabbath breaking, intemperance [and] profaneness"—conditions the young minister was prepared to change.

Between 1830 and 1833, Ansel Bridgman rode a monthly circuit to every settlement in the area, even during the most severe winter months. Fighting constantly against "great influences in the spread of error and immorality," it was, he acknowledged to friends back east, a difficult task.

"The field of my labours is extensive ... the trials of a faithful missionary are great— sometimes they appear almost overwhelming." However, his mission was clear. Like many other men and women of the era, he could reasonably assume that humanity was intended by God to live in peace, plenty, and morality; if they did not, whatever interfered with God's plan—poverty, injustice, ignorance, sin, sickness—must be eliminated.

> It was the duty of ALL to actively labor to make the world a better place.

By 1805, a map of Michigan included representation of Detroit and the state's many rivers, indicative of the importance of water travel in that day. (Courtesy of State Archives of Michigan)

"The cause in which [I am] engaged, I feel to be a good one, and [I] am willing to spend [and] be spent for its promotion," he wrote.

Like Bridgman, thousands of men and women established and joined a host of voluntary societies. They were incredibly ambitious and achieved an easing of social ills and immorality with new experiences, new environments, new ideas, new philosophies. In a way, they were to their time what the 1960s activists were to the twentieth century. The reform movement tackled everything from dietary changes to women's rights, and even led to the creation of several experimental "utopian societies," such as Brook Farm in New England, the Oneida community in New York, and the Alphadelphia community near Kalamazoo.

Alphadelphia, largely the brainchild of Dr. H.R. Schetterly of Ann Arbor, was created in 1844 on more than 1,000 acres of land in Comstock Township. The community's founding philosophy was based on the principles of a Frenchman, Charles Fourier, who advocated the formation of small communities with common ownership of land, sharing of duties, and equal distribution of the fruits of the group's labor. Although admirable in its aim, "Fourierism," as it came to be known, generally failed to

The 500-pound Alphadelphian Society Bell is the last remnant of a utopian community founded near Kalamazoo in 1844.
(Courtesy of Kalamazoo Gazette)

take one important element into account: human nature. Alphadelphia, for example, failed in less than four years, despite having as many as 188 residents in 1845. Historian Willis Dunbar notes that members of the community were assigned various jobs, ranging from printers to blacksmiths, but that "jealousies crept in and inequalities were charged in the assignment of work." The utopian society's community house burned in 1846; by 1848, the community's last member had moved and the property was sold.

In addition to communes, the Second Great Awakening spawned a variety of new religions, including the Church of Jesus Christ of Latter-day Saints (the Mormons) and the Seventh-Day Adventist Church, the latter of which was, for all intents and purposes, headquartered in Battle Creek by 1860. The reform movement also produced two particularly ambitious endeavors: the battle against alcohol, and the battle against slavery. The first ultimately would lead to prohibition laws in a number of states, including Michigan (where it was largely unenforced). The second ultimately would lead to something far nobler—and far bloodier.

The Seal of Michigan Territory, 1814, was controlled by the Secretary of the Territory and affixed to all official documents as a symbol of authenticity.
(Courtesy of State Archives of Michigan)

Walter Harper & Nancy Martin

Harper Hospital, Detroit, 1864. Walter Harper and Nancy Martin donated land for the institution, which was founded by a group of citizens interested in establishing a hospital for sick and wounded soldiers in the state. (Courtesy of State Archives of Michigan)

Few in Detroit had heard of Walter Harper (1789-1867) before he donated 944 acres to the city fathers in 1859. He gave them freedom to use the land, or sell it to fund other projects, as they saw fit, stipulating only that they would oversee "the erection and maintenance of a hospital for the benefit of the sick and aged poor" in Detroit.

Ten days later, the newspapers reported another surprise. Harper's former housekeeper, Nancy Martin (1799-1875), added 20 acres of her own to Harper's gift. She asked that his hospital be built on a portion of this land, a beautiful site dotted with oak and hickory.

Surprisingly, no suggestion of hanky-panky ever surfaced between the pair. (And in the then-small town, a scandal would not have gone unnoticed.) Residents were more interested in what prompted their gifts. For Martin, the likely cause was a good soul and lack of heirs. Harper had heirs aplenty, but apparently didn't like any of them. We have no way of knowing for sure whether his gift sprang from humanitarian impulse or from disappointment in his children.

He fathered six of them before moving his family from Philadelphia to Detroit in the early 1830s. He came to town with money in his pocket, both from years of work as a coachmaker and from investments in real estate. And he spent most of it, buying up land for less than two dollars an acre.

But Harper's life was not a settled one. He returned to Philadelphia, became a widower, remarried, fathered another child, and moved again to Detroit, this time bringing along the servant girl, Nancy Martin. Within a few years, the stern man with a long nose and piercing eyes became a widower a second time and parted—angrily, completely, and for unknown reasons—with his children. He retired by age 50 and lived the rest of his life in virtual seclusion.

Nancy Martin was everything Harper was not: a coarse, exuberant character well-known in the community. She began life in a Philadelphia slum, married twice, was twice widowed, and had a daughter, who died at the age of 4. She left Harper's household shortly after arriving in Detroit and built up a loyal clientele selling vegetables door-to-door.

Later, Martin went into business as a green grocer and, in her stall at the public market in Cadillac Square, came to know everybody who was anybody in Detroit. As historical accounts explain, regulars at the market expected a joke from Martin, who was considered a "huckster" with "a large vocabulary of plain Saxon words, more expressive than elegant."

After business hours, Martin enjoyed strong spirits, sometimes in sufficient quantity to land her in jail. But in spite of a notable lack of refinement, this woman of great heft, firm jaw, and missing teeth was one smart businesswoman. Her profits bought a comfortable home and the acreage she donated to the city.

In the late 1850s Harper and Martin shared a roof again, this time hers. (Records suggest she acted as his nurse.) Both lived to see Harper Hospital open its doors, and after Harper died, his long-time acquaintance took a room there. She would sit in the hallway outside her door to banter with the medical students and engage passersby in loud and salty conversation. Though she embarrassed the administrators, they took good care of her until she died, nearly a decade later. Today, the hospital she helped build remains one of the Motor City's significant medical centers.

Fighting Demon Gin

By comparison to the Civil War, the fight over temperance seems a minor skirmish. Still, it reached a feverish pitch across various parts of the country, including Michigan, and by the 1830s was at the center of the philanthropic agenda. Reforming the drinker of spirits, you see, wasn't merely a movement against alcohol; in large part, alcohol was demonized and held forth as the symbol of so many social woes: crime, immorality, poverty.

Alcohol, reformers believed, destroyed individual lives and weakened or wrecked family ties. From pulpits across the state, the warning was simple and clear-cut, as one clergyman said in an address to his congregation in 1833: "Drink in all its combinations, add(s) to every trouble … destroying the home, and cursing the young lives of the children."

Action, therefore, needed to be swift and immediate. "Women of Battle Creek," a temperance leaflet of the 1840s asked, "shall husbands, sons and brothers go down to drunkards' graves and we sit with folded hands, making no effort to remove temptations from their pathway?" Through meetings, pamphlets, songs, and hundreds of societies, reformers argued the sinfulness of drinking and the need for moral restraint.

The pattern for temperance activity had been set in Michigan as early as 1830. At Dexter, in Washtenaw County, a temperance society was organized in January of that year. Hindered originally by the sparseness of its population—since drunkenness and opposition to it generally require both alcohol and people—the Reverend C.G. Clarke reported a year later that the village "now has over 100 members … with a second Society about to be organized." At last, the village had enough people to preach and be preached to.

Starting in scattered localities and then growing in numbers, temperance societies sprang up in almost every town and settlement. Banning alcohol, reformers argued, was moral progress and would save the individual, the family, and the nation. It didn't, of course, then or decades later when the United States experimented with Prohibition. Enforcement was too great a challenge. In addition, Americans in the 1800s would see their concern over drinking supplanted by concern over slavery and the destruction of the Union.

Abolition Movement Grows

As popular as the temperance movement was, the antislavery crusade was even more so. Opposition to slavery began in the colonial period and developed slowly in the early

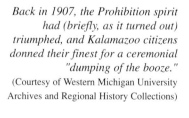

Back in 1907, the Prohibition spirit had (briefly, as it turned out) triumphed, and Kalamazoo citizens donned their finest for a ceremonial "dumping of the booze."
(Courtesy of Western Michigan University Archives and Regional History Collections)

nineteenth century. Abolitionists and missionaries brought the issue of slavery before the public and pointed out the brutality of the "peculiar institution." They preached that slavery was a sin, a sin against God and man.

One of slavery's earliest important enemies was Benjamin Lundy, a Quaker, who founded the *Genius of Universal Emancipation* newspaper in 1821. An itinerant lecturer and organizer of abolition societies, he was the first antislavery editor to employ a woman, Elizabeth Margaret Chandler, as a regular correspondent.

Raised in Philadelphia, Chandler was a prominent figure in the female antislavery circles of that city. A brilliant scholarly writer, she moved to Michigan in 1830 and continued to write for Lundy's newspaper. She looked upon the "agitation of emancipation" as one of women's duties, and her work led to the first abolitionist organization in Michigan, the Logan Female Antislavery Society, established in 1832 near Adrian.

Antislavery societies increased until there was scarcely a county that did not have at least one, and sometimes more. By 1838, only a year after Michigan had achieved statehood, Detroit had 19 local societies, and Lenawee County 15. Most of what the antislavery societies did at the start was pure propaganda—oration, newspaper articles, and religious and political debate. But not every abolitionist was happy to fight against slavery with mere words, and their interest in actually doing something led to the formation of Michigan's Underground Railroad.

Highly organized in Michigan, the Railroad helped escaped slaves make their way across the state to Canada. It was operated generally by deeply religious people, such as the

STOCKHOLDERS
OF THE UNDERGROUND
R. R. COMPANY
Hold on to Your Stock!!

The market has an upward tendency. By the express train which arrived this morning at 3 o'clock, fifteen thousand dollars worth of human merchandise, consisting of twenty-nine able-bodied men and women, fresh and sound, from the Carolina and Kentucky plantations, have arrived safe at the depot on the other side, where all our sympathising colonization friends may have an opportunity of expressing their sympathy by bringing forward donations of ploughs, &c., farming utensils, pick axes and hoes, and not old clothes; as these emigrants all can till the soil. N. B.—Stockholders don't forget the meeting to-day at 2 o'clock at the ferry on the Canada side. All persons desiring to take stock in this prosperous company, be sure to be on hand. By Order of the

Detroit, April 19, 1853. **BOARD OF DIRECTORS.**

Detroit was a terminus of one line of the Underground Railroad. From there fugitive slaves were transferred to Canada—and freedom. (Courtesy of State Archives of Michigan)

The home and store of Erastus Hussey, on Michigan Avenue in Battle Creek, was a busy "station" of the Underground Railroad. This structure was long since demolished when the W.K. Kellogg Foundation relocated its headquarters to the site in 1991, but the Foundation asked a community committee how it should commemorate the connection. The committee recommended a sculpture, and the result is this striking piece by African-American artist Ed Dwight. (Courtesy of W.K. Kellogg Foundation)

Quakers, who provided escaped slaves with food, clothing, shelter, and guidance from one "station" to the next. Cassopolis, Schoolcraft, Battle Creek, Coldwater, Jackson, Detroit—these were just a few of the stops on the Michigan "line."

As charity work, the Underground Railroad was incredibly dangerous, expensive, and tedious: clothes and food had to be found, transportation arranged, schedules adhered to, secrecy maintained. But as an opportunity to put one's religious, political, and moral beliefs into action, it was vastly rewarding: escaped slaves were helped to freedom for the first time in their lives, often with their families and children. Abolition no longer was a mere ideal.

Unfortunately, the institution of slavery was too well-entrenched and too powerful to be shaken from the local level. The challenge called for a united, well-organized effort throughout the state. In the summer of 1836, Michigan antislavery groups organized the Michigan Antislavery Society, believing that, united, they could accomplish their mission more effectively. In this they were not mistaken. Michigan became a hotbed of antislavery activity, especially for the Underground Railroad, many of whose most effective conductors (such as Battle Creek's Erastus Hussey) had prices put on their heads by enraged slave owners.

Practicality Replaces Piety

It is telling that, despite their religious roots, the abolitionist reformers eventually took this turn toward the pragmatic and political. As the country grew larger, so did its troubles. As the troubles grew larger, more wholesale political and businesslike approaches became necessary for Michigan philanthropists. For example, when severe economic conditions caused starvation and homelessness for many Grand Rapids children in the 1850s, an orphanage was founded. "The cry of the needy has sounded continually in our ears," said Mrs. J.D. Atwater, secretary of the orphanage's Ladies' Committee. "We, of course, will remember them in our prayers; however, we must also do so much more of a practical nature."

Charity reformers were beginning to perceive that the consequences of urbanization, and not mere moral depravity, played a major role in the growth of neediness. The nature of the social and economic problems that plagued Michigan at midcentury were, of course, not entirely new. In the early decades of the nineteenth century, the acceleration of urbanization in Detroit had caused a multitude of woes. By 1850, these problems had increased tremendously not only in Detroit, but across the state in Grand Rapids as well, causing unprecedented levels of unemployment, vagrancy, crime, and disease.

Part of the difficulty stemmed from Michigan's rapid population growth, first as a territory and then as a state. While the flood of new residents might have been a source of pride for Michiganians, it also created an increased demand for emergency relief that strained an already overtaxed public and private relief system. The stress was exacerbated by an economic depression that lasted from 1854 to 1858. A number of economic shocks that precipitated depression conditions caused one charity worker in Grand Rapids to comment: "In consequence of the general stagnation of trade, hundreds who are accustomed to earn their daily bread, have either been discharged from employment, or are put on short allowance." Hungry men roamed the streets, and at times, by necessity, abandoned their families to charity. The number of those out of work and impoverished reached unprecedented levels.

Grand Rapids' Monroe Street in 1831. The Baptist missions in the background were typical of early, religious philanthropic organizations. In the foreground, Chief Noonday's hut is at the left, and the old Indian Trail leads to Louis Campau's Trading Post—the three log cabins on the right. (Courtesy of Local History Department, Grand Rapids Public Library)

      The unemployed crowded with penniless newcomers into an increased number of slum areas and shantytowns, making it impossible for the residents of Detroit and Grand Rapids to escape daily reminders of widespread poverty. Detroit's residential sections were surrounded by slum areas. Stables were converted to rooming houses; mansions were divided and subdivided into warrens. Dozens of people lived in space originally meant for a single family. On the outskirts of Grand Rapids, squatters lived in hastily erected shantytowns with grossly inadequate sewage facilities.

      Faced with a mounting crisis, charity workers looked increasingly outside the framework of organized religion and moralistic methods of reform, and sought new, practical tactics and approaches to eliminate poverty. An example is the Young Men's Benevolent Society, formed in Detroit in 1848, when the reform movement was finding its feet. The Benevolent Society's membership, drawn from the city's business and professional ranks, was decidedly secular. They were not interested in the spiritual condition of the poor—that was the church's province. Nor would they concern themselves with "paupers whose bad habits were the cause of their poverty." Instead, their aim was to help a new category of unfortunates: the growing class of hardworking, thrifty men and women—the worthy poor—thrown upon the dole by economic hard times.

...charity workers looked increasingly outside the framework of organized religion....

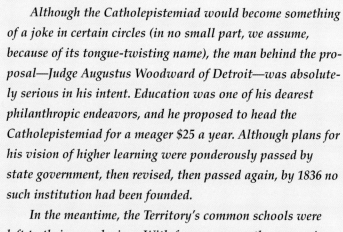

Education in the Michigan Wilderness

Investigating the history of education in Michigan is nothing if not a test of one's spelling ability. Take the state's Catholepistemiad, for example. In 1817, the Legislature passed an act to establish "the Catholepistemiad, or University of Michigania," a system of academies, universities, museums, and libraries with 13 professorships for subjects including Anthropoglossica (literature), Iatrica (medical science), and Diegetcia (historical sciences).

This depiction of a one-room schoolhouse is based on the Scotch Settlement School built in 1861 in Dearborn. It is by no means the typical school of the time, which, in out-state communities, was often a shack furnished with crude benches, a Bible, and a dictionary.
(Courtesy of State Archives of Michigan and *A History of Michigan in Paintings*, Ameritech Michigan)

Although the Catholepistemiad would become something of a joke in certain circles (in no small part, we assume, because of its tongue-twisting name), the man behind the proposal—Judge Augustus Woodward of Detroit—was absolutely serious in his intent. Education was one of his dearest philanthropic endeavors, and he proposed to head the Catholepistemiad for a meager $25 a year. Although plans for his vision of higher learning were ponderously passed by state government, then revised, then passed again, by 1836 no such institution had been founded.

In the meantime, the Territory's common schools were left to their own devices. With few resources, the mere existence of schools was a tenuous proposition. Still, exist they did, in schoolhouses built of logs with oil-paper windows and rough-hewn benches. Many settlers from New York and New England, especially, were educated, and they wanted learning for their children, even if it meant they would trace their letters in a box of dampened sand—money for luxuries such as blackboards was scarce. By way of pay, teachers received room and board at student homes, an occasional bushel of vegetables, and four or five dollars a month.

Understandably, many of the state's earliest charity efforts focused on education. Almost from the start, children from poor families were allowed to come to school for free, but many were too proud to accept. (The first truly free schools didn't appear until 1842 and then only in Detroit. It took another 30 years before poor children in other parts of the state could come to school without feeling they were "charity cases.") In some instances, children who didn't attend didn't miss much: the small, township schools often were open only two or three months a year.

The big city did afford more education options, but even in Detroit a large number of children did not attend school. An 1836 census counted 3,000 children of school age, but only 600 of them actually enrolled. While education was important to citizens there and elsewhere in the Territory, folks couldn't quite figure out how to organize it or make it accessible to all children. Sweeping solutions would not come until much later.

In a way, this leads us back to Judge Woodward and his Catholepistemiad. Obviously, Michigan was ready for neither the complex system of higher learning he envisioned, nor the then-radical notions he championed: state-provided education, non-sectarian schools, and tax subsidization. Most of Woodward's ideas would become staples of public education, but not until many years after his death. While it's likely he was ahead of his time, we'll never know what might have happened had he simply called his idea "a plan for higher education in Michigan."

By 1850, as the need for relief was about to soar, the Society had set its policies into action. Relief to the needy was given on a one-time basis and then only to help an individual gain employment. Most of the people helped by the Society lacked either job skills or a knowledge of where employment might be found, or both, and were forced to enter an already overcrowded, unskilled labor market. The results were low wages and frequent unemployment. To help these individuals find work, the Society established employment offices where jobs were offered. Fees paid by employers financed the service.

But employment offices were only part of the reform program initiated at this time; charity workers' most ambitious efforts were in the area of child welfare. "Here begins a life ...," wrote one relief worker, "which is black with unimaginable horrors."

In 1846, a group of women in Grand Rapids met at the Prospect Hill schoolhouse to form the Grand Rapids Union Benevolent Association. Initially, the ladies set out "to aid, according to the discretion or deliberate judgment of its members, such sick and needy persons as may be reported." Their focus was gradually narrowed to encompass women and children only.

Like most charities, the Grand Rapids Union Benevolent Association started "conspicuously handicapped by lack of funds." Determined to do what they could with what little they had, members channeled practical relief to the neediest poor. Clothing, donated from the community, was mended at meetings and dispensed as needed. Books were purchased so children could attend school. Furniture from members' homes was loaned. In February of 1850, a "Mrs. S.," newly arrived in Grand Rapids, destitute and with two small children, "was loaned sheets, pillows, furniture, and a stove to heat her small shanty." In every case a member visited the relief recipient's home and dutifully reported her findings to the membership. The secretary carefully recorded each report of assistance.

As the 1850s progressed, the carefully kept books of the Association filled with references to women "abandoned" by husbands, "destitute," "unemployed," and sick. "Mrs. B. [was] in want of clothing" after her home burned. "Mrs. L. whose husband left ... and took everything, including the blankets." Mrs. C. "recently moved in the village ... alone ... trying to raise twelve children in a small shanty." Precarious, indeed, were the lives of women and children in the nineteenth century.

During the hard times of 1857, two members of the Association's visiting committee, while making their rounds in the district of "the shanties," came upon a "Mrs. W." The young

The Grand Rapids Union Benevolent Association was begun by women, served women and children, and sought change in county laws for their betterment. They later built this hospital. (Courtesy of Local History Department, Grand Rapids Public Library)

woman was found "roaming the street, destitute and delirious, having no food for her family for several days." Hungry, sick, and unable to do her customary work by which she had, during the winter, supported her family, she told of watching her eldest child die from hunger two weeks earlier. When the visiting committee found the mother, she was carrying her youngest child, still a baby and already dying, through the streets in her arms. After calling an emergency meeting, the Association women arranged for a doctor and paid for his services from their own pockets. "It was too late," the secretary recorded in the minutes. "He arrived to pronounce the child dead." The women arranged for burial, sewed a funeral shroud, and prayed for the child's soul. It was, they conceded, "too little, too late."

It was this tragedy of the children in the streets without even the "most basic of needs met" that compelled the Association to seek a change in the county poor laws. The usual practice of sending poverty-stricken youngsters to the public poorhouse greatly disturbed them. They knew that almshouses were horrible environments for adults, let alone children. Some, such as in Ingham County, were so verminous that despite "eternal vigilance, the beds [were] occupied by creatures other than the sleeper"; others, such as the Eaton County poorhouse, were so decrepit that the inmates had to haul water from two miles away.

The unsanitary conditions, compounded with the practice of mixing children with adults, appalled the women. In 1848, the Kent County Poor Farm housed inmates who were "destructively inclined," "uncleanly," and "epileptic," as well as subject to violent outbursts. In short, it was no place for children.

To combat this problem, the Association petitioned the Poor Master and won an important change in the county bylaws, one that formally sanctioned the placing of destitute children directly in their care. This access to the children was an important victory. Reformers were certain that the child in the street and the orphan out begging were training for a future of ignorance and crime—an assumption particularly astute for an era that predates formal social work. The street, reformers knew, exposed children to thieves, drunks, and prostitutes, all of whom offered a substantial lesson in the ways of the city's dark side. Often, the children's home lives weren't any better.

With the new law, the women could remove children directly from the street and their families before the young souls had "fully assimilated the deviant values of the parents and evil companions." The era of the asylum was under way. Between 1840 and 1860, Michigan

St. Vincent Orphan Asylum of Detroit, c. 1870. One of the early institutional answers to a critical problem in large cities across the country. (Courtesy of Detroit Public Library Burton Historical Collection)

Judge Hall's wife had to be plucky: life was hard for the Michigan settlers. But women of the 1800s had more going for them than one might expect. It's true that they did not have the opportunity (until 1851) to pursue a college degree in the state, nor the right (until 1855) to inherit and control property, nor the right (until 1920) to vote in a national election. But neither were they the mythic "barefoot and pregnant" victims of male oppressors.

For starters, the pioneer woman was the family's protector. She worked hard to make their rough cabin a warm and welcoming refuge in the often-inhospitable new land. She was also the family accountant, running the household industriously and thriftily, believing "it isn't what you make, but what you save, that helps you get ahead." And, of course, she shouldered all the other responsibilities one might expect: most accounts tell of women "cheerfully" going about their baking, cleaning, nursing, and sewing; their bargaining with the local cobbler or cabinetmaker; and their planting, weeding, harvesting, "putting down," cooking, and serving vegetables from their gardens.

Most significantly, a woman was also the family insurance agent and financial planner. She was the one who made arrangements—to the extent possible—for her husband's and children's survival through the next (inevitable) crisis. A woman did this by maintaining strong ties with kin nearby and back home in the east, for she considered them as much her family as her own husband and children. If parents or sisters lived far distant, she wrote frequent letters and made long journeys to visit them, not only out of familial love and loyalty but because she knew her nuclear family might need to rely on her kin for financial support some day. In that era, no single household could guard against death, illness, or financial disaster (for example, nearly 20 percent of children lost a parent before they reached age 15). There was no government program to tide a family over in hard times; the generosity of relatives was the tenuous safety net that saved them.

To a degree, a woman settler considered her entire community "family." She sent food to families struck by tragedy, nursed kin and neighbors when they were sick, and joined other women to sew clothing or quilts for those in need. Most of her charitable deeds were unrecorded or, at most, recorded under her husband's name—"Mrs. John Smith"— a practice that continues among many women today.

Early Michigan women acted as protectors of home and family not because their husbands browbeat them into it—at least not usually—but because it was the role expected and accepted by both genders in that day. In fact, if a female settler ever even thought about an independent existence, it was probably as something to be avoided. For her, autonomy would have been synonymous with loneliness and powerlessness. To be sure, women suffered from their lack of civil rights in the nation's early days—enduring such atrocities as wife beating and spousal rape without the legal recourse and support networks available today. Still, familial "connections" often gave women a different kind of power than that granted by universities or legislation, and many women derived both satisfaction and security from their hard and busy lives.

> *"After six months' hard toil in the woods, I got the ague, and was sick for several weeks, and at last got discouraged and disheartened. Money about all gone, no one but myself with my bare hands to provide for my family, I gave up, and told my wife I would settle our claim, and we would go back to Vermont. But that plucky little wife of mine came to me, and, putting her hand on my shoulder, said, 'You will do no such thing. You will get over the ague. All you need is courage. We are going to stay here. I will stand by your side, and we will fight the battle out, here in the woods, and secure a home.' This cheered me up. I stayed. And for all that I possess, or have accomplished in Michigan, I am indebted to that resolute little woman."*
>
> —Judge Tolman W. Hall of Battle Creek, date unknown

philanthropists wholeheartedly embraced the notion of institutions. They endowed and founded orphanages, asylums, temporary homes, "final resting places of the aged," industrial schools, and child-placement societies. They helped the sick and aged, "fallen" women, neglected children, and the mentally unbalanced. In short, there wasn't much that the reformers believed an institution couldn't make better.

In many cases, they were right. With regard to the mentally ill, for instance, medical care in Michigan and elsewhere in the early 1800s was nonexistent at best and barbaric at worst. In 1843, Massachusetts schoolteacher Dorothea Dix revealed that the nation's mentally ill citizens were being grossly mistreated. As Michigan historian Willis Dunbar has noted, victims often were locked into attics, pens, and cellars. By 1848, however, Michigan had become one of 11 states to agree with Dix's recommendation that asylums for the insane (as the institutions were known) should be established. It wasn't until 1850, however, that a formal committee of Michigan legislators selected Kalamazoo as the site for the state's first mental institution. Kalamazoo residents enthusiastically supported the idea, and donated money and land for the building. (The land, however, eventually was sold and the institution built on another site in 1859.)

As the move toward institutions indicates, private benevolent societies had become distinctly more secular by the middle of the century. (To be sure, though, the evangelical ethos remained an important influence.) The benevolent societies had also become more efficient. While the moral-uplift effort of the 1820s and 1830s featured haphazard "friendly visiting" by part-time volunteers, the charitable efforts of the 1850s featured genuine networking, communication, and transportation systems. Organizations tried with considerable ingenuity to adapt their techniques and goals to urban realities. The men and women who founded asylums, created depots, and organized soup kitchens did so to address the desperation of the times.

While earlier endeavors had (rhetorically at least) included the entire city within their sphere of concern, the newer philanthropic organizations targeted more specific geographic areas and population strata. They defined their respective groups of aid recipients with considerable precision and brought a new level of professionalization to philanthropy.

But much more important, their actions revealed a growing awareness that economic and social conditions played a crucial role in creating poverty. With the coming of the Civil War, this new practicality was about to face its gravest challenge.

1861-
the early
1890s

War, Charity,

and the Gospel of Wealth

2

September 1862

"I send you these words in health, cheerfulness and contented in my way. I ... hope that God will support me spiritually and physically, that He may cause me to walk with joy."

—a member of the 25th Michigan Infantry, in letters to his family, prior to his departure from Kalamazoo for the Civil War battlefields.

July 1863

"If there is no money to buy [food], we steal.... We do not starve ourselves anymore; we have been soldiers too long. I do not suffer hunger even if the people give us dirty looks. The revolver is on my hip and that is it."

—the same member of the 25th Michigan Infantry, in letters to his family, after being in battle and on the march for many months.

(Chapter overleaf photos courtesy of Detroit Public Library Burton Historical Collection and State Archives of Michigan)

Chapter Two

War, Charity, and the

Gospel of Wealth

1861-the early 1890s

One of the great truths about war is that humanity is rarely prepared for the horror of it. History is dense with tales of people who beat the drums, gathered arms, invoked God's name, reassured themselves that they were doing the honorable thing ... and then went off to a miserable fate they had scarcely imagined.

In this regard, the Civil War was no exception. It was a horrible, bloody catastrophe of a war in which soldiers fought not only each other, but inadequate clothing and shelter, hunger, and disease. Despite the prewar hype, the Bible-thumping, the political skirmishes, and the North's righteous goal of justice and unity, the extent of the suffering brought about by the war likely surprised almost everyone (with the possible exception of the *Detroit Free Press*, which predicted doom, despair, and destruction even before Michigan soldiers headed south).

Certainly, the war's nastiness surprised a fair number of charity workers, particularly those who had banded together to send soldiers off to war with handmade quilts and lovingly prepared preserves, neither of which would stand up to the requirements of battle.

But perhaps it's to mankind's credit that war is something for which we aren't instinctively prepared. If it's tragic to enter a war without being fully primed for the horror of it, so, too, is it tragic to know the extent of the human degradation that is about to ensue and then to choose war anyway.

Looking back on Michigan's philanthropic effort during the Civil War, then, is a matter of recalling first the charity workers' inability to prepare for war's horrific reality and then their extraordinary ability to become utterly and efficiently practical when they realized that

Church leaders often pooled their resources to conduct early missionary work in frontier settlements of the west. This small Isabella County Church was dedicated in August of 1898 by a growing congregation. They had outgrown the smaller log cabin church on the right.
(Courtesy of State Archives of Michigan)

compassion and good intentions (and homemade quilts) could not combat the nightmares of the battlefield.

The wartime effort put forth by Michigan relief workers was astounding. From Houghton to Tecumseh, from Detroit to Grand Haven—and in every village, town, and city in between—volunteers sprang into action when President Lincoln called men to battle in the spring of 1861. They met in churches, schools, and homes, beginning a sewing frenzy that would produce everything from clothing to tents to battle flags, sometimes finishing items mere hours before Michigan soldiers marched south. Historical texts and journals make it easy to imagine a soldier fumbling with his rifle, his boots, and the buttons on his just-completed shirt as he hastened to get out the door to battle.

In the early, heady days of the war, before months of sickness, hunger, and battle had decimated the Union troops, and before bone-numbing fatigue and lack of adequate resources had sapped the optimism from many a volunteer, relief workers feverishly sewed, rolled bandages, and gathered supplies to send to local men. Although relief groups generally held formal meetings once a week, many women sewed every day, wherever they could—in church, at the town hall, in the parlor at home.

This early relief work was vital: when the Civil War began, Michigan's financial cupboards were mostly bare. Although mining had started in the Upper Peninsula in the 1840s, and the timber industry was showing the first signs of an economic force in the making, the state was still primarily a rural, farming region when the war began. Its militia groups—which were local organizations, not state-funded institutions—generally consisted of men who had

Troops of the 2nd Michigan Infantry in 1861. Michigan soldiers were the first troops west of the Alleghenies to arrive in the nation's capital. President Lincoln is said to have exclaimed, "Thank God for Michigan," reassured by their arrival that the western states would remain loyal to the Union. (Courtesy of Detroit Public Library Burton Historical Collection)

Laura Smith Haviland

The dogged independence of Laura Smith Haviland (1808-1898) ruffled feathers on both sides of the Mason-Dixon Line. She far overstepped the role of the typical female Underground Railroad worker concerned chiefly with rustling up food and clothing for fugitives hidden in her husband's barn. Furthermore, Haviland ignored the Railroad's usual modus operandi, in which it conducted its work collectively and in secret. Haviland operated out in the open and, usually, alone.

During the first three decades of her life, Haviland was busy marrying a farmer, moving from New York State to the Raisin River in Lenawee County (near today's Adrian), and bearing eight children. She was still a young woman when the antislavery movement spread into Michigan in the early 1830s, after the arrival of abolitionist writer Elizabeth Chandler. The pair became friends, and Haviland headed Chandler's local antislavery society, the Logan Female Antislavery Society (the first of its kind in the state), when the writer died a few years later. Haviland's involvement with the group didn't sit well with her fellow Quakers; although most of them were steadfast in their opposition to slavery, they believed it would end naturally, whenever other Christians got around to emancipating their slaves. Haviland eventually left the Quaker sect, but stuck close to its pacifist precepts.

Haviland next opened the Raisin Institute in 1837. There, girls learned sewing and housework and boys learned how to farm. Significantly, Haviland didn't distinguish between the races. Hers was the first Michigan school to admit African-American children.

In 1845 tragedy struck. An epidemic claimed much of Haviland's family, and afterward, she was haunted by dreams of a slave at her door, feet bloody from the shackles on his ankles. She became convinced that the dream was calling her to a more active role in the antislavery movement.

The new widow's first priority was to help protect the escaped slaves and freedpeople living in and near the

(Courtesy of State Archives of Michigan)

Raisin community. Under a system she devised, any lurking slave catchers were greeted by a blast from a tin horn, which summoned help from sympathetic neighbors. When the horns didn't scare these hunters away, she escorted former slaves to one of the state's many Underground Railroad stations. From there, they could escape to a safer spot in Michigan, or to Canada.

Haviland traveled even greater distances to take on slave catchers face-to-face. On one journey to Ohio, she ferreted out a trap set for a freedman who had farmed on her property. She sprang the trap successfully and then stared down the angry, pistol-waving slave catchers on the train ride home.

Eventually, Haviland made her way to Cincinnati to work beside Levi Coffin, reputed president of the Underground Railroad. She nursed sick fugitives and taught African-American children in the basement of the Zion Baptist Church, a busy Railroad station. She often ventured alone outside the relative safety of those walls to take fugitives to Canada and lead slaves out of Kentucky, Tennessee, and Arkansas.

These exploits and her brazen, condemnatory letters to slave owners made Haviland so infamous in the South that Tennessee slaveholders offered a $3,000 reward for her capture, dead or alive. She had a similar shortage of friends in the North, where some clergymen and others felt the place for a woman, even a Railroad woman, was in the home.

Undaunted, Haviland established a school for escaped slaves in Windsor, Ontario, in 1852. A decade later, she was immersed in teaching, clothing, and feeding the freedpeople ignored by most Civil War relief efforts. And in the years before her death, still other causes—the need for orphanages, women's rights, and prohibition—captured the attention of the feisty little woman, remembered by Adrian residents as "Aunt Laura."

joined at least as much to socialize as to learn military drills. For many of them, the adjustment to military life was difficult. The Civil War journal of soldier Charles B. Haydon, for instance, notes that one day early in 1861 when Michigan's first regiments—still stationed in Detroit and consisting primarily of former store clerks, bookkeepers, students, and the like—were served rice pudding for dessert instead of pie, a small riot ensued.

To be fair, though, Michigan's regiments were as tenacious and enthusiastic as the state's relief workers, and included just enough members who had some military training or experience to serve as examples for those who didn't. The state's troops ultimately would become some of the nation's best and most relied-upon, with more than 20 percent of our men marching off to war, including more than 1,600 African-Americans—almost 24 percent of the state's total African-American population—and 181 Jewish soldiers, at a time when the state's entire Jewish population consisted of approximately 150 families. About 14,000 Michigan men would die.

Clearly, energy, devotion, and commitment were not in short supply in Michigan. Philanthropy here was not only alive and well, but a bit less morally judgmental than it had been decades earlier. But per-

The "Aid Society" meets at the Baxter home in Van Buren County, c. 1895. Across the state, generous souls like these worked to meet the particular needs within a community. (Courtesy of Western Michigan University Archives and Regional History Collections)

haps because they were swept up in the noble sentiment of their cause, Michigan volunteers did not always score a practicality bull's eye. Down-filled pillows, quilts embroidered with lines of poetry or scripture, very-breakable jars of jam, and encyclopedia-size Bibles were just a few of the items men toted as they left for war.

The errors became quickly apparent. Many of the unwieldy items were returned, given away, or simply dumped. Even Michigan soldier John Anthony Wilterdink, an intensely religious man, returned his Bible and religious books to his family and asked them to send, instead, "a small Testament or Psalm book." Military leaders were increasingly frustrated with abandoned camps strewn with the debris of "fancy work, fruitcakes, and whatnots"—as one report from the front described.

However, it would be harsh to dwell on the flaws of war relief work, particularly in light of the good intentions and hard work involved and the fact that so many other educated

African-American churches had been key centers of resistance to slavery before the Civil War, and became important sources of support for the war effort. Pictured is the African Methodist Episcopal Church in Detroit, 1882. (Courtesy of Detroit Public Library Burton Historical Collection)

Sarah Richmond and other young Grand Rapids women sewed and baked for the men of the 3rd Michigan Infantry. Her diary records the patriotic enthusiasm of the Civil War's early days—excitement that lasted until the fighting claimed its first casualties. (Courtesy of Local History Department, Grand Rapids Public Library)

and well-informed people also underestimated the demands of the war. (Lincoln himself originally summoned men to volunteer for a 90-day tour of duty; that span soon was upped to three years.) Besides, much good was achieved. The strong-minded individuals who focused on war relief were scrappy and dedicated. If they made mistakes, they quickly addressed them.

"The amount of work we have accomplished is a wonder to ourselves," one Kalamazoo woman wrote to a friend in 1861, "[but it still] impressed many with the feeling that regular systematic effort for the relief of soldiers when sick or wounded would be necessary." Military leaders agreed. "What is needed," said one military report early in the summer of 1861, "is trustworthy information from some recognized authority … as to the real wants of the soldier, and judicious advice as to the best mode of supplying them." In other words, the Union war effort needed an organization that would step forth boldly and say: "Send dried vegetables, not fruitcake."

The United States Sanitary Commission was just such an organization. Formed in June 1861 through a voluntary citizen effort, the Sanitary Commission would be the nation's first centralized, quasi-public charitable association. Through a network of regional branches and local auxiliaries, the Commission attempted to unite and systematize all benevolent efforts for the Union troops. Soon, more than 7,000 local soldiers' aid societies throughout the North joined the network, including just under 400 societies in Michigan alone.

Interestingly, nothing similar to the U.S. Sanitary Commission developed in the South, possibly due to the Confederacy's philosophy toward states' rights—that is, each state was an island of self-rule. The South also suffered from critical supply shortages, transportation problems, and financial chaos, among other things, but its philanthropic hands were, to a large extent, tied behind its back.

By contrast, the North had not just one national war relief group, but two. About a year after the United States Sanitary Commission was formed, the United States Christian Commission also went to work. The two groups competed fiercely in raising funds, collecting supplies, and winning the loyalty of the women volunteers who did most of the local work. The groups also had vastly different missions. The Sanitary Commission was founded primarily to help prevent the disease that would kill more than two enlisted men for every one killed by battle injuries. The Christian Commission, which represented YMCAs; Bible, temperance, and Sunday School societies; and many Protestant evangelical churches, was founded to guard morals and save souls.

Before Michigan's late nineteenth century industrial boom, agriculture was the basis of both the state's economy and philanthropic generosity. (Courtesy of Clements Library University of Michigan)

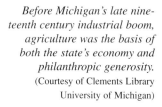

Ultimately, each group modified its mission to appeal to the average person on the street, who was more interested in donating material goods and sending them to the local boys than in saving souls and preventing disease. Perhaps as a result, neither organization was particularly successful in generating the exclusive devotion of the local relief societies. Tellingly, the Ladies Soldiers' Aid Society of Kalamazoo, which organized a massively successful fundraiser in 1864, the Kalamazoo Sanitary Fair, donated equal portions of its profits to the Christian Commission and to the Michigan branch of the Sanitary Commission. A share of the proceeds also was sent to the Michigan Soldiers' Relief Association in Washington, D.C., which maintained a hostel there, called the Michigan Soup House, for soldiers on leave. The Kalamazoo group also used Fair profits to purchase and distribute many supplies on its own.

Inasmuch as any war relief group can be termed a success—hundreds of thousands of people still died in the Civil War, after all—the U.S. Sanitary Commission was arguably the more successful of the two national relief organizations. Before the end of the first year of war, and before the Christian Commission was really up and running, the public already viewed the Sanitary Commission and its auxiliary soldiers' relief groups as the principal agent and almsgiver to the Union forces. Coordinating the work of the smaller societies, the Sanitary Commission set up supply stations and hospitals, provided aid for the sick and wounded during warfront emergencies, hired and trained nurses, and organized the collection, shipment, and distribution of donations. The Sanitary Commission also sent inspectors to Union hospitals and taught troops in camp how to cook their food properly and how to prevent the spread of disease.

By the second year of the war, with the Sanitary Commission's advice, civilians had a better understanding of what the soldiers needed—hospital supplies and food essentials. Efficiency in supplying these essentials became the order of the day. Women could clear a house and put its rooms to work as sewing factories on scarcely a moment's notice—and then keep the house in that disheveled condition for weeks if they had to.

Actually, the effect of the war relief effort on women was one of the largest cultural ramifications of Civil War philanthropy. Women not only learned how to be dispassionately efficient, they learned how to be businesslike. Michigan women organized relief groups, drafted constitutions, elected officers, collected dues, raised money, assigned work, scheduled

One of Marquette's most prominent citizens, George Shiras III, was the father of wildlife photography and also an internationally known naturalist and conservationist, author, lawyer, and member of Congress. He was also a philanthropist, founding the Shiras Institute to finance recreational, civic, and beautification projects throughout the Upper Peninsula. (Courtesy of Marquette County Historical Society)

At this rented brine well in Midland, Herbert Dow developed a new way to produce bromide through an electrical reaction. His supply of raw material was virtually unlimited, and one of many natural resources that would create industrial fortunes, and tremendous philanthropy, in Michigan. (Courtesy of Midland County Historical Society)

"God's own blessing, we trust, will rest on all men, women and little children of Michigan who may be thus inclined to strengthen the hearts and hands, and encourage the valor and patriotism of the fathers and husbands, and brothers and sons, who have manfully resisted the overthrow of that government which good men of olden time established, and which we humbly pray a right-eous God may ever preserve."

So ended an 1864 plea from the Ladies Soldiers' Aid Society of Kalamazoo for merchandise, produce, livestock—in short, anything the women could get their hands on—to sell at the Kalamazoo Sanitary Fair. Proceeds from their ambitious, four-day fundraiser would benefit the state's sick and wounded Civil War soldiers.

Word of the ladies' request spread across the state, thanks to newspaper notices and soldiers aid societies in other cities. Thousands responded, with donations of everything from silverware and pianos to horses and barrels of fruits and vegetables. Widowed mothers whose sons had been killed in battle sent humble contributions. A small child from another county sent a few cents with an earnest message that she wished it were more. Her sentiment surely tore at the ladies' heartstrings: her family was poor, her mother was ill, and her father and brother were off fighting the war.

As donations poured in, the ladies busily prepared for their event. They rode herd on the crew hired to erect an exhibit hall and dining room on grounds rented from the Kalamazoo Horse Association—a feat of construction that amazed at least one onlooker: "It will be noted that a very brief period elapsed between the time that the idea of holding the 'Fair' was first entertained and its occurrence.... Considering the fact that the lumber was to be brought by teams a distance of 28 miles, the circum-stances seemed to be embarrassing." But the ladies were a determined lot, and their buildings were finished on time.

The fair opened on September 20, 1864, and Michiganians from a dozen counties traveled to Kalamazoo to see the goods exhibited in the great Sanitary Hall. The Adjutant General's office supplied the items that drew most attention: tattered, battle-scarred banners borne by Michigan regiments of the Army of the Potomac or the Army of the West.

Even with those reminders of the war, the event was upbeat, likely the biggest doings the town had seen since Abraham Lincoln spoke in Kalamazoo during an 1856 political rally. It was also hugely successful. Visitors listened to speakers and music and, as was the hope of the relief society, bought the goods that had been contributed. In one instance, a knickknack donated by a child was sold and returned by purchasers again and again, until it finally produced a "handsome" (unfortunately unrecorded) amount toward the ladies' grand total: $9,618.79. Most of today's Rotarians and Junior Leaguers would be more than happy if their fundraisers earned as much.

This flier, announcing a wartime fundraiser organized by the Ladies Soldiers' Aid Society of Kalamazoo, helped draw citizens from every corner of the state to a worthy cause. (Courtesy of Western Michigan University Archives and Regional History Collections)

MICHIGAN STATE SANITARY FAIR!

TO BE HELD ON THE
STATE AGRICULTURAL FAIR GROUNDS,
KALAMAZOO, MICHIGAN,
ON THE
20th, 21st, 22nd and 23rd of September, 1864.

The Ladies Soldiers' Aid Society, of Kalamazoo, invite the various Aid Societies, Sanitary and Christian Commissions, in the State of Michigan, to join them in a

Grand Michigan State Sanitary Fair!

In aid of our noble Soldiers in the hospitals and fields, as above stated. We believe that a large amount may be raised for these objects, and that great good may be done.

CONTRIBUTIONS

Of all classes of Goods, Merchandise, Produce, Implements, Works of Art, indeed *everything* that can be converted into money, are respectfully solicited from individuals, companies, shops and societies, in this State, and from abroad.

meetings, and gathered enough real-world business acumen to cause a moment or two of fore-boding among those who believed in a male-dominated social order. All of these skills would later play a role in the suffrage movement and in the work of women's clubs that began seek-ing—and achieving—wholesale social improvements near the end of the century.

Despite their new skills, however, and the marked improvement in war relief efficiency, volunteers soon discovered that their enthusiasm was in greater supply than their resources. By the fourth year of war, the lack of money had become a critical issue, and many women felt a need to seek funds more aggressively. Some of them, well-dressed and proper, resorted to standing on street corners to solicit donations. As shocking as it must have been (this was, after all, the middle of the Victorian Era), the street-corner tactic generated only modest amounts of cash, and soon women were looking for other strategies.

In Kalamazoo, one of those new strategies was the previously mentioned Sanitary Fair, which cleared more than $9,000 in profit. According to economist John J. McCusker, that figure translates into $77,400 in 1991 dollars, a remarkable take for a village of fewer than 10,000 souls.

From War to Depression

The war relief effort demonstrated that small groups of volunteers could bring about massive social change, if they were united and properly organized under a larger authority. In this sense, the Civil War gave philanthropy a shot in the arm, a chance to display its true power. The nation barely survived its incomprehensible destruction, even with a massive mobilization of volunteers; without Civil War charity, we can reasonably wonder whether the country would have survived at all.

The significance of that achievement did not go unnoticed. As America buried its dead and started clearing the debris, the era's philanthropists—now aware that they could tackle mammoth challenges—began switching gears. Though the war was over, there was still work to be done. The conflict left in its wake thousands of disabled veterans, destitute widows, and helpless orphans. Michigan citizens from all walks of life worked to relieve this human misery, creating numerous new organizations, such as the Ladies' Society for the Support of Hebrew Widows and Orphans in the State of Michigan, which was organized in Detroit in 1863.

By the time the depression of the 1870s rolled around, relief agencies had become ubiquitous. Detroit and Grand Rapids city directories of that era describe dozens of associa-tions that alleviated misery, combated pauperism, and addressed every imaginable emergency.

In the early years at Michigan State University (founded in 1855 as the Agricultural College of Michigan), all students were required to work three hours a day in the farms or gardens to assist with their expenses and to aid in the development of the young institution.
(Courtesy of Michigan State University Archives and Historical Collections)

During the Civil War, Michigan sent more troops to serve the Union (on a per capita basis) than any other state. About 14,000 Michigan men would die from battle injuries and disease.
(Courtesy of State Archives of Michigan and *A History of Michigan in Paintings,* Ameritech Michigan)

Unfortunately, the depression that afflicted much of the country between 1873 and 1878 overwhelmed even this generous outpouring of charitable sentiment and activity. Though even more agencies were created during the depression—soup kitchens, bread lines, free lodging houses, and distribution centers for coal, food, clothing, even cash—the economic times left thousands without food or adequate shelter and disheartened thousands more. As much as $20,000 ($246,000 in 1991 dollars) in some form or another of charitable relief was distributed in Detroit alone during the winter of 1875, but unemployment and destitution remained firmly entrenched, particularly in urban centers. "Humane men look in vain for an effective mode of solving this painful problem," one disheartened charity worker wrote.

Discouraged and overwhelmed by their inability to banish poverty, many charity workers of the 1870s began to change their mind-set. At the risk of oversimplification, the essence of the new ideology was this: If charitable people couldn't make poverty disappear through hard work, dedication, and a multitude of relief efforts, then something must be wrong—not with those who were providing the aid, but with those who were receiving it.

This floral display at Grand Rapids' John Ball Park, c. 1885, was made possible by time, money, and materials generously donated to demonstrate community pride.
(Courtesy of Clements Library University of Michigan)

By the time Sojourner Truth (1799-1883) moved to Battle Creek at age 57, she was on career number three. In a life filled with struggle, this African-American orator transformed herself again and again, each time into whomever the times needed her to be.

Born Isabella Baumfree in Ulster County, New York, Truth belonged to several owners before she was emancipated by state law in 1827. A year later, she found herself in New York City with a new last name (Van Wagenen, courtesy of her last owner) and an ability to draw audiences as a preacher and singer.

Sojourner Truth

Isabella began traveling as Sojourner Truth, itinerant preacher, in 1843, and a few years later became an antislavery lecturer. But thanks to her famous 1851 "Ain't I a Woman" speech, Truth's new neighbors in Battle Creek likely thought of her as a feminist, the role that springs to mind today.

The "Ain't I a Woman" incident wasn't planned. It happened at a women's rights conference in Akron, Ohio, where, for more than a day, Truth listened to ministers blast the notion of equal rights for women. On the second day, she stepped forward to speak, uninvited, in defense of all women:

"Dat man over dar say dat womin needs to be helped into carriages, and lifted over ditches, and to hab de best place everywhar. Nobody eber helps me into carriages, or ober mud-puddles, or gibs me any best place! And a'n't I a woman? Look at me! Look at my arm! [She bared her right arm to the shoulder, revealing tremendous muscles.] I hab ploughed, and planted and gathered into barns, and no man could head me! And a'n't' I a woman? I could work as much and eat as much as a man—when I could get it—and bear de lash as well! And a'n't I a woman? I have borne thirteen children, and seen 'em mos' all sold off to slavery, and when I cried out with my mother's grief, none but Jesus heard me! And a'n't I a woman?"

Actually, Truth had appropriated her mother's tragic experience. She had only five children herself, and none of them were sold permanently into slavery. The details didn't matter. Truth's listeners were riveted, and her reputation spread.

During the Civil War, she went to Washington, D.C., to help African-American refugees fleeing the warfare in Virginia. She saw that handouts of old clothes and hot soup didn't address the real problem—a lack of paying jobs—so she set up a program that matched refugee workers with employers in New York and Michigan. She also asked Congress to set aside land in Kansas for a freedpeople's settlement. Lawmakers refused, but Truth saw scores of African-American southerners who shared her vision move to "Free Kansas" before she died in Battle Creek.

(Photo courtesy of State Archives of Michigan)

The problem wasn't the serious economic depression, argued charity reformers, but too much charity. Too much relief money made paupers out of decent people. Too much reliance on charity was a sign of moral failing. What the poor needed wasn't jobs, food, or coal, but the advice and guidance of a good, decent, morally superior "friend."

If all of this sounds remarkably familiar, one need look back no further than the early 1800s to find the matching ideological shoe. Philanthropy in Michigan had metamorphosed from the religious, high-minded moralizing of the 1810s and '20s, to the more sympathetic practicality of the 1850s and '60s, and back again … sort of. Actually, to be historically accurate, Michigan philanthropy has never been any one particular thing. It was, and is, a mixture of approaches, forces, and philosophies all working together (or sometimes not working together), with a few emerging as prominent enough to provide a sense of philanthropic gestalt. In the 1870s, that sense of gestalt, we can fairly say, took a tilt back toward philanthropy as a moral, though less religious, crusade.

This time, however—thanks to the reform movements of the 1840s and '50s and the Civil War—charity workers had a more vigorous sense of practicality and businesslike efficiency. They didn't simply drop in to instruct the poor on morals as they had earlier in the century; now they used carefully planned and documented techniques. ("Endeavor to foster 'pride of home,' by helping to make the dwelling bright and cheerful, with the gift of such articles as cannot possibly pauperize, but will elevate and refine the taste."—item number 16 on the Detroit Association of Charities' list of General Hints and Suggestions to Visitors.) This time, when charity workers gathered information about the lives and habits of the poor, they placed it into files that were centralized, systematically accumulated, arranged, stored, and—when prospective philanthropists asked about a particular family—carefully disseminated.

Getting Charity Organized

Such tenacious commitment to organization and efficiency was one of the hallmarks of what became known as the charity organization movement. With its roots in the well-publicized London Charity Organization Society founded in 1869, the U.S. charity organization movement focused on ways to bring order out of the chaos that was private charity. During the 1870s, organizations patterned after the London Society were set up in large cities throughout the United States. By the early 1890s, both Detroit and Grand Rapids had charity organization societies of their own.

Philanthropy in the United States, the movement posited, did a disservice to the truly

Peck's Camp, established in 1883 in what would become the mining town of Ironwood. Men arrived to explore for ore, found it in abundance, and opened Pabst Mine, one of the richest in the history of the Gogebic Range. (Courtesy of State Archives of Michigan)

needy by squandering its resources on fraudulent requests and by needlessly duplicating services. Charity reformers accused philanthropic societies of dispensing money to the poor indiscriminately, thereby discouraging paupers from ever working at all. Levi L. Barbour, president of the Detroit Association of Charities, noted in 1885 that he had personally seen a vagrant receive $2.50 for a few hours of begging. What possible incentive, Barbour wondered aloud, would a beggar ever have to work at a real job all day long for the comparatively meager sum of $1.25—a typical day's pay—if he could make twice as much, much more easily, by begging? As long as reckless, misinformed philanthropists made vagrancy profitable, pauperism would surely flourish, Barbour said.

Barbour and others who shared his view did have a point. Michigan philanthropy, although widespread, had become less than perfectly efficient. So many new private charities sprang up in the 1870s that overlapping services and lack of communication among the various groups were genuine problems. As the charity reformers saw it, such disarray only made it easier for the ever-greedy pauper to extract handouts from many philanthropic groups simultaneously.

Public philanthropy was no better, detractors said, and they criticized the growing cost of government aid and the resulting higher taxes. The government, charity reformers argued, should not be in the business of providing charity. Instead, private benevolence could and should assume complete responsibility for the poor. However, private charity came with a catch: charity organization societies prided themselves on the fact that they were *not* primarily relief-giving agencies. In Grand Rapids, for instance, the charity organization's president assured the city that the agency helped the poor become useful members of society by providing not food, shelter, or jobs, but counsel, advice, and friendship. Charity reformers successfully reduced public relief in many cities, even as they were ending, or at least reducing, private relief.

The charity organization movement's opposition to almsgiving was one of its most defining characteristics and actually was quite fierce. Just like their counterparts in the moral reform societies of the 1810s and '20s, charity reformers of the 1870s were convinced that people who suffered from poverty usually were deficient in some way: moral, mental, or physical. They also took it for granted that no one would work if he didn't have to. As Alfred Crozier of the Grand Rapids Charity Organization Society said in 1893, "If you pay a man to work, he'll work; if you pay him to beg, he'll beg."

A Chippewa Indian Women's Club near Lake Superior, c. 1890. In every chapter of Michigan's history, residents have banded together to share individual resources for the common good. (Courtesy of State Archives of Michigan)

Marquette, 1881. The number of mines on the Marquette Iron Range had vastly increased since the 1860s. Railroads brought ore from mines in the west to docks at Marquette, where it was loaded for shipment to the mills. (Courtesy of Clark Historical Library Central Michigan University)

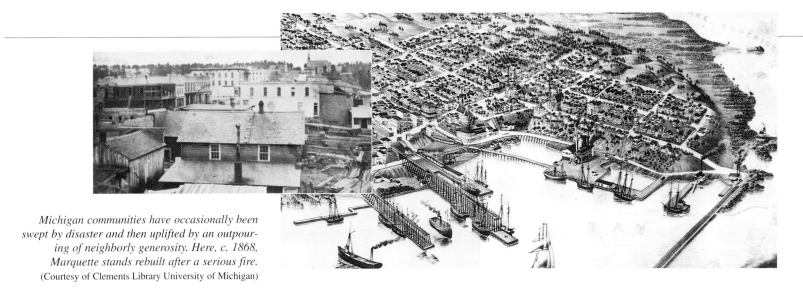

Michigan communities have occasionally been swept by disaster and then uplifted by an outpouring of neighborly generosity. Here, c. 1868, Marquette stands rebuilt after a serious fire. (Courtesy of Clements Library University of Michigan)

Crozier, as well as many others in the charity organization movement, believed that to be kept at work the poor had to endure deprivation—in the form of unpleasant working conditions if they were not "ambitious" enough to work anywhere but in a workhouse, or in the form of a dismal, cold-and-hunger-filled existence if they "chose" not to work at all. When the pressure of necessity was relaxed, the poor would start goofing off, or so the reformers assumed. In some places in the United States, the opinion manifested itself as a conscious decision to make workhouses unpleasant; if the poor wanted "pleasant," the reasoning went, they could work harder and find better jobs. One leader of charity organization thought, Josephine Shaw Lowell of New York, actually advocated the establishment of labor colonies for the poor. Others in the movement, inspired by Lowell's severity, supported such measures as flogging and imprisonment of the vagrant poor.

With such a stigma attached to poverty and charity (not to mention the startlingly comprehensive files maintained on those who sought relief), we can only assume that many poor people, when faced with a choice between being poor and silent or being less-poor but ostracized, looked at the dwindling amount of relief available through the charitable organization societies and said, "No thanks." (The amount of relief available, requested, and distributed in New York City dropped sharply after the city's Charity Organization Society formed. The group's leaders considered the drop to be evidence of the fraud that had been perpetrated in the past by paupers.)

A quintessential philanthropic act: the neighborhood barn raising. These acts of voluntary philanthropy occurred throughout the state. This one took place near Brown City. (Courtesy of State Archives of Michigan)

Though weeding out frauds and loafers was the charity reformers' initial task, the movement's aims eventually became more interventionist. By the late 1880s and early 1890s, charity workers began using their vaults of accumulated information to help the poor change

Mary Sagatoo was nothing if not the very image of a proper Victorian Era woman. Devoutly religious, kind, and charitable to a fault (some of her philanthropic instincts would cause difficulties for her), Sagatoo was different from her genteel Boston counterparts in one significant way: she married a Chippewa chief and moved to Michigan.

No doubt shattering the stereotypes of the day, the young Chippewa, Joseph Cabay, was university educated and, in fact, met his future wife while he was studying at Harvard. Married in Boston in 1863, the newlyweds were struck by tragedy while en route to Joseph's native Michigan— he became sick and died. Mary continued the journey, settled among the Chippewa, and began a religious school. Eventually, she married her husband's cousin, Peter Sagatoo, and undertook a variety of efforts to help the Chippewa who were settled near the former village of Saganing, north of Bay City. (The tribe later was moved to a reservation near Mount Pleasant.)

Mary Sagatoo

Sagatoo lived with the Chippewa for decades. Her charitable work included teaching; collecting food supplies and clothing; obtaining medical help during epidemics; soliciting money from friends and relatives in Boston to help build a church; and traveling to Washington, D.C., to seek financial support for church construction from the U.S. Secretary of the Interior. For her trouble, she was not only turned down by the Interior Secretary, but chastised for having married not one, but two Native Americans. Instead of lambasting the Secretary, the ever-gracious Sagatoo (as she notes in her 1897 book Wah Sash Kah Moqua, or 33 Years Among the Indians) merely pointed out that she had married her Native American husbands one at a time.

> "The Indian heart is ever open to acts of kindness,"
>
> – Mary Sagatoo, Wah Sash Kah Moqua, 1897.

Although Sagatoo's efforts did ultimately provide a church, medical care, and food and clothing for those in the tribe who couldn't afford it, her philanthropic work did not always progress smoothly. After using all of her own money to travel to Bay City and purchase clothing, she realized she had provoked jealousy by not distributing new clothing to every member of the tribe. Another time, she and her husband used proceeds from the small store he operated to fund her travels to seek donations for the church; the store was forced to close as a result.

Sagatoo, however, remained relentlessly gracious, despite living in near-poverty, experiencing charitable failures, and being once (wrongly) accused by a tribesman of stealing from the church fund. Her devotion to religion is likely the reason.

"The Indian heart is ever open to acts of kindness," she wrote in her book. "They are not the brutal race they have been depicted. They possess traits of humanity which vie with those of their white brothers.

"Had the white man come to these shores in the same spirit of love and peace as did William Penn, Elliott, and other humanitarians who saw the image of God in the poor red man as in the white, how much suffering for both races might have been saved.

"Had the white man in all his dealings only been governed by Christian motives."

their lives. Once a needy family had been investigated, its moral flaws diagnosed, and a file established, charity workers could go about the task of effecting transformation.

Instead of feeding the vices of poor people by giving them money and resources they didn't earn, charity reformers argued, better to advise and counsel the poor so that they could become better—that is, middle-class and working—people. "Let there be a direct and personal helpfulness that usually leaves out of the count all financial dealings," the Grand Rapids Charity Society advised. "You are to give—what is far more precious than gold or silver— your own sympathy, and thought, and time, and labor."

Similarities to the "NO ALMS!" reformers of the beginning of the century are obvious, but the charity reformers of the 1870s were, in fact, different. They intentionally sought to separate philanthropy from the realm of the spiritual. The constitution of the Grand Rapids Charity Organization Society actually said as much: "The Society is to be kept free from all questions of religion." This extraction of religion from charity probably had much to do with the charity organization movement's goal of clearheaded, efficient, scientifically-applied philanthropy.

Though charity reformers duplicated the philosophy of the earlier reform movement by relying on the influence of a "friendly visitor," this era's visitor usually came with some training, or at least a list of rules and helpful hints to guide her (for indeed she usually was a she, and from a middle- or upper-class family). Ultimately, the charity organization movement would lead to the school of thought that conceived "friendly visitation" as a profession, laying the groundwork for the modern social worker.

Interestingly, although the reformers shared their earlier counterparts' belief in the friendly visitor's influence, they also shared the less moralistic view—seen in Detroit in the 1830s to 1850—that city life itself was partly to blame for poverty. Life in urban areas, they believed, was responsible for separating the urban poor from the social ties and neighborliness that might have provided a moral uplift outside the city.

There was, indeed, room to point a waggling finger at Michigan's cities, if for no other reason than that there were suddenly so many of them. After the Civil War ended, the state, like the rest of the country, went back to the business of growing, and cities popped up all over. Sometimes the growth was too rapid, and a city's ability to keep pace—in terms of housing, food supplies, jobs, and health standards—was lacking.

Besides poverty, Michigan cities had many other problems. Near the top of the list were poor or nonexistent streets, inadequate sewage treatment facilities, and crime.

The Ladies Library Association of Kalamazoo erected the first building in the United States built specifically as the headquarters of a women's club. The 1879 structure remains the Association's home today. (Courtesy of Western Michigan University Archives and Regional History Collections and the Ladies Library Association)

Contaminated water supplies were a growing concern and often contributed to regional epidemics. East Saginaw alone would spend more than $500,000 on sewage facilities between 1866 and 1889.

Mind-boggling for its time, the size of that figure illustrates the incredible population and economic growth in the Saginaw area as a result of the state's burgeoning agricultural business and lumber industry. Michigan had long been agricultural, but agriculture was beginning to be recognized as a source for profit, not merely the foundation for self-sufficiency among the pioneers. And no recounting of the state's history would be complete without a mention of the lumber industry.

When Pine Was King

Once the eastern states were stripped of white pine, Michigan became the leading supplier of the lumber much beloved by the nineteenth-century building industry. In a single year—1870—the value of the state's timber products was $32 million. Three years later, Michigan was home to some 1,600 sawmills, with a combined annual production of $40 million. More than 24,000 people were working in the state's lumber industry by 1880 and, a decade later, Michigan led the nation in all areas of lumber production.

Because both peninsulas were so forest-rich, little of the state escaped unscathed. Although Saginaw became a major trade center largely because of the lumbering done in that vicinity, the timber industry was going wild everywhere, creating new cities and residential centers even in the previously underdeveloped northern Lower Peninsula and Upper Peninsula. The lumber barons marched their troops across the state, leaving behind ghost towns and vast fields of stumps where virgin forests once stood. By the turn of the century, Michigan's forests were so heavily logged that the industry was forced to move on to new stands of tall trees in the Northwest.

Many fortunes, and much philanthropy, have been carved out of Michigan forests. To accommodate the country's insatiable appetite for lumber, timbermen worked year-round. Logs were piled on sleds and pulled out of the woods over iced trails. Here, horses draw a towering load to Wisconsin Land and Lumber Company in Hermansville in the 1880s. (Courtesy of State Archives of Michigan)

In Carnegie's Footsteps

This is not to suggest that all of those in the lumber industry were robber barons. The industry employed thousands of people and accounted for much of the growth in civic works that occurred across the state during that time. In addition, many of the men who grew rich from Michigan timber believed in a type of public stewardship best reflected by steel baron Andrew Carnegie's "Gospel of Wealth." Carnegie believed that the rich had an obligation to share their wealth in ways that benefited the public. However, he was most decidedly not a socialist or a communist or a radical anticapitalist. On the contrary, Carnegie believed that the concentration of wealth in the hands of a few leading industrialists (such as himself) was "not only beneficial but essential to the future of the race." Those most fit to receive this boundless wealth (as selected through a type of social Darwinism) would, he said, bring order and efficiency out of the chaos of rapid industrialization.

Unlike earlier philanthropists, Carnegie and those who subscribed to his views envisioned a society held together by institutions bestowed by the rich and patronized by the "fit." The endowment of libraries, universities, art galleries, public parks, and concert halls all fell within the patron's sphere. If great wealth were properly administered, Carnegie claimed, "the ties of brotherhood may still bind together the rich and poor in harmonious relationship."

Marquette's Peter White was closely associated with banking, insurance, mining, shipping, railroads, higher education—in short, almost every venture that brought growth and development to the city and region. (Courtesy of Marquette County Historical Society)

Lumber and shipping were among the Michigan industries in which early fortunes were made, thanks to the state's abundant natural resources. Shown here is the schooner Day Spring of the Buckley and Douglas Lumber Company of Manistee. (Courtesy of State Archives of Michigan)

"Soon the news of 'Half the State of Michigan on Fire' called us to action on our own laws of civil relief," wrote Clara Barton in 1881. She was referring to a fire that devastated St. Clair, Lapeer, Tuscola, Huron, and Sanilac counties in the Michigan Thumb that year. The catastrophe prompted the first-ever disaster relief project of the American Red Cross, the agency organized just weeks before by Barton in her hometown of Dansville, New York. The fledgling organization sent eight boxes of clothing, a little money, and its first field representative, Dr. Julian B. Hubbell, to survey the fire relief work. (The bulk of the assistance to victims came from state relief organizations, particularly the Port Huron Relief Committee.)

The calamity to which Barton responded was not really a "natural" disaster. It was helped along by an industry run amok. Logging in the Thumb had peaked in the early 1870s, with sawmills chewing up hundreds of thousands of acres of towering virgin forest. Left in the lumbermen's wake was a desolate landscape dotted with stumps and 15-foot high piles of "slashings," the logs and branches rejected by the logging company inspectors. The slashings became tinder for horrendous fires that raged through the state many times in the next decade.

After a dry summer in a logging region, any spark could ignite the piles of bone-dry branches. And, many summers, sparks did just that—wiping out whole towns in Michigan and Wisconsin. But for Thumb residents, the worst came in September 1881, after a hot summer with little rain. Small fires were burning throughout the denuded forests of the area when, on September 5, a southwestern gale whipped the flames out of control.

Darkness fell over settlements in the inferno's path, but then the smoke was chased away by "a solid wall of flame from 50 to 100 feet high," one witness said. Another remembered the wind "increased to a hurricane, and … with a horrible roaring bore the insatiable flames with the speed of a race-horse."

The fire engulfed the region for three days, and Bad Axe, Ubly, and Huron City were destroyed. To escape the smoke and flames, people hid in wells or lay covered with wet blankets in the fields. Some fled to Lake Huron and spent the night immersed in the water.

Many did not escape. The fire killed more than 280 and, in destroying 3,400 buildings, left 15,000 people without homes. It also wiped out telegraph poles and rail lines, leaving water the only conduit for communication. Ironically, a shortage of lumber forced families to bury children together, two or three to a coffin.

The tragedy was a metaphor for the fate of the state's timber industry. In only a few short years, Michigan would be so heavily logged that timber barons would move on to greener pastures, and the residents who stayed behind would be left to contend with its unfortunate—and munificent—legacies.

MICHIGAN'S
TERRIBLE CALAMITY.

DANSVILLE SOCIETY OF THE

RED CROSS.

A CRY FOR HELP!

The Dansville Society of the Red Cross, whose duty it is to accumulate funds and material, to provide nurses and assistants if may be, and hold these for use or service in case of war, or other national calamity—has heard the cry for help from Michigan. Senator O. D. Conger wrote on the 9th of September that he had just returned from the burnt region. Bodies of more than 200 persons had already been buried, and more than 1500 families had been burned out of everything. That was in only twenty townships in two counties. He invoked the aid of all our people. The character and extent of the calamity cannot be described in words. The manifold horrors of the fire were multiplied by fearful tornadoes, which cut off retreat in every direction. In some places whole families have been found reduced to an undistinguishable heap of wasted and blackened blocks of flesh, where they fell together overwhelmed by the rushing flames. For the dead, alas ! there is nothing but burial. For the thousands who survive, without shelter, without clothing, without food, whose every vestige of a once happy home has been swept away, haply much, everything, can be done. The Society of the Red Cross of Dansville proposes to exercise its functions in this emergency, and to see to it that sympathy, money, clothing, bedding, everything which those entirely destitute can need, shall find its way promptly to them. But the society is in its infancy here. It has in fact barely completed its organization. It has not in possession for immediate use the funds and stores which will in future be accumulated for such emergencies. It calls therefore upon the generous people of Dansville and vicinity to make at once such contributions, money or clothing, as their liberal hearts and the terrible exigency must prompt them to make. Our citizens will be called upon for cash subscriptions, or such subscriptions may be left with James Faulkner, Jr., Treasurer of the Society, at the First National Bank of Dansville. Contributions of Clothing and Bedding may be left at 154 Main street, Maxwell Block, Sewing Machine Agency of Mrs. John Sheppard.

A special agent of the Society will be dispatched with the money and goods to see to their proper distribution. Please act promptly.

EXECUTIVE COMMITTEE RED CROSS.

Dansville, Sept. 13, 1881.

DANSVILLE ADVERTISER STEAM PRINT.

(Photo courtesy of State Archives of Michigan)

In a somewhat more condescending vein, Carnegie said, "The millionaire will be but a trustee for the poor, entrusted for a season with a great part of the increased wealth of the community, but administering it for the community far better than it could or would have done for itself."

Carnegie's Gospel of Wealth is best summarized in the following quote from his 1889 "Wealth" article: "The man who dies thus rich dies disgraced." While Carnegie did not die a poor man, he left a splendid legacy in literally thousands of public library buildings across the United States and assorted Carnegie foundations and endowments for benevolent purposes.

Carnegie's views inspired many who carved their fortunes from Michigan's white pine forests: Charles Hackley of Muskegon; Katherine Bonifas of Escanaba (whose wealth came from her husband); and Wellington Burt, Arthur Hill, Aaron T. Bliss, and Arthur Eddy, all of Saginaw. Certainly, there were others. Today, their legacies live on—among them are Alma College; Bay City's Sage Library; Saginaw's Hoyt Library; and, in Muskegon, many parks, hospitals, schools, a library, and an art gallery. The lumbermen may have devastated the state's forests, but they did penance in community good works.

Their Gospel of Wealth, however, would not end poverty, which was about to worsen considerably as the country was devastated by another economic depression. Tens of thousands would be left jobless, poverty-stricken, and starving as a result of the Panic of 1893. That depression, the greatest the nation had seen thus far, would be an important benchmark for philanthropy, social thought, and politics. In short, philanthropy was about to change again. Call it progress. Or call it the Progressive Movement.

1890s-1918

Decades of Transition:

Depression, Progressivism, and the Great War

3

"In a progressive country, change is constant and inevitable."

—Former British Prime Minister Benjamin Disraeli

Families like the Gnageys of Pennsylvania moved to Michigan soon after a tornado wiped out their barn, c. 1895. (Courtesy of Gnagey family collection)

(Chapter overleaf photos courtesy of State Archives of Michigan)

***N**ot long after Disraeli uttered these words, change did to the United States what a tornado can do to a barn: set the stage for something new, while making one heck of a mess.

In U.S. socioeconomic terms, the "tornado" was the financial Panic of 1893, which appeared on the horizon suddenly (although, in retrospect, some warning signs had existed). One day in May of that year, a major railroad filed for bankruptcy. Next, the stock market tumbled. Soon, banks and businesses were collapsing across the country—an inexplicable occurrence to many who still considered the United States the land of opportunity. Others, however, such as gloom-and-doomsayer Henry Adams, saw the Panic as evidence that the nation's business magnates were attempting to establish a tyrannical food chain, with themselves at the top and ordinary working citizens at the bottom.

For most, it didn't much matter whether the Panic was a temporary aberration or a symptom of deep-seated injustice; the net effect was the same. Businesses closed, people lost their jobs, banks failed, industrial production plummeted, and fear of a currency shortage swept the nation. By winter, a full-fledged depression had settled in. Unfortunately, it didn't appear to be going anywhere in a hurry, and the winter of 1893-94 proved to be a long, dark one. Relief agencies across the country suddenly found themselves overwhelmed by the thousands of honest workers and their families left unemployed, homeless, and destitute. It soon became apparent to many that the charity reform movement's disparaging view of almsgiving, if not fundamentally flawed from the beginning, was at least outdated. The Panic and ensuing depression afflicted millions without prejudice: rich, poor, middle-class, charitable, greedy, hardworking, lazy.

Kalamazoo immigrants of Dutch heritage could seek assistance from the Holland American Aid Society in the case of sickness, accidents, or death. Organized in 1904, the society also promoted "social relations" among its members. (Courtesy of Western Michigan University Archives and Regional History Collections)

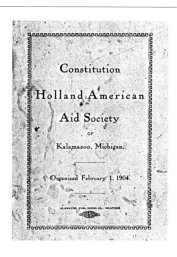

Constitution

Holland American

Aid Society

OF

Kalamazoo, Michigan.

Organized February 1, 1904.

KALAMAZOO PUBLISHING CO., PRINTERS

Residents of Bruce Crossing, a tiny community in the Upper Peninsula, gather for the train's arrival. At the turn of the century, the railroad was an important link to the rest of the world. (Courtesy of State Archives of Michigan)

So all-encompassing was the crisis that it ultimately shook many people's belief in good, old-fashioned American opportunity. As one political journal noted, even many of those in the European press jumped on the U.S. Doom-and-Despair Express; one London business publication, for example, termed the Panic "a fiasco unprecedented even in [the United States'] broad experience," and proceeded to rip our fine country's economic system, financial institutions, building practices, and trade policies into a pile of inferior American shreds.

Unfortunately, the economic chaos of 1893 came on so quickly and with such wide-reaching effect that charitable organizations had little time to adapt. About the best they could do was give out as much relief as they could, as quickly as they knew how. For some of those in the charity organization societies, which for years had preached that almsgiving aided primarily the fraudulent and the lazy, the depression must have been a tad embarrassing.

In 1919, with medical care for African-American families poor to nonexistent, the Detroit Urban League established a baby clinic at its community center. Trained personnel taught mothers better methods for caring for their children.
(Courtesy of State Archives of Michigan)

For several years after 1880, Detroit was recognized as the stove-making capital of the world. The giant stove displayed at the Detroit-Michigan Stove Company on Jefferson Avenue was constructed for the Chicago Columbian Exposition of 1893.
(Courtesy of Detroit Public Library Burton Historical Collection)

52

Caroline Bartlett Crane

Imagine the looks that passed among Kalamazoo's burly street cleaners: a certain middle-aged woman had just dropped by again, at 3 a.m., to make sure their technique was up to par. Undoubtedly, the men knew she was no one to be trifled with; Caroline Bartlett Crane (1858-1935) had earned quite a reputation in the city (and state and nation, for that matter) as America's Public Housekeeper.

Crane personified the Progressive Movement. Her no-nonsense life was committed to social justice and a more cleanly, orderly world. She began her crusade from the pulpit, as a preacher ordained by the Iowa State Unitarian conference. (The Iowa Unitarians were no fools. They welcomed women ministers, who would settle for low salaries and small churches in frontier towns.) Crane preached for a while in Dakota Territory before coming to the First Unitarian Church in Kalamazoo.

When she arrived in 1889, she found a divided congregation chiefly interested in her ability to perform funeral ceremonies. She soon inspired the parishioners to unite in a cohesive, enthusiastic group—a significant feat, given that her nondenominational congregation included liberal and orthodox Christians, Jews, Moslems, Christian Scientists, and Spiritualists. She led them in local charity work that included distributing food and clothing to the needy, ousting a crooked county official, organizing a study club for African-American women, and forming a local women's labor union.

The preacher shocked everyone when, at 38, she married a local doctor 10 years her junior, Augustus Warren Crane, M.D., one of the nation's pioneer radiologists. Her numerous roles—wife, community activist, pastor—were exhausting, and Crane resigned her pastorate in 1898. That freed her to go full-throttle at what she called her "civic ministry."

In 1901, Crane's report on conditions at Kalamazoo slaughterhouses led to passage of a state law that allowed local governments to enact ordinances for meat hygiene. She led an inspection of poorhouses the same year, and put a statewide plan in place to provide better medical care for poorhouse residents. Her efforts to clean up the streets of downtown Kalamazoo gained national attention: by day, sanitation workers in white suits and brooms patrolled the byways; at night, the city's firemen hosed down the streets.

A few years later, President Theodore Roosevelt asked Crane to critique new federal meat inspection regulations. She reported that the new guidelines were useless and alleged a conspiracy between meat packers and federal meat inspectors, making public secret USDA documents to back up her claim. The USDA emerged tarnished, but little changed by Crane's allegations. (Meaningful reforms in meat inspection weren't passed until 1967 and 1972.)

Crane's most ambitious project took place between 1906 and 1916, when she was invited by 62 cities in Michigan, Kentucky, and Minnesota to investigate their social and sanitary conditions. She systematically observed each community's water supply, sewers, street sanitation, garbage collection, milk and meat supplies, schools, poorhouses, hospitals, prisons, orphanages, and other institutions. Her findings were described in public speeches and were often published as guidelines for reform.

When the United States entered World War I, Crane registered 900,000 women for volunteer service in her office as president of the Michigan Women's Committee of National Defense. Her patriotic dedication to this post was belatedly repaid a few years later: in 1920, at age 62 and after decades of service to her city, state, and country, the Twentieth Amendment to the U.S. Constitution allowed Crane to vote in a national election for the first time.

Now they were dispensing relief to people even *they* had to admit were decent, hardworking folk. Small wonder that the charity organization societies went about the business of giving with little fanfare. They distributed only a limited amount of relief (they had not, as you'll recall, been organized with any structure for acquiring funds for distribution), and generally did so quietly and after only cursory investigations.

Michigan relief agencies that had not previously fallen under the umbrella of the charity organization movement did the best they could to increase the amount of aid they provided. Private associations started soup kitchens and inexpensive or free lodging houses. In Kalamazoo, an extraordinary woman named Caroline Bartlett Crane, who was minister of the

Detroit Mayor Hazen S. Pingree (second from left) helped battle the Panic of 1893 by giving unemployed citizens vacant land for gardens. Here, he inspects one of the "Pingree Potato Patches" that won him enormous popularity with voters. (Photo courtesy of *Detroit News*)

city's People's Church (Unitarian), helped organize the collection and distribution of food and supplies for the needy. Even newspapers across the state got into the act, creating special relief funds and distributing food and fuel. *The Evening Press* in Grand Rapids, for example, opened a supply warehouse where donations for the needy could be dropped off and distributed and also operated a cart to pick up donated supplies. "Anything, everything is needed," the newspaper reported in December of 1893. "Get it out, take it to a *Press* station and the 'Good Cheer' cart will call for it. Food, too, is in demand—anything that will stave off hunger and cold."

Despite this patchwork of efforts, the scope of the depression overwhelmed charitable organizations and agencies. Michigan philanthropy, like charity across the country, had not been prepared—psychologically or materially—for such wholesale need. For the first time on a large scale, public works projects were organized to help fill

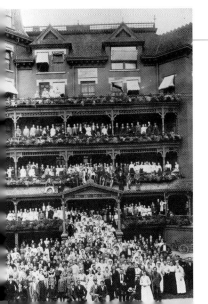

The Battle Creek Sanitarium, founded by the Seventh-Day Adventist Church as the Western Health Reform Institute in 1866, was transformed into a major health "spa" after 1875 by Dr. John Harvey Kellogg. Dr. Kellogg, remembered today primarily because his younger brother Will Keith founded the Kellogg Company and the W.K. Kellogg Foundation, was a health reformer who believed in the efficacy of a vegetarian diet, regular exercise, and fresh air long before the rest of the medical profession embraced these principles. (Courtesy of Willard Library Local History Collection)

Hazen S. Pingree

(Photo courtesy of State Archives of Michigan)

Few politicians have been as good a friend to the common man as Hazen S. Pingree (1840-1901), three times mayor of Detroit and twice Michigan's governor. He was a Republican who had the foresight to be one of government's earliest advocates of such reforms as a graduated income tax, an eight-hour workday, and direct election of U.S. senators—all of which became law well after he left office. He was, however, best known nationwide for a much smaller project: Pingree's Potato Patches.

"Ping" was elected mayor after running Pingree and Smith, a successful shoe manufacturing company, for many years. This businessman was accustomed to getting his money's worth on any investment, and he felt the citizens of Detroit should expect no less. His all-out attack on municipal abuses targeted shoddy street paving, gouging by the local utilities, inflated street railway fares, and ridiculously low tax assessments for business properties.

Poor Ping was surprised when prominent citizens—the very people who urged him to seek public office—turned against him, snubbed him socially, and opposed his re-election. Of course, his former friends owned stock in the utilities and the lightly taxed properties.

But the common folk recognized a friend when they saw one and re-elected Ping three times. He made the gas company lower its rates, and, when he couldn't force the electric companies to do the same, built a new power plant that saved the citizenry an enormous $104 per lamp per year.

When the Panic of 1893 put thousands out of work, Ping borrowed vacant lots and suggested that residents use them to grow their own vegetables. He even sold his favorite horse and donated the proceeds—$380—to the seed fund. Ping's gardens flourished and other cities adopted the mayor's plan.

In 1896, Ping was elected governor. In Lansing, his reformist agenda was opposed tooth and nail. His struggle with the railroad lobby is one example. Ping thought the wealthy, well-established railroads no longer deserved tax-exempt status. His proposal to tax the railroads was blocked repeatedly by state senators and the state Supreme Court but it eventually made it to the ballot and was passed by a majority of the voters. Still the Senate balked, refusing to implement the amendment until after Ping left office.

Disillusioned, Ping retired after two terms as governor. In a bitter final address to the Legislature in 1901, he said, "It is your special privilege and duty to bring the so-called 'merchant princes' and 'captains of industry' in this country to a realization of the fact that our laboring men are something more than tools to be used in the senseless chase after wealth."

The same year, he went off to hunt elephants in Africa, bagged one, traveled on to visit friends in London, and died there. A huge public funeral in Detroit must have convinced lawmakers that Ping was no longer a threat; they passed a resolution in praise of his sterling character.

the gap. Various local governments created centers for woodcutting and stone-breaking, and sewing shops to provide for the poor. In addition, many special projects were implemented to give jobs to unemployed workers—street sweeping, sewer construction, road paving, and building construction.

By the onset of the Panic, Detroit had grown into an industrial powerhouse and was a major producer of railroad cars, stoves, pharmaceuticals, and ships. Because industry was particularly hard-hit by the depression, Detroit's citizens suffered acutely. One business after another slashed its employment rolls or closed its doors. Even the local Pullman railroad car production plant shut down completely at the height of the depression. Though the plant was relatively small by Pullman standards, the railroad car business had been so entrenched in Detroit, and Pullman was such an icon in the railroad car industry, that the closing struck a dismally symbolic chord.

In the midst of all of this, Detroit Mayor Hazen S. Pingree came up with the idea of allowing the city's poor and unemployed to plant their own gardens on vacant city land, free of charge. Potatoes were among the more popular crops, and Pingree sold one of his own horses to help raise money for seeds. Although the garden plot plan was not a major remedy for the devastation of the depression, we can safely assume that the people who benefited from the program were less concerned with its effect on economic indicators than with its effect on their stomachs. Pingree's plan was a catchy idea, perhaps because of its practicality and

In the 1890s, more than one of every 10 Michiganians lived in Detroit, which would become the thirteenth largest city in the United States by 1900. Here, open-air streetcars, horse-drawn vehicles, bicycle riders, and pedestrians move at a leisurely pace through downtown Detroit's Cadillac Square. (Courtesy of *Detroit News*)

low overhead, and many cities across the country emulated it—Buffalo, Brooklyn, New York City, and Toledo, to name a few.

With the mayor of the state's largest city encouraging hungry people to plant potatoes on vacant lots, it's apparent that things were bad, indeed, between 1893 and 1897. Still, it's important to note that this particular depression was not as severe as the one that hit the United States in the 1870s. *The Journal of Political Economics* notes that major economic activities fell about one-fourth during the 1893-97 depression, compared to one-third during the depression in the 1870s (and about one-half during the Great Depression, which would begin in 1929).

Why was it that the depression of the 1890s, if not as severe as that of the 1870s, caused so much more panic, self-doubt, and philosophical convulsions? Possibly it was because the generation of the 1870s still recalled the privations of the Civil War, while that of the 1890s had been used to much higher standards of health, welfare, and economic activity. In any case, while life at the turn of the new century was no picnic for the average worker, neither was it as bleak as the public sentiment suggested. Also, the wealth that had been accumulated by ever-increasing numbers of people in the 1880s did not stay under lock and key during the depression. In New York City alone, up to $5 million in relief funds was distributed in 1893-94.

A New Philanthropy

Admittedly, philanthropy was unable to keep pace with the need created by the depression, but it's difficult to find any point in U.S. history when charity was able to meet all needs. At least as significant as the increased demand for relief was the change in the philanthropic point of view. After depression struck in the 1870s, philanthropy believed the needy were deficient or fraudulent. When depression came again two decades later, these attitudes were challenged, debated, and ultimately considered by many to be lacking in compassion and understanding. This is not to say that everyone was sold on the idea of charity, even with a larger-than-life depression in progress. Many charity reformers still stepped up to the lectern to denounce almsgiving; Josephine Shaw Lowell continued to advocate low-paying, unpleasant working conditions for public warfare projects; and many business leaders feared that too much generosity might lead to socialism and ruination for the country.

However, as the "temporary" distress of the winter of 1893-94 grew into a long-term crisis, as years went by without a significant solution to the unemployment problem,

The arts were supported by many in the state's largest city. In 1898, fire destroyed the Detroit Opera House, which brought to that city a continuous series of popular plays and musicals. The reconstructed building is illustrated here on the cover of its weekly program booklet. (Courtesy of Detroit Public Library Burton Historical Collection)

Natural disasters like the tornado that demolished Fowlerville in 1909 brought "everyday philanthropy"— neighbors helping neighbors—to the fore. Here, the community's Catholic Church is roofless and heavily damaged, but still standing. (Courtesy of State Archives of Michigan)

the phrases "self-help" and "self-made man" began to sound hollow. Public officials, private philanthropists, ordinary citizens, and even many in the charity organization movement began to believe that poverty was not a *cause* of social problems and injustices, but a *result*. For instance, Margaret Stansbury, president of the Detroit Day Nursery, a charity organization, stated in 1893 that she thought the social order needed to be examined. "Progress for the whole community" had to be considered as a treatment for pauperism, she said.

At the time, this was a radical notion. But Stansbury was about to have a lot of company. By the time the depression eased in 1898, newer and younger charity workers were decrying the repressive attitudes of their elders. They took new social science classes at universities and spurned the survival-of-the-fittest philosophy of social Darwinists. Instead, they embraced an emerging philosophy that sought to use human intelligence to help as many people as possible survive and thrive, and they prompted educators, workers, and private citizens to fight against the inequalities in society. Progressivism was fanning out across the country almost as rampantly as the Panic had before it.

But to call Progressivism a purely social or philanthropic phenomenon would be inaccurate. It also was a political event: political parties and alliances changed their platforms and goals as the result of progressive thinking. Widespread tax reform was one of the outcomes, leading to the nation's first income tax in 1913. In 1917, Congress would allow for the deduction of charitable contributions, setting the stage for wholesale growth in the number of nonprofit institutions and foundations.

At the turn of the century, the Northeastern Michigan Development Bureau worked to bring business and industry into one of the state's less-populated regions. (Courtesy of State Archives of Michigan)

Other political manifestations of the Progressive era included public ownership of many utilities and improvements in government health standards. Caroline Bartlett Crane, for example, would fight tirelessly for stricter inspections in the meatpacking industry. Corruption in politics and business had led to epidemics, such as typhoid, in some U.S. cities where privately-owned water companies had lobbied for and obtained political approval—formal or otherwise—for lax water-quality standards. Progressivism was, in part, the public's way of saying it had had enough of government's failure to act.

But Progressivism also was a phenomenon related to class struggle—labor unrest and unionization became widespread during the Progressive era, as indicated by the bloody Pullman strike in Illinois and the numerous strikes and labor disputes that erupted during and after the depression. Mostly, however, Progressivism was a way of thinking—a public realization that a new era was dawning.

During World War I, most Fisher Body employees were female—proof that women worked in factories long before Rosie the Riveter became a World War II icon. (Courtesy of Bentley Historical Library University of Michigan)

In the philanthropic arena, the depression helped solidify the notion of charity as social responsibility, as opposed to religious duty—an idea that helped create the settlement houses. Originating in England, the concept of a settlement house, in which charity workers would take up residence in a neighborhood of poor people and immigrants, emerged in the late 1880s. By the turn of the century, settlement houses had opened in most large U.S. cities. Their purpose was to give the financially secure an opportunity to gain new insight into poverty by establishing relationships with them and by, essentially, sharing their lives. The goal was to help and learn simply by being a good neighbor. Although Jane Addams, one of the founders of Hull House in Chicago, was among the most prominent of the settlement house workers, Michigan was not left out of the movement. Grand Rapids, for example, had the Bissell House, which opened in 1897, and Detroit was home to the Hannah Schloss Settlement, which was started in the early 1900s as a community center and charity headquarters for the city's Jewish residents, primarily immigrant families. The Schloss Settlement hosted a variety of programs, including a day nursery for working mothers, social and cultural programs, a boys club, and classes in English, stenography, and domestic science. The settlement also offered a library, gymnasium, and bathing facilities; provided medical and legal services; and distributed relief.

Bissell House, constructed in 1897 in one of Grand Rapids' poorest neighborhoods, was typical of the settlement houses organized at the turn of the century. Residents came to the Ottawa Avenue house for classes, social gatherings, fresh water, and bathing facilities.
(Courtesy of Local History Department, Grand Rapids Public Library)

Across the country, the new progressive philanthropy also worked to help poor people "get ahead." In Michigan, for example, several charities organized "Success Clubs." As the president of the Lansing Bureau of Charities explained it, the clubs sought "to enable a youth to do well and fully the particular thing he is interested in, even though it be a mere fad." In the late 1890s, some charities started "Penny Savings Societies" to encourage thriftiness and financial independence among the poor. In Kalamazoo, hundreds participated in the program; by 1904, the society's total deposits had reached $5,000. However, one charity administrator's comments indicate that, Progressivism notwithstanding, some of the middle- and upper-class women in charge of the program still had no true grasp of deep-seated, day-in and day-out poverty:

"[The $5,000] represents pennies, nickels and quarters, which might have been given to the candyman, the saloon-keeper, etc., but which was saved with a definite purpose

This World War I poster, c. 1917, urged Americans to do their part for one of the nationally organized wartime causes.
(Courtesy of Western Michigan University Archives and Regional History Collections)

Jewish Philanthropy

Michigan's philanthropic heritage has been broadened by almost every group that has lived within the state's borders: Native Americans, Europeans, Catholics, Puritans, African-Americans, Latinos, Asian-Americans, and more. Yet another significant charitable tradition in the state is Jewish philanthropy.

By 1850, about a dozen Jewish families had arrived in Detroit from Germany—enough to form the city's first synagogue, Beth El. At the time, 21,000 people lived in the city. By the end of the century, thanks to the tremendous influx of Jewish immigrants from Eastern Europe, Detroit's Jewish community increased to 5,000 in a city of 300,000.

As with many of America's earlier immigrants, Jewish families came to the new world to escape restrictions in their homeland. For people of Judaic beliefs, however, the restrictions were particularly harsh—they could not own land, attend universities, or practice certain trades. As Jewish immigrants poured into Detroit (and Cleveland, Atlanta, and Milwaukee), the problems of adjustment and relief grew apace. Many immigrants were poor and didn't speak English well, if at all. They needed shelter, clothing, medicine, jobs, and most important, to feel welcomed by others of their faith.

Responding to the need, and continuing a strong tradition of caring for their own, Detroit's Jewish community formed charitable groups centered in its synagogues. Typical was a group of Beth El choir girls, who began sewing clothing for immigrant children in 1889. One of the congregation's older women suggested teaching the children to sew for themselves and, by 1904, the Beth El Self-Help Circle was teaching not only sewing but cooking, cleaning, and English to more than 200 students.

This focus on building self-sufficiency was typical of charitable work among Jewish residents. Also typical was a fervent belief in Americanization, frequently the subject of sermons and articles and the theme for social

United Jewish Charities brought philanthropists from many organizations together to provide a broad range of programs for youth. (Courtesy of Jewish Federation of Metropolitian Detroit)

and even religious events. Hanukkah parties for children included "Red Riding Hood" lantern shows, Passover became an occasion for sermons about George Washington, and congregations held large prayer meetings on America's national holidays.

Despite their increasing acculturation, however, most of those in Detroit's Jewish population wished to retain their religious and cultural identity. Philanthropy was one way to do that, and their enthusiasm created an abundance of independent groups that often duplicated each other's efforts and competed for limited funds. To make better use of the community's resources, Rabbi Leo Franklin of Beth El convinced the Beth El Hebrew Relief Society, Hebrew Ladies' Sewing Society, Self-Help Circle, and Jewish Relief Society to join together in 1899 as United Jewish Charities (UJC), the city's first central Jewish philanthropic organization.

Over the years, UJC ran child-care programs, foster-care services, orphanages, employment bureaus, old-age homes, and clinics. It gave funds for burial services and interest-free loans, took children on day outings, and ran a camp on the shores of Lake St. Clair. ("Except for the delousing procedure performed at the start of each camping session, the children apparently had a wonderful time," one Jewish history book recounts.) The organization also offered classes in English, sewing, dancing, music, and manual training; held dances, concerts, and lectures; and sponsored a variety of youth and adult clubs. The UJC Relief Committee gave immigrants emergency money for food, rent, medical care, legal aid, and child care.

Funds for this work came from private donations and from money allocated by the temples. While the men determined how much of the temple's resources could be given to charity, the women decided where and how the money would be spent. UJC operated until 1926; it ultimately evolved into the Jewish Federation of Metropolitan Detroit, which thrives today.

Roberta Griffith

Practically everyone has heard of Helen Keller. It's likely far fewer have heard of the remarkable woman who said, "Anyone can do what Helen Keller did. Hard work, intelligence, good teachers, and proper facilities are all that a blind or seeing person requires."

Those are the words of Roberta A. Griffith (1870-1941), whose advocacy for the blind in Grand Rapids made an impression on a society that didn't much expect women—especially a blind woman—to make their own opportunity in the world, much less create opportunity for others. Left sightless by a childhood illness, this Philadelphia native wasn't satisfied with her education from schools for the blind in Michigan and Ohio. She won a scholarship from Western Reserve University in Cleveland and was admitted as its first blind student on a one-week trial basis. She quickly proved to her professors that she could cut it academically, then worked as a newspaper writer and music teacher to supplement her scholarship income before graduating with high honors.

Griffith arrived in Grand Rapids in 1900 to be near her elderly mother, whom she supported by working as a successful magazine writer and real estate agent. She lived on Sheldon Street, in a home that eventually became the headquarters for the Association for the Blind and for Sight Conservation, which Griffith founded in 1913. A score of women volunteers helped her complete a census of blind residents in Grand Rapids and then charted the state's first program in blindness prevention.

By 1922 the Association had served more than 1,400 people, some blind, some with seriously curtailed sight, some who needed blindness prevention services. Over the years, the Association's projects included providing sight-saving classes in the public schools, raising funds to purchase eyeglasses for needy children and adults, and conducting eye-health institutes for nurses, social workers, and teachers.

Recognizing that social events were as important to a sightless person as to anyone else, Griffith organized luncheon clubs for older men and women and convinced community groups to throw parties for her protégés. Her more serious work included authoring, in 1913, a bill for the Michigan Legislature that mandated the use of nitrate of silver in the eyes of newborn infants, a law that has saved the sight of thousands. Griffith also helped form the American Association of Workers for the Blind, compiled a six-volume dictionary for the blind, and worked to develop a single Braille print system for the United States.

On the home front, Griffith focused on finding jobs for people (mostly men) who were sightless. She also placed blind men in charge of news and concession stands at factories and public buildings. In her obviously limited spare time, Griffith penned a romance novel and took several transcontinental vacations alone.

In 1963, years after her death, Griffith's Association moved to Grand Rapids' Mary Free Bed Hospital to coordinate its efforts with other local programs. Renamed Vision Enrichment Services, the agency is active today, sponsoring, among other projects, a successful glaucoma screening program and a low-vision clinic that helps people use their remaining sight effectively.

for shoes, clothing, rent, a brace for a cripple[d] child and many other wise purposes. The result is plainly seen in my work in [the] District among the people who save. These people no longer come to me for a pair of shoes or a half ton of coal, instead they ask the Penny Savings collector to cash their books for the amount needed."

Helping the poor to save money, even pennies, was certainly a laudable cause. Still, mere pennies could not help those entrenched in poverty make it through a winter of unemployment, and setting money aside was likely an absurd notion to those who couldn't feed their children.

It makes sense, however, that some of the charitable programs and ideas that arose during the Progressive era would be less than perfect, simply because so many new activities, programs, and organizations were popping up. Philanthropists, to their credit, were trying novel things.

A New Voice for Women

Women's clubs were among the more pervasive new charitable forces during this era, and they sprang up across the United States and Michigan in impressive numbers. *Michigan History Magazine*, for example, notes that Jackson alone had more than 20 active women's clubs, while in Grand Rapids about 6,000 women participated in club activities in the late 1800s and early 1900s. Although women had long been involved in charity, and had long been active in women's clubs, the nature of the clubs' activities changed significantly during the Progressive era. Before, women attended meetings to discuss books and cultural issues. Now they gathered to plan charitable activities, discuss municipal failings, establish libraries, and make plans to improve the local educational systems. They also heard speakers on all sorts of issues, from health improvement and financial independence for women to socialism and anarchy. These activities must have surprised those husbands who thought their wives were off debating the literary merits of the various Brontë sisters.

While women's clubs tackled a wide array of social and philanthropic causes, municipal issues such as health, education, and general welfare were their universal concerns. In Lake Odessa, for example, club members persuaded the city

In 1920, after women gained the right to vote, members of the League of Women Voters became active in voter registration drives and in discussions of political issues. (Courtesy of Public Museum of Grand Rapids)

Salvation Army bell-ringers collecting coins and currency for the needy were (and still are) a common sight in Michigan cities. (Courtesy of Salvation Army National Archives and Research Center)

council to enact a curfew ordinance; in Dowagiac, women transformed an old cemetery into a park and playground; in Eaton Rapids, women brought about a city ordinance against spitting on the sidewalks; and clubwomen across the state, in such places as Battle Creek, Saginaw, Pontiac, and Royal Oak, engaged in community beautification projects.

Often, however, the women's efforts were stymied by their inability to vote. They could effect only those changes they could persuade men to sanction through city ordinances and state legislation. This limitation prompted many women to add "win suffrage" to their list of things to do. Although Crane and other suffragists convinced the Michigan Legislature to approve, in 1893, a bill allowing women to vote in local elections, the state Supreme Court threw it out. As was typical of the Progressive era, continuation of an injustice merely strengthened the reformers' resolve. In the case of suffrage, women who had been thwarted in their lobbying efforts now turned their eyes toward changing the basic laws and Constitution that allowed such discrimination. By the 1920s, as the Progressive Movement wound down, suffragists would win at the national level.

African-American Philanthropy

Although women's clubs seemed to have a gift for detecting social ills, one particular injustice—racial discrimination—failed to capture their attention to any significant degree. Generally, the state's white charitable organizations did not provide relief to African-Americans. African-Americans, however, began forming their own charities and social organizations during the Progressive era, including the national Sigma Pi Phi fraternity, founded in 1904 by a group of African-American men in Philadelphia, and a variety of clubs for African-American women in Michigan. The In As Much Circle of King's Daughters and Sons Club, founded in Detroit in 1895, is believed to have been the first African-American women's club in the state. Mary McCoy, wife of inventor Elijah McCoy, was one founder of that club, which dealt with such concerns as homelessness, poverty, and young motherhood. By 1920, Detroit would have at least eight clubs for African-

The Detroit Urban League provided much-needed recreational facilities for the city's African-American residents. Here, young men gather at the reading room in the League's community center in 1919. (Courtesy of State Archives of Michigan)

Here, c. 1930, the congregation of the St. Luke African Methodist Episcopal Church poses in front of the oldest African-American church in Grand Rapids, founded in 1863. During the Great Depression (and still today), small congregations willingly shouldered the burden of assisting those in need. (Courtesy of Local History Department, Grand Rapids Public Library)

These words attest to a significant development in philanthropy at the turn of the century: African-American women were organizing to take on the newest challenges to their race.

During the Progressive era, thousands of African-Americans left farms in the South and streamed into the growing cities of the North. Despite segregation and discrimination, some of them prospered, and a middle class emerged. Like their white counterparts, these African-Americans of more comfortable means lived in a social climate that encouraged service to others. And there were plenty of folks who needed that service; the main-stream, white, Christian charities of the day typically provided little, if any, aid to those of other races or religions.

To fill this void, African-American women banded together locally and, eventually, nationally to provide organized assistance. The National Association of Colored Women (NACW) boasted 1,000 clubs with 50,000 members by 1916. (This group was formed after African-American women's clubs were excluded from the General Federation of Women's Clubs, which, in the 1890s, became the national umbrella for white women's clubs of all kinds, such as literary guilds, church auxiliaries, and suffragist groups.)

The ladies of the African-American clubs were successful with sizable projects, including the organization of settlement houses, hospitals, day nurseries, and homes for children, working women, and the elderly. In Detroit, clubs such as the In As Much Circle of King's Daughters and Sons Club, the Lydian Association of Detroit, the Guiding Star, and the Willing Workers also responded to cases of individual need referred by other charities in the city.

One of the founders of the In As Much Circle club was Mary McCoy, wife of inventor Elijah McCoy (whose much-copied products, such as lubricating devices for steam engines, are responsible for the phrase "the Real McCoy"). Although Mary McCoy was a community leader and was the only African-American charter member of one of Detroit's most prestigious women's clubs of that era—the Twentieth Century Club—little is written about her. The absence of historical information about McCoy surely attests to the near-invisible status of African-Americans in Detroit at the turn of the century, and probably says something about the status of women generally, as well.

African-American women were acutely aware that they faced a societal double whammy: prejudice that sneered at both race and gender. True to their motto, "Lifting as We Climb," the clubs took a special interest in helping women in the laboring class. Fanny Barrier Williams explained the challenge of their mission: "Among colored women the club is the effort of the few competent in behalf of the many incompetent…. Among white women the club is the onward movement of the already uplifted."

During World War I, African-American women organized to conserve food and sponsor bond drives. With energy left over, they worked to improve health and safety in their own communities. Typical was the Detroit Colored Women's War Council, which organized food conservation programs and Patriotic Leagues for young African-American women. Its members also launched a "suppression of liquor campaign," arranged lodging for soldiers' families, and campaigned for better sanitation, police pro-tection, and street lighting.

In 1920, eight clubs in Detroit joined together as the Detroit Association of Colored Women's Clubs. When the group incorporated 20 years later, its president, Rosa Gregg, mortgaged her home, her car, and her husband's business to make a $2,000 down payment on a house that would become the association's permanent home. It was located on an all-white street, so the members were forced to put in a new door on a side street and change the building's address. This discrimination notwithstanding, the Detroit associa-tion reached peak membership in 1945, with 73 clubs and nearly 3,000 members.

> "*The old notion that woman was intended by the Almighty to do only those things that men thought they ought to do is fast passing away. In our day and in this country, a woman's sphere is just as large as she can make it and still be true to her finer qualities of soul.*"
>
> – African-American club member and lecturer Fannie Barrier Williams, 1904

American women. They addressed the same issues taken up by white women's clubs—urban strife, poverty, health problems, and unemployment—but in relation to African-Americans as the particular victims and beneficiaries.

City life took an especially hard toll on African-Americans. Many had fled the South for better jobs and living conditions in Michigan as the state grew into an industrial power before the Panic of 1893. Between 1860 and 1880, the state's African-American population grew from 6,799 to 15,100. Because of discrimination, they generally were less valued than whites in the workplace: African-Americans were almost always the first to lose their jobs in an economic recession and among the last to be re-employed when times improved.

After the Panic, and after the turn of the century, even more African-Americans flooded into the state. New factories were demanding new sources of labor, and Michigan was about to ride the Progressive era into a giddy, albeit temporary, Industrial Nirvana. The ride would come complete with gas-powered wheels.

Michigan Industry Booms

When the depression of 1893-97 lifted, the state's auto industry still was in its infancy. But the future looked bright. A number of men—Ransom Olds, Henry Leland, Will Barbour, John and Horace Dodge, and Henry Ford, among others—were busy perfecting their plans for gasoline-powered vehicles. Ford, of course, would go on to

Ransom E. Olds drives his gasoline-powered vehicle through the streets of Lansing in 1896. Until Henry Ford found success with his assembly line, Olds was the best-known automaker in Michigan. The vehicle pictured here was eventually given to the Smithsonian Institution. (Courtesy of State Archives of Michigan)

achieve incredible success and wealth after his company's moving assembly line became a fixture in the auto industry.

Despite its starring role, the auto industry was only a part of the state's rapidly expanding economic base. In the last half of the nineteenth century, such companies as Dow Chemical, Parke-Davis, and Upjohn (now Pharmacia & Upjohn), to name a few, burst upon the scene and, after the depression, experienced explosive growth. The Postum Company and the Battle Creek Toasted Corn Flakes Co. (today's Kellogg Company) started making cereal in Battle Creek in 1898 and 1906, respectively. Grand Rapids was becoming the country's furniture capital. The Detroit suburbs were producing giant cement and chemical companies, many of which obtained their supplies from northern lower Michigan and the Upper Peninsula (and established a variety of plants in northern Michigan in the process). Paper companies were springing up in the Kalamazoo area. Bay City was becoming a shipbuilding power. Flint was becoming an industrial powerhouse. All in all, the Progressive era was a time of tremendous business growth in Michigan.

This growth was particularly crucial to the state's philanthropic history. Suddenly, Michigan was home to a lot of people with a lot of money, and numerous affluent businessmen and women put their funds into good works in the state. As we will see in later chapters, the groundwork for large-scale corporate philanthropy and the development of large foundations in Michigan was being laid during the Progressive years, for the simple reason that significant sources of capital were being accumulated. As a result of its grand economic growth in the Progressive era, Michigan would become home to many of the nation's pioneering philanthropists and leading foundations.

Among the early (and somewhat unsung) philanthropic leaders in Michigan was Ransom E. Olds, founder of the Reo Motor Company. Although happy to promote his image as a penny-pincher, Olds—a devout Baptist who never smoked or drank—donated to numerous causes he and his wife believed in, including the YWCA and YMCA, and Kalamazoo College, a Baptist-affiliated institution. The Oldses also donated their summer home as a camp for the Lansing YWCA in 1908, purchased Lansing's old Sparrow Hospital for use as a day nursery for children of working mothers in 1912, and provided the land and building for the Ladies' Library and Literary Club in Lansing in 1914.

Most significantly for the future, however, Olds also created Michigan's first private foundation, the Ransom Fidelity

In 1913, Henry Ford's introduction of the moving assembly line cut in half the time it took to assemble a chassis. His innovation was the ultimate mass-production advance of the times. (Courtesy of State Archives of Michigan)

To help stamp out a dangerous disease, the Grand Rapids Anti-Tuberculosis Society killed and collected thousands of flies in 1916. (Courtesy of Local History Department, Grand Rapids Public Library)

Company, in 1915. Chartered for the purpose of supporting higher and secondary education, hospitals, youth agencies, cultural programs, churches, and animal welfare, it is today a family foundation with more than $4 million in assets.

As economic prosperity brought an increase in individual philanthropy in Michigan, it made its mark on organized charity, as well. Michigan, for example, was one of the first states in which a community foundation was established. (Cleveland, Ohio, was first in 1914, and still has one of the country's largest community foundations.) The Detroit Community Trust, established in 1915, was largely aimed at civic improvement projects. The Trust later became a private foundation and was eventually dissolved into the Community Foundation for Southeastern Michigan, which was legally established in the 1980s. The first community foundation in Michigan that has provided continuous service since its founding was the Grand Rapids Foundation, organized in 1922. The Kalamazoo Foundation followed five years later.

Michigan also would be one of the first states in which charitable organizations banded together to conduct joint fundraising efforts and to avoid duplication of services. For instance, between 1913 and 1917, the Associated Charities and the Board of Commerce of Detroit would work together to coordinate charity organizations. In 1917, benevolent societies in both Detroit and Grand Rapids launched what would later be known as "community chest" efforts, in which various charities were funded through a central organization. (At the national level, this cooperative approach would evolve into the modern United Way.)

War Relief In Michigan

Progressivism, and the new ideas it engendered, were about to run into a brick wall, or more specifically, a trench. In 1917, the United States joined the Great War, which had already left millions of soldiers dead in grisly warfare on French soil. Michigan industry retooled for the production of military equipment.

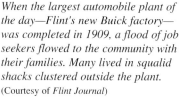

When the largest automobile plant of the day—Flint's new Buick factory— was completed in 1909, a flood of job seekers flowed to the community with their families. Many lived in squalid shacks clustered outside the plant.
(Courtesy of *Flint Journal*)

BE A VOLUNTEER

How to become a Fourth Liberty Loan Volunteer has been fully explained in the various issues of the Tribune and it is now up to the people of South Haven to make this plan a success.

The TRUE VOLUNTEER is the man or woman who makes immediate response to our government's appeal for funds with a subscription that represents the very limit of his or her financial resources or earning powers.

REMEMBER, you are not giving a penny, but are lending your money to THE BEST GOVERNMENT on EARTH which offers you the very highest security, both for your money, and for your person and property.

NEXT SATURDAY, SUNDAY and MONDAY ARE VOLUNTEER DAYS

WE ARE COUNTING ON YOU

South Haven War Board

During World War I citizens were urged not only to conserve food and to donate time and goods to the war effort, but also to loan money to Washington. Here, the South Haven War Board promises that the "Best Government on Earth" offers "the very highest security" for the donor's funds.
(Courtesy of *Photographic Memories - South Haven* by Richard Appleyard)

The state's charity organizations had begun contributing to the war effort when the slaughter began in Europe in 1914. Horrified by tales of atrocities—the "rape of Belgium" in particular inflamed sentiment in Allied countries—Michigan groups sent huge quantities of food to European refugees, war widows and orphans, and to injured soldiers. The Grand Rapids chapter of the Daughters of the American Revolution supported 10 French orphans throughout the war and sent money to pay for Sunday dinners for a Belgium orphanage. The Branch County Women's Club sewed and knitted more than 2,000

The Ann Arbor chapter of the Daughters of the American Revolution was typical of wartime charities that sent handmade clothing and other essentials to troops and refugees during World War I. (Courtesy of Bentley Historical Library University of Michigan)

African-American draftees at Camp Custer near Battle Creek were required to patronize only the "colored club," to live in "colored barracks," and to serve in segregated units. (Courtesy of State Archives of Michigan)

Katherine and Tracy McGregor

" ...to relieve the
misfortunes
and promote
the well being
of mankind"
—McGregor Fund Mission Statement

Work and contemplation: the pursuits that make us whole. This philosophy informed the work of a Michigan philanthropist who provided for the most basic needs of Detroit's sick and poor, and tried to feed their minds and souls, as well. A booklet published by the American Historical Association in 1937 notes that Tracy McGregor (1869-1936) felt, "if you can give a man a thought or idea, it may be as important as giving him a square meal or a new suit of clothes."

Between 1891 and 1935, more than 700,000 men received a hot meal, new duds, and a place to sleep at McGregor's mission, the McGregor Institute, on Larned Street. They also got a work assignment, encouragement to stick to the straight and narrow, and a bit of enlightenment. The booklet continues: "Often, during the past thirty years, [McGregor] could have been found on an evening in a mission in Detroit, reading aloud to derelict men, chapters or poems from his favorite books. What is more important, the unfortunates were listening."

Undoubtedly, they had little choice, but their benefactor's intentions were good. By all accounts, McGregor was a generous, modest, soft-spoken man with a knack for drawing others to his causes. Luckily for Detroit's poor, he moved in influential circles, partly because of his marriage to Katherine Whitney, daughter of a wealthy local businessman. They wed shortly after McGregor arrived in the city at age 22. An Ohio native, he dropped out of Oberlin College to move to Detroit when his father, who founded the then Helping Hand Mission, died suddenly.

McGregor changed the mission's name and was still operating it successfully when, in 1912, he called close associates together for another project, the Thursday Group. He proposed a weekly luncheon and discussion of the city's social problems and stressed that theirs would be a "doing" group: "We will put in our brains and hearts, and, when needed, our money, and will stand together for any good thing that seems possible and advisable to do."

In the years preceding World War I, the Thursday Group was responsible for effecting many "good things," including dramatic improvements in the court system, better care for people with epilepsy, and new city building codes. McGregor was also behind the formation of the Detroit Community Fund and Community Union—both predecessors of today's United Community Services. His goal was foresighted: bring the city's charities together to eliminate overlapping efforts, operate more economically, and plan for the common good.

Over the years, Tracy and Katherine contributed generously to higher education and to causes that benefited women and children, people with epilepsy, and people with developmental disabilities. In 1925, they established the McGregor Fund with a gift of $5,000. In the years before the McGregors' deaths, the fund supported the University of Michigan, the Wayne County Home for Feeble Minded, the Merrill Palmer Institute for women, and many other local and national charities. All told, the McGregors would give $10 million to the fund. Today, it has assets of more than $150 million.

Toward the end of his life, McGregor shared his lifelong love of books and early U.S. history with college libraries, making funds available for rare source books in American history. His own collection of rare books was donated to the Alderman Library at the University of Virginia upon his death.

garments for French and Belgian school children, while the Huron County branch, which was headed by the wife of Governor Albert Sleeper, sent a shipload of Christmas toys to Belgian and French children.

Once the United States entered the war in 1917, however, the state's charities expanded their efforts. As was often the case, particularly in war charities, women were the philanthropic workers (the men were off at battle). Called upon by National Food Administrator Herbert Hoover to pledge their help in conserving food to meet the war's demand for supplies, Michigan women (like women across the United States) went into a food-conservation frenzy. Petition drives, in which women signed their pledges to conserve food, were especially popular. Every single woman in Ontonagon County signed such a petition and, eventually, Michigan would secure more pledges than any other state. Posters everywhere bade women to make "Every Garden a Munitions Plant" and to remember that

In 1917, the YMCA conducted classes in French at Battle Creek's Camp Custer to help the troops prepare for their imminent arrival in Europe. (Courtesy of Western Michigan University Archives and Regional History Collections)

"We Can Can Vegetables and the Kaiser Too." Women volunteers held food conservation meetings and offered prizes for the best wheatless, meatless menus. Almost every community had a canning center where women could bring their produce. One woman in Isabella County even established a canning center in the middle of her flower and vegetable garden, where a "community canning" was held every Thursday morning.

In these efforts, war relief workers demonstrated two attributes—community-mindedness and cooperation—that have always led to the best sort of philanthropy. For example, high school students in Grand Traverse County volunteered to help tend the area's cherry crops, and in Van Buren County in October of 1917, schools were closed for three weeks so that students could harvest the region's fruit crops. Elsewhere, students, Camp Fire Girls, Boy Scouts, even firemen kept busy knitting garments to send to military personnel and refugees.

The state's African-American population was extremely active in the relief effort, despite the cruel discrimination they faced before, during, and after the war. African-American women organized to provide supplies and sponsor war bond drives. The Detroit Colored Women's War Council, for example, initiated food conservation programs, launched a "suppression of liquor campaign," organized community and camp entertainment, and offered lodging to soldiers' families, in addition to its extensive community work.

Blessedly, World War I ended only a year and a half after the United States began its official involvement. Michigan charity workers turned their attentions to peacetime efforts, though they would, as they had after earlier wars, tend to those widowed, orphaned, or disabled by the bloodshed for years to come. Life as everyone had known it returned just in time to be knocked on its ear—first by the turbulent age that became known as the Roaring Twenties, and then by the Great Depression of the 1930s. Amid such upheaval, modern Michigan philanthropy would be born.

The Roaring '20s, the Hungry '30s,

and the Birth of Modern Michigan Philanthropy

4

Chapter Four
The Roaring '20s, the Hungry '30s,
and the Birth of Modern
Michigan Philanthropy
1919 - 1939

Before we plunge headlong into the roller coaster ride that was the Roaring Twenties, let's stop for a moment to examine where we've been. We've seen Michigan as a wilderness inhabited by Native Americans and the occasional French fur trader; we've seen the area become a popular destination for pioneers from New England; and we've seen Michigan grow into a relatively populous and somewhat urbanized, but still largely rural, state.

Michigan was poised, however, to launch into a vortex of urbanization. Near the turn of the century, as the automotive industry was gearing up, the state's very essence was about to change. By 1920, industry of all sorts would mushroom across the Great Lakes State, and for the first time, Michigan would have more urban residents than rural.

This urban industrial growth occurred almost exclusively in the southern half of the Lower Peninsula; in part, because the Upper Peninsula's two staple industries—lumber and mining—were dwindling. Between 1910 and 1920, Michigan's population grew by 30.5 percent, most of it south of a line drawn from Muskegon in the west to Bay City in the east. Most significant amidst this growth and development was the rise of the auto industry. This fair state—the former "land of ills, ague, fever, and chills"—was producing a shiny new export, one that turned heads across the nation.

In 1901, the entire auto industry produced only a few thousand cars. By 1919, more than 6.5 million cars were on the road. As impressive as that growth was, even better times were ahead. As the Roaring Twenties took hold, U.S. residents collectively fell head over heels in love with the new mode of transport, buying more than

(Chapter overleaf courtesy of Bentley Historical Library University of Michigan and Local History Department, Grand Rapids Public Library)

By 1912, Lansing (along with the rest of Michigan and the United States, for that matter) had fallen head over heels for the automobile. (Photos courtesy of State Archives of Michigan)

23 million cars by 1929. In fact, one small, unscientific survey done in a U.S. town in the early 1920s revealed that its residents were almost twice as likely to have a car as a bathtub.

Many men around the globe had been working to develop gasoline-powered vehicles, but for a variety of reasons—many of which add up to chance—Michigan won the automotive sweepstakes. Ransom E. Olds, Henry Ford, Will Barbour, Charles King, Henry Leland, John and Horace Dodge, William Murphy, David Buick, James Whiting, Charles Stewart Mott, and William Durant are but a few of the Michigan men who plowed into uncharted territory to create a thriving new industry and a national phenomenon.

Many of these men would prove as vital to Michigan philanthropy as they were to the auto industry. Mott, for example, earned most of his fortune by successfully operating a company that manufactured automotive parts and then selling it to General Motors in 1913, in the form of a stock exchange. With the automotive industry

Charles Stewart Mott's interest in young people and education prompted the Mott Foundation to support the growth of the community education movement, first in Flint, then across the nation. (Courtesy of Charles Stewart Mott Foundation)

The Oliver Mining Hospital in Ironwood likely served not only that western Upper Peninsula community, but also citizens in neighboring counties. (Courtesy of State Archives of Michigan)

The Lithuanian-American Mutual Aid Group was typical of fraternal organizations of the 1930s, which provided both assistance and social interchange for immigrants with shared ethnic roots. Here, the group poses at Sts. Peter and Paul School on Quarry Street in Grand Rapids. (Courtesy of State Archives of Michigan)

Katherine and Bill Bonifas

(Photo courtesy of Delta County Historical Society)

Practically from the time he was born in the 1860s, Bill Bonifas, the "Timber King," knew how to pinch a nickel. Whenever the millionaire traveled on business, his wife packed him a lunch. By the time he died in the 1930s, he had amassed a fortune that may have topped $20 million. Luckily for the residents of Escanaba, Bill's widow, Katherine, put the Bonifas fortune to wide use in their Upper Peninsula community.

Undoubtedly, Bill Bonifas kept tight hold of his money because he "came up the hard way." Born in Luxembourg, he came to the United States as a young man, landing in New York City with a too-small suit and only a few dollars to his name. He headed west, planning to work in the wheat fields of South Dakota. Somewhere along the way, he caught the wrong train and ended up in Green Bay, Wisconsin. He made his way to Escanaba and went to work cutting swamp timber into railroad ties and fence posts.

Soon, Bill had saved enough to bring seven brothers and sisters from Luxembourg. The sturdy Bonifas clan set up a lumber camp for 40 men at Garden, near Escanaba, and began sending posts and ties to Wisconsin, Illinois, and Detroit during the height of Michigan's lumber boom. When his "jacks" had stripped the swamps at Garden, Bill moved his operation west, where he had bought up great tracts of virgin pine, cedar, and spruce for as little as 65 cents an acre.

Business boomed and "Big Bill," as he was known, employed hundreds of men in several camps. The burgeoning cities of the Midwest demanded lumber, the railroads bought ties by the millions, and the new paper industry gobbled up as much pulpwood as it could get. As the state's forests toppled, the Timber King's investments in automobile manufacturing, paper, and oil contributed to a fortune of substantial proportions.

By the early 1930s, Big Bill had withdrawn from lumber operations. It would be unfair to say he spent most of his time warding off supplicants; he did make sizable gifts to the Catholic church and a gymnasium, now the Bonifas Art Center, in Escanaba and to Marquette University in Milwaukee. But the bulk of his fortune was intact when he died in 1936.

His wife was not pleased about having to contend with Big Bill's money. Like her husband, Katherine Bonifas came from modest means; she was an immigrant fresh from Ireland when she hired on as a maid in the Garden lumber camp. Unlike Big Bill, Katherine was shy and retiring, a homebody who, even with millions, scrubbed her own floors and darned her own stockings.

The Bonifases had no children, and Bill left his wife everything. Katherine was quite embarrassed and more than a little flummoxed by the size of their fortune. Colleges and churches, beggars, neighbors and friends all hounded her for donations. She hated to be asked directly for money, and eventually sought help from John A. Lemmer, a respected school superintendent in Escanaba. As the Lumber Queen's financial adviser, he helped her investigate charities that wisely refrained from asking directly for assistance. If a cause was worthy, Katherine wrote a check.

Lemmer's influence is evident in Katherine's many gifts for education. She funded a technical school, a new public elementary school in Garden, a Catholic high school, a public senior high school, a junior college, and a school for handicapped children. The Bonifas fortune also helped build a combined city hall/county courthouse and recreational facilities in Escanaba, and left a legacy that continued after Katherine's death in 1948. According to one history book, her will left $2.5 million to "many charities, members of her family, the city and schools, and Catholic churches and projects."

yet in its infancy, Mott's decision to exchange his company for GM stock was something of a gamble. Obviously, his faith in the staying power of automobiles paid off. At the time of his death in 1973, Mott's fortune was believed to have been about $1 billion. Fortunately for Michiganians, Mott took great interest in charitable causes; much of his fortune was given to philanthropic endeavors across the state and country.

Mott, however, is significant not merely because of his economic savvy and munificence, but also because, like fellow Michigan businessmen Henry Ford, Sebastian S. Kresge, and W.K. Kellogg, he was in the vanguard of a new charity movement that created large, private foundations.

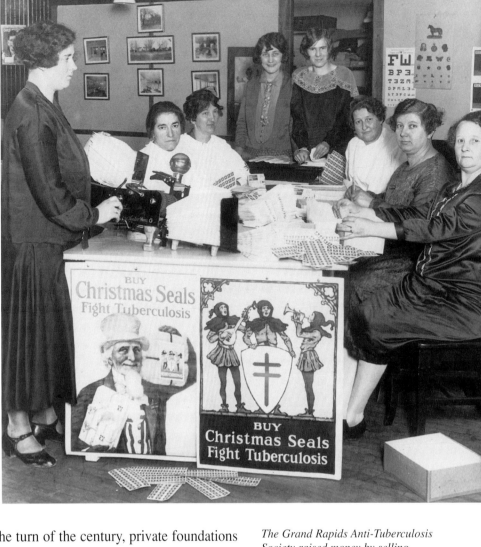

The Grand Rapids Anti-Tuberculosis Society raised money by selling Christmas Seals in 1927. As was typical then (and in many cases, still today), women were the "doers" of most front-line charity work.
(Courtesy of Local History Department, Grand Rapids Public Library)

Today, foundations seem to us to be indispensable institutions. But just after the turn of the century, private foundations were few and far between. Only a handful existed before the 1920s, and most of those were relatively new.

Among the more obvious reasons for the growth of private foundations after World War I was—as mentioned in chapter 3—the significant creation of capital that had occurred after the turn of the century when the nation's, and Michigan's, economy flourished. Another important development was a change in the tax laws. As we've already seen, the 16th amendment to the U.S. Constitution cleared the way for a progressive income tax in 1913, and Congressional action in 1917 allowed for the deduction of charitable contributions. In addition, a 1930 legal decision allowed corporations to deduct donations to charitable organizations, and a 1935 law established a tax rate of 70 percent on estates of more than $50 million; tax exemptions, however, were allowed for donations to nonprofit organizations. The 1989 book *The Third America*

The Henry Ford Hospital was built in 1915 with $10,750,000 donated by the Ford family. Associated with the hospital is the Henry Ford Hospital School of Nursing and the Edsel B. Ford Institute for Medical Research.
(Courtesy of State Archives of Michigan)

In 1910, a citizen's committee in Grand Rapids formed a Boy Scout organization to give young males healthy experience in outdoor life and community service. Here, the Boy Scouts advertise the 1927 Christmas Seal campaign. (Courtesy of Local History Department, Grand Rapids Public Library)

Henry Ford

(Photo courtesy of State Archives of Michigan)

The man who, in 1936, started one of the country's largest foundations wrote, in 1922: "I have no patience with professional charity or with any sort of commercialized humanitarianism. The moment human helpfulness is systematized, organized, commercialized, and professionalized, the heart of it is extinguished and it becomes a cold and clammy thing."

To be fair, Henry Ford also wrote, on the same page of his book, **My Life and Work**, "Heaven forbid we should grow cold to a fellow creature in need." Still, he felt personal charity—taking care of one's own family, friends, and neighbors—was more humane than "professional charity," which, he wrote, "degrades the recipients and drugs their self-respect."

The apparent schism within this legendary figure is typical: most accounts agree that Ford was an enigma, a man who championed many unpopular ideas (such as the "Peace Ship" he sent to Europe in an effort to end World War I) and who chalked up many achievements less well known than his success with the Tin Lizzy. For example, Ford was a pioneer commercial aviator (he built the Trimotor, America's first commercial airliner), successful coal and iron miner, and innovative forester. He was also the second-largest glass manufacturer in the country, one of the largest farmers in Michigan (tilling 10,000 acres), a linen and cotton weaver, newspaper publisher, coal distiller—and holder of a $200 million bank account by 1927.

Ford managed all of those things with no regular office and no regular office hours. He conducted business when and where he happened to be and preferred to spend most of his time at home, surrounded by 25,000 rose bushes and 500 birdhouses. On his estate, the fruit trees were reserved for the birds. A visitor reported: "Mr. Ford won't let us touch a single cherry. He says, 'What do you want them for—to can? I will buy you a carload of cherries, or two or three carloads, but please leave the ones on the trees for the birds.'"

Ford cared little for art, books, religion, politics, or club life and even less for the kind of history that marked centuries by their wars, dynasties, or kings. Of such accounts, he sputtered, "History is bunk." Yet he had a deep love of the history of everyday people, particularly those who had carved a country out of the American wilderness. Ford profoundly affected the historic preservation movement when he founded the Edison Institute in 1929. It grew into the Henry Ford Museum-Greenfield Village complex in Dearborn—one of the country's most extensive exhibits of American history.

But he hated to be called a benefactor or philanthropist, saying, "I give nothing for which I do not receive compensation." One example was his Henry Ford Trade School, which, beginning in 1916, taught young men to be tool and die makers, and in the process helped ease a serious labor shortage in the auto industry.

Ford's greatest philanthropic legacy was the Ford Foundation, established in Dearborn in 1936, during the depths of the Great Depression. Despite his distaste for professional philanthropy, the foundation that bears his name quickly became the largest grantmaking charity in the United States—a final paradox in a life replete with contradictory achievements.

contends that the new estate tax law was specifically aimed at the Ford Motor Company and the Ford family fortune. The new legislation provided encouragement for Ford and other successful capitalists to dedicate a portion of the wealth that they had created to philanthropic purposes, and he did exactly that when he established the Ford Foundation in 1936.

Henry Ford himself, however, had pursued charitable interests on his own well before that time. For example, he was instrumental in establishing Henry Ford Hospital in Detroit in 1919. According to his 1922 book *My Life and Work*, the hospital was designed as one that would serve not specifically the rich or the poor, but those in between "who can afford to pay only a moderate amount and yet desire to pay without feeling that they are recipients of charity."

Ford also started the Edison Institute, which includes Greenfield Village and Henry Ford Museum, in 1927. His "great museum would display the artifacts of American culture, and out the door a village would preserve the community setting of long ago," as one publication put it. The village and museum, which Ford opened to local school children right from the start, eventually grew to include a great variety of machinery and buildings from American history—including, perhaps, the most famous: Thomas Edison's Menlo Park laboratory. Both the Henry Ford Museum and Greenfield Village attract visitors from around the world to this day.

Given Ford's track record, then, one can see that while the new tax laws might have provided an incentive for creating a private foundation, they were far from the only impetus for the family interest in philanthropy.

A ride on the Greenfield Village train was a most popular attraction at the outdoor historical museum, c. 1965. The complex, with its extensive exhibits of American history, grew from the Edison Institute, which Henry Ford founded in 1929. (Courtesy of the collections of Henry Ford Museum & Greenfield Village)

"We are a company of dedicated people producing quality products for a healthier world," said W.K. Kellogg, pictured here in his factory, circa 1930. The cereal-maker and W.K. Kellogg Foundation founder cared deeply about the health and welfare of others. (Courtesy of Kellogg Company)

Other Michigan industrialists similarly began putting their philanthropic instincts to work. They were aided by the fact that the stage had been set for philanthropy on what was essentially a corporate scale. Many people in the United States had become very wealthy right about the time that Progressivism was spent as a political movement. Although Progressivism dissolved, many of the country's newly wealthy businessmen liked some of its philosophies, particularly the idea of using organized, scientific approaches to better mankind. The appeal of that philosophy would spur philanthropists to fund research in such areas as social welfare, government economic policies, and medicine.

This is not to say, however, that the megaphilanthropists of the early twentieth century were a pack of raving progressives. On the contrary, many of them were very able to separate their charitable and business lives. Andrew Carnegie and

In the 1950s, the Kellogg Experimental Farm and Forest near Richland demonstrated uses for land that could not support field crops. (Courtesy of W.K. Kellogg Foundation)

One of the world's largest grantmaking foundations was established by a self-described "poor man" and "selfish person." Will Keith Kellogg was born in Battle Creek during the last antebellum year, and lived until the first year of the "Police Action" on the Korean Peninsula. His life can be divided neatly into two acts. For the first 46 years of his life, he was a faceless amanuensis of his eminent older brother, Dr. John Harvey Kellogg, director of the internationally renowned Battle Creek Sanitarium. For the final 45 years, he became a global captain of industry, and a philanthropist of epic proportions.

From 1880 until 1906, Will labored as many as 80 hours per week in the San's service, discharging duties that ranged from managing the institution's business affairs to chasing down escaped patients in the dead of night. For his Herculean labors, Will collected wages from his famous brother that kept his family perpetually impoverished. Will confided to his diary, "…am afraid I will always be a poor man the way things look now."

And so he may have been, had not the Kellogg brothers, who were ever in search of ways to jazz up the San's strictly vegetarian fare, discovered the process of flaking grains into delicious, ready-to-eat cereals. Will recognized the commercial potential of the new products immediately, but Dr. John was concerned that hucksterism might damage his standing in the nation's medical community. He sharply limited the marketing of the cereals outside of the San's confines; even after 1897, when a recent San patient named C.W. Post rapidly made millions by pedaling cereals and coffee substitutes, the good doctor was adamant in restraining his younger brother's cereal selling efforts.

*Finally, with middle age hard upon him, Will left Dr. John's employ, and founded the Kellogg Company. The early years were tenuous. He had to fight for the right to use his own surname (Dr. Kellogg felt that he was **the** Kellogg, and sued Will, unsuccessfully, for christening the company with the family name). The entrepreneur also battled back from tight credit and a devastating fire, and before the First World War broke out, he had joined C.W. Post among the millionaires.*

"I do not intend to spoil my children by making them wealthy," declared Will Kellogg, and he was true to his word. He was, however, anything but callous toward young people. In fact, it was a tragedy that struck his grandson Kenneth Williamson—paralysis caused by tumble from a second-story window—that induced Will to establish the W.K. Kellogg Foundation. Between 1930 and his death in 1951 he endowed the foundation with nearly all of his ownership of the Kellogg Company, thus launching one of the world's largest grantmaking foundations.

To the end, Will Kellogg would accept no accolades for his extraordinary generosity. "A philanthropist," he said, "is one who would do good for the love of his fellowmen. I love to do things for children because I get a kick out of it. Therefore, I am a selfish person and no philanthropist." Michigan—and the rest of the world—could certainly do with a few more people as "selfish" as Will Keith Kellogg.

W.K. Kellogg

(Photo courtesy of
Kellogg Company)

John D. Rockefeller, for example, donated millions to help "uplift" the less fortunate, even as they contended with their own workers, who complained about working conditions and wages and tried to unionize.

The Rise of Private Foundations

Their practical differences with Progressivism notwithstanding, the captains of industry began looking for new, scientific methods to improve the welfare of mankind. One approach that proved popular was the establishment of private foundations. Philanthropists such as Carnegie and Rockefeller had done so long before the estate tax law of 1936 had provided an incentive to establish private foundations. Now, in addition to that motivation, donors were coming to realize that creating private philanthropic institutions allowed them to personally explore, direct, and influence new avenues of charity, such as research and education.

Michigan, with its base of wealth, particularly in the auto industry, was a likely home for many of the foundations that followed: the Kresge Foundation in 1924, founded by retailing magnate Sebastian S. Kresge; the Charles Stewart Mott Foundation, founded by Mott in 1926; the W.K. Kellogg Foundation, founded by cerealmaker Will Keith Kellogg in 1930; and the Ford Foundation, established in 1936 by Henry and Edsel Ford. They remain among the country's largest foundations, each with assets in excess of one billion dollars. (The Ford Foundation, which had the highest asset base of any American grantmaking foundation for most of the twentieth century, moved its headquarters to New York in the 1950s.)

In the years before the Great Depression, Michigan's foundations put a variety of philanthropic plans into action. The Kresge Foundation, for example, initiated a long-term relationship with the Methodist Children's Home of Detroit. (The Foundation would donate more than $2.7 million to the home between 1927 and

In 1922, Lee M. Hutchins, president of a local pharmaceutical company, founded the state's oldest continuously operating community foundation, the Grand Rapids Foundation, with a $25 gift from S. George Graves, president of the Grand Rapids Association of Commerce.
(Courtesy of Grand Rapids Foundation)

"For assisting charitable and educational institutions; for promoting education; for scientific research; for care of the sick, aged, or helpless; for the care of children; for the betterment of living and working conditions; for recreation for all classes, and for such other public, educational, charitable or benevolent purposes as will best make for the mental, moral, and physical improvement of the inhabitants of the County of Kalamazoo . . ."

FROM THE DECLARATION OF TRUST OF THE KALAMAZOO FOUNDATION, AUGUST 24, 1925

1953.) And even before the establishment of his foundation, S.S. Kresge made substantial gifts, including a new gymnasium, to Albion College in the early 1920s when his son, Stanley, was a student there. The patriarch, a devoutly religious man who supported Prohibition, had a particular interest in the small, private college because of its emphasis on Christianity.

At the same time, the Mott Foundation wasted no time in providing grants to children's camps, churches, and a crippled children's program, all in Michigan. Also noteworthy is the fact that the Foundation was only two years old when it made its first grant for international (and environmental) purposes, in 1928: $500 for the University of Michigan's "Greenland Expedition." According to the Foundation, the primary purpose of the expedition was to study air circulation patterns on the Greenland ice cap with kites and balloons.

The 1920s also saw more community foundations appear in Michigan, in such places as Grand Rapids in 1922 and Kalamazoo in 1925. Again, business leaders usually were involved.

Though setting up foundations was the trend, many of Michigan's major philanthropists would not stop there. Besides establishing the W.K. Kellogg Foundation in 1930, Kellogg also endowed the Kellogg Biological Station and provided the campus for the California Polytechnic University at Pomona. And Upjohn Company founder W.E. Upjohn, whose donation in the 1920s led to the creation of the Kalamazoo Foundation, would be so moved by the tragedy of the Great Depression that in 1932 he would create the W.E. Upjohn Unemployment Trustee Corporation (today known as the W.E. Upjohn Institute for Employment Research).

In the 1920s, nothing seemed so far off as a Great Depression. Granted, agriculture didn't share in the prosperity that swept much of the nation, and seasonal unemployment in the automotive and construction industries remained a concern. But life, for the most part, was on the upswing across Michigan and the rest of the country. Large-scale

In 1927, the Kresge Foundation provided major funding toward the purchase of land and construction of an administration building and equipment for the Methodist Children's Home Society of Detroit. This project was typical of the Foundation's focus on bricks-and-mortar projects. (Courtesy of Kresge Foundation)

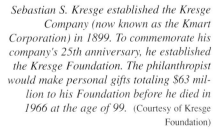

Sebastian S. Kresge established the Kresge Company (now known as the Kmart Corporation) in 1899. To commemorate his company's 25th anniversary, he established the Kresge Foundation. The philanthropist would make personal gifts totaling $63 million to his Foundation before he died in 1966 at the age of 99. (Courtesy of Kresge Foundation)

charity efforts continued to be the trend. Community fund drives (often known as the "community chest") became even more organized, in no small part due to corporate annoyance at the number of charitable requests distracting their workers.

In Michigan, the automotive industry helped the push toward United Way-style fundraising by insisting that charities unite to make a single request of workers. In some cases, charities that didn't participate in the cooperative effort weren't allowed to solicit donations from workers; those that did participate could collect donations through a single paycheck debit (marking the birth of the corporate payroll deduction for charity). The result was disgruntlement and disagreement on the part of some fund solicitors; health-oriented charities, in particular, remained aloof from the forced unification. And in some instances, local agencies disagreed with their national affiliates about whether to participate in local cooperative fundraisers. The fact that a local charity would be affiliated with a national parent, much less agree to consult with it, was indicative of that fact that philanthropy's scope was broadening, from local to state to national to international.

Also broadening was support for the temperance movement, which had drawn fervid volunteers to its ranks since the nation's early days. Antidrinking sentiment grew so strong in the state, in fact, that Michigan enacted its own prohibition legislation about a year before the U.S. Constitution was amended and nationwide Prohibition declared. In 1918, the Great Lakes State suddenly became a very dry place. At least in theory. In practice, bootleggers operated an armada of boat traffic to and from Canada's alcohol-bearing shores. Temperance activists discovered that enacting Prohibition and enforcing it were two very different things. Nonetheless, the law wouldn't be repealed nationwide, and the saloons legally opened again, until 1933.

Curiously, while Michigan was one of the first states to go dry, it was the first to vote for the repeal of the Eighteenth Amendment in 1933. (The state had repealed its own prohibition law a year earlier.) By then Michigan residents probably had more

The Community Fund in Flint ran this newspaper ad in 1930 to urge donations—however small—for charity.
(Courtesy of State Archives of Michigan)

A trust established by Minnie C. Blodgett through the Grand Rapids Foundation provided funding for the Blodgett Clinic for Infant Feeding in the 1930s.
(Courtesy of Public Museum of Grand Rapids)

James Couzens

In the 1930s and '40s, children in Michigan received tremendous gifts from a man whose generosity was in league with that of Kellogg, Carnegie, Rockefeller, and Kresge—philanthropists whose names are familiar today. But you may never have heard the name Couzens, for James Couzens (1872-1936) wanted it that way. When he formed the Children's Fund of Michigan in 1929, he forbade inclusion of his name in its title.

Couzens' name is also missing from his other great legacy: Ford Motor Company. He worked side by side with Henry Ford to found the company and build it into a billion-dollar empire. While Ford tinkered with new inventions, Couzens minded the "front office," establishing innovative programs for purchasing, labor, sales, and distribution. His strait-laced, hard-driving ethic made him few friends, but a great pile of money: his initial $2,500 investment ultimately earned nearly $30 million. Couzens left Ford in 1915 for a second career in politics, becoming mayor of Detroit and a U.S. Senator.

This stony-faced businessman had a soft spot for children. By one account, he had such difficulty whenever he saw a sick or suffering child that he couldn't bring himself to walk through an orphanage or hospital ward. The $10 million fund he established (one of the 15 largest in the United States at that time) would support county health departments, rural pediatric clinics, oral health projects, expanded public health nursing and education, guidance clinics, and summer camps—all for children, and all in Michigan.

Couzens was especially interested in bringing information about children's health into rural communities where knowledge (or the resources to apply it) was nonexistent. He cautioned his trustees not to consider requests from individuals, but instead to focus on mass needs: "When a new Ford car did not work," he told them, "we didn't assign an expert mechanic to fix that one car. We studied the problem as a whole to see what was wrong with the manufacturing process so we would not make the same mistake twice."

An interesting thing about the Children's Fund of Michigan is that it no longer exists: Couzens stipulated that its capital and earnings be spent entirely within 25 years. He wished to maximize the foundation's impact over the short term, and directed his trustees to fund programs that would stand on their own after the mother fund closed down, confident that each community would muster the resources necessary to carry worthy projects forward.

With the clock thus ticking, Couzens' trustees set out aggressively to spend the money, ferreting out areas of need and programs that could fill them. By 1945, the money was indeed spent as Couzens had directed, and the Fund was dissolved. The trustees even gave away two buildings and a summer camp the Fund had erected.

In one sense, nothing was left of Couzens' gift. After all, had Couzens allowed his fund to live on, it would have grown manyfold by the end of the twentieth century, and still be generating grants forever. In another sense, everything was. Of this man's distinctive philanthropy, a Detroit newspaper noted: "Senator Couzens endowed his good works with something more than millions. He endowed them with self-sufficiency. The Children's Fund blazed a trail; then left to posterity the dignity of following that trail on its own feet on its own strength."

Philanthropist James Couzens worked side by side with Henry Ford to build a billion-dollar automotive empire. His early investment in Ford Motor Company allowed Couzens to donate millions to projects benefiting Michigan children.
(Courtesy of Detroit Public Library Burton Historical Collection)

Camps sponsored by the Children's Fund of Michigan were a summertime treat for thousands of underprivileged children in the 1930s and '40s.
(Courtesy of Bentley Historical Library University of Michigan)

Louis Kaufman

"I have attempted to build an institution, not for today or tomorrow, but for generations to come." Millionaire Louis Graveraet Kaufman was speaking of the ornate marble and bronze of his new bank building in 1927, but this New York financier could have been describing far loftier endeavors. He is remembered in his hometown of Marquette as one who was unfailingly loyal and generous to young people in that community. Tellingly, this man who was worth $150 million before World War II had a brass quartet from Marquette High School play at his funeral.

In the early 1890s, then barely out of his teens, Kaufman was a fast-rising star in the banking business. At the Marquette County Savings and First National Banks, he climbed through the ranks with amazing speed—messenger, teller, cashier, manager, vice president, president, and chairman of the board. In 1910, Kaufman caught the attention of Judge Elbert Gary, president of United States Steel Corporation, who asked him to come to New York and see what he could do with the staid but stagnant Chatham National Bank. Kaufman did plenty, merging it with Phoenix National to form one of the largest banks in New York (now Chemical Bank). He's also famous for introducing branch banking—at the time a startling new concept for a national bank.

Interestingly, Kaufman never gave up his presidency of the First National Bank in Marquette, gaining a special government clearance to head both institutions. In 1926, he donated land for a new bank in his hometown and took great pride in building a Roman Corinthian showplace.

In a sense, Kaufman also was a builder of cars, helping to pull General Motors out of severe financial difficulties in 1916 as chairman of its finance committee. And he helped erect the world's most famous skyscraper, serving on a four-man team that arranged financing for the Empire State Building.

What endeared Louis Kaufman to the citizens of Marquette, however, was the banker's dedication to building educational opportunities for local children. In 1926, he donated money for land for a new high school, and shortly thereafter, established the $100,000 Kaufman Endowment Fund, the first high school endowment in the United States. In its early years, the Fund paid for famous figures in drama, art, and music to travel to the Upper Peninsula and perform for schoolchildren in the ornate high school auditorium—also built by Louis Kaufman.

The Kaufman Fund has grown significantly, thanks in part to the sale of an interesting portion of the endowment—one of the finest privately held collections of rare coins in the country. Instead of locking them away in "National" coin albums, Kaufman displayed the coins for public enjoyment, first at the New York bank and later at First National in Marquette. And when they were offered for public auction by the Rare Coin Company of America in 1978, the auction catalogue warned that many were marred by the glue and tacks that had affixed them to the display boards. Obviously, the collector was less concerned about resale value than about sharing his numismatic interests.

In the 1980s and 1990s, Kaufman's endowment has funded a school planetarium— the only one in the Upper Peninsula—school computers, and renovations to the school auditorium he built, plus scholarships, sports team awards, and scores of smaller youth education projects within the Marquette school district.

important things on their minds than legal access to drink—problems like the Great Depression and the state's nonagricultural unemployment rate of around 34 percent. Under the circumstances, the goals of the Prohibition Party must have seemed frivolous.

The Depression notwithstanding, Michigan foundations continued their programming efforts. For example, the W.K. Kellogg Foundation, created even as the Great Depression was settling in to stay awhile, carried forth the philanthropic priorities of founder Will Keith Kellogg, proprietor of the Kellogg Company. "W.K.," as he was known, was a serious man who had endured a difficult childhood. (His father's first wife and one of his own sisters had both died of illness.) Kellogg, who was working part-time in his father's factory by the age of seven and as a broom salesman with his own territory by age 14, once acknowledged that he had never learned to play. Not surprisingly, two of his most intense areas of charitable interest were youth and health care.

Health programs for children were widespread in public schools during the 1930s, thanks to support from many Michigan organizations. Here, youngsters line up for a TB check. (Courtesy of W.K. Kellogg Foundation)

His foundation addressed children's welfare by providing financial support in the 1930s to school consolidation and modernization projects in seven Michigan counties; youth recreation projects, particularly in Battle Creek, the Foundation's home base; and a scholarship program to send rural youth to Michigan State University for agricultural classes. In the area of health and medicine, the Foundation supported a large, collaborative initiative known as the Michigan Community Health Project (MCHP). Started in 1931, the project was aimed at helping local counties organize, consolidate, and expand their health services. The project initially started in Barry County, then was expanded over the next five years to include Allegan, Eaton, Van Buren, Hillsdale, Branch, and Calhoun counties. It trained local authorities to determine what medical services were most needed, and then helped them to organize those services and obtain the necessary equipment, which typically included diagnostic fundamentals such as X-ray machines.

In the 1930s, the Upper Peninsula Development Bureau was dedicated to drawing attention to the natural treasures of northern Michigan. (Courtesy of State Archives of Michigan)

In the 1920s, African-Americans were not the only minority to suffer discrimination in Michigan. Mexican laborers brought in to work the sugar beet farms in the eastern part of the state toiled for pitifully low wages, and lived in miserable conditions. (Courtesy of State Archives of Michigan)

Depression Devastates the State

Despite the best efforts of organized philanthropy, Michigan was hit hard—and early—by the Great Depression because of the state's reliance on manufacturing, particularly in the auto industry. Nationwide, unemployment began to climb immediately after the stock market crashed late in 1929; still, joblessness wasn't catastrophic at the national level until mid- to late-1931. In Michigan, however, at least 18 percent of the state's nonagricultural workers were unemployed as early as 1930. At times during the depression, the state's unemployment rate ran almost 10 percentage points ahead of the national average. In short, things were looking grim, indeed.

Quickly, the Great Depression touched off a firestorm of political debate. Many people, including President Herbert Hoover and a series of Michigan governors—such as Wilber Brucker—believed that government intervention in the unemployment problem was not only unnecessary, but wrong. Others, such as Detroit Mayor Frank Murphy, believed that governmental action was not only warranted, but vital to the state's survival. Local governments and charities could not handle such a crushing problem on their own, they argued, pointing to the growing unemployment rate and accompanying human misery. (By 1931, Ford Motor Company had slashed its payroll by 75 percent from its 1929 level.)

As the debate raged and unemployment dragged on for years, municipalities and charities across the country struggled to provide local relief, then collapsed under the demand. City after city faced bankruptcy, and local charities all but ceased to be of significant help, since they had no influx of donations to distribute. Just when the number of needy was skyrocketing as never before, the depression was putting the squeeze on local charitable resources. In 1931, when the Detroit Community Chest fund drive fell significantly short of its goal, about 45,000 families were on the city's

With donations at cardboard chimney collection sites across Grand Rapids, charitable souls brightened Christmas morning for children of the city's unemployed. (Courtesy of Local History Department, Grand Rapids Public Library)

In 1899, a group of concerned citizens in Grand Rapids organized the City Mission at Market Avenue and Louis Street. It ran revival meetings and crusades to rescue the destitute from the "demon rum." (Courtesy of Local History Department, Grand Rapids Public Library)

relief rolls. With more than 485,000 Michigan residents jobless, the state's local charities must have felt they were fighting a raging wildfire with a leaky squirt gun.

But fight they did, only to encounter many of the same problems that had cropped up in the depressions of the 1870s and 1890s; charities by and large were structurally, psychologically, and materially unable to cope with massive numbers of healthy, able—and unemployed—individuals. The only area in which they could fairly be expected to succeed was in helping the sick, young, aged, and poor who typically needed aid even when the economy was bright. In Flint, for example, the local community chest coordinated Depression-Era fundraising and made sure that only bona fide "needy" people received aid.

Recognizing that private charities simply were not up to tackling the nation's most devastating depression all by themselves, local municipalities across Michigan implemented a number of relief programs. Some cities acted more quickly than others. In Flint, municipal assistance to the needy was limited until at least 1933, when federal financial aid began. In Ann Arbor, Grand Rapids, and Detroit, assistance for the unemployed began almost immediately, and often took distinctive forms. In 1930, for example, Detroit's Mayor Murphy implemented a citywide registration of the unemployed to determine the exact scope of the problem, then followed up by appointing a special committee on unemployment and offering a free job placement bureau. But these activities, and even $14 million a year in relief expenditures, weren't enough. By 1932, Detroit officials were among those actively promoting federal intervention in the unemployment problem.

Officials in Ann Arbor and Grand Rapids joined in the plea at about the same time. Both cities had valiantly worked to provide relief on their own, largely by establishing "workfare" programs that paid workers in scrip that could be used at the city store or to pay for city-provided utilities. Local merchants, in dire need of business themselves, had loudly protested the establishment of city stores. Also, in Grand Rapids, many residents had grown tired of the extraordinary efforts that City Manager George Welsh claimed were needed, or at least had grown tired of Welsh's brashness

The most basic form of charitable giving helped ease hunger pangs for thousands of families during the Great Depression. Here, the City Welfare Department of Grand Rapids operates a collection and distribution center for donated canned goods. (Courtesy of Local History Department, Grand Rapids Public Library)

During the Great Depression, Grand Rapids residents worked for scrip (currency substitute) at city-sponsored workfare programs, such as this potato distribution center. Scrip could be traded for goods at the city store. (Courtesy of Local History Department, Grand Rapids Public Library)

From the start, natural resources have been fundamental to Michigan's allure: Native Americans lived off the land; trappers sought the state's abundant wildlife; farmers settled here to till fertile soil; and miners and timber barons harvested vast mineral and lumber treasures. It's not surprising, then, that much of the state's philanthropic history is tied to the land.

In 1915, for example, the state Legislature exhibited a great deal of foresight by granting the Public Domain Commission the authority to accept "gifts, grants, and devises of real property" to be preserved for "public park purposes." The action really didn't bear fruit until the 1920s, when the state's first parks commission began work. Strapped for cash and land, and spurred by public enthusiasm for the state park concept, the commission eagerly sought gifts. Individuals and corporations responded with land contributions that created 59 of the first 64 state parks.

In the early years, these small parks were battered by overuse. While the state parks hosted 220,000 visitors in 1922, the number increased to nearly 9 million just eight years later. Michigan realized it needed to acquire larger tracts of land to prevent destruction of the very natural features the parks sought to preserve. In most cases additional lands were eventually acquired to create larger, more usable parks from the original gifts.

Among the first donations:

- D.H. Day State Park, from Grand Haven resident and Michigan State Park Commission Chairman David H. Day. His gift of 700 feet of Lake Michigan shoreline is now part of Sleeping Bear Dunes National Lakeshore.
- Brimley State Park on Lake Superior, which began with a gift of 38 acres from the businessmen of the Brimley Commercial Club in 1922. Today, visitors come to the 151-acre park to watch freighters navigate the Soo locks.
- J.W. Wells State Park on Green Bay, which grew from land donated by Ralph Wells, son of pioneer lumberman John Walter Wells, in 1925. Today, 974 acres of lakeshore and woods lie inside its boundaries.
- Hartwick Pines State Park in Grayling. The economic Panic of 1893 saved the trees that are the focal point of this now 9,238-acre oasis. Karen Michelson Hartwick, daughter of a lumber pioneer, gave 3,182 acres—including the island of primeval forest—to the state in 1927.
- P. H. Hoeft State Park, made up of 301 acres donated by lumber baron Paul H. Hoeft of Rogers City. Visitors enjoy its sand dunes, inland woods, and Lake Huron shoreline.
- Ludington State Park on Lake Michigan, founded in 1927 by the citizens of Ludington, whose efforts and dollars acquired all of its 4,514 acres.
- Charles Mears State Park and Silver Lake State Park, both on Lake Michigan in and near Pentwater. The land was donated by Carrie Mears, daughter of entrepreneur Charles Mears.
- Dodge Bros. No. 4 State Park, on Cass Lake near Pontiac. A posthumous gift of 78 acres from Horace and John Dodge has grown to a 138-acre park. (The Dodge land had been among parcels donated by the Dodge Company directors after John and Horace Dodge's deaths.)
- Highland Recreation Area in Milford, which comprises the 114-acre Dodge Bros. No. 10 State Park and the country estate of Edsel and Eleanor Ford.
- Warren Dunes and Warren Woods State Parks in Sawyer, where visitors enjoy Lake Michigan beaches, sand dunes, and 200 acres of virgin beech and maple forest donated by Edward K. Warren of Three Oaks.

Land donations such as these do more than open Michigan's natural beauty to the public (although that philanthropic end is, in itself, welcome). Rather, they say something about our state and its history, and point to a type of philanthropy that is quintessentially Michiganian.

(Photo of Hartwick Pines, courtesy of State Archives of Michigan)

in tackling the unemployment problem on his own. He once illegally used city funds to purchase 27,000 bushels of potatoes for distribution to the city's needy. Welsh also used the city's snow removal budget to hire local unemployed men to shovel snow, and appropriated money generated by a bond issue for sewer work to hire scrip workers for the project. As you might expect, the city's private excavation contractors were not at all pleased.

Solving the huge unemployment problem through municipal action, then, proved virtually impossible. Local governments' attempts to make more efficient use of the funds they did have began a vicious circle: the very efforts that sought to help the unemployed hurt the ability of local businesses to hire workers. Numerous charities and state and local government leaders pleaded to the federal government for assistance.

But President Hoover (as well as most Michigan governors during the depression years) remained steadfast in their belief that the government should not get involved in private-sector economic matters such as unemployment. Although Hoover eventually did partially capitulate and implement some limited federal loan and aid programs, his action was viewed as too little, too late by too many voters. In 1932, they elected Franklin Delano Roosevelt. Michigan's Governor Brucker, who was a great admirer of Hoover, shared the president's noninterventionist stance and was also voted out of office that year. (Apparently, it had not escaped voters' attention that a state unemployment commission appointed by Brucker had no real power and had been reduced to issuing such vacuous boosterisms as "The only adequate remedy for unemployment is employment.")

Roosevelt, of course, implemented the much-praised and much-maligned New Deal, which directed massive federal intervention in the economic and unemployment woes plaguing the country. These relief programs generally were welcome at the local level, even if residents resented the federal government's

President Franklin Roosevelt's New Deal provided massive federal relief programs that created work for hundreds of thousands. Pictured here, a Detroit street repair project in the mid-1930s. (Courtesy of State Archives of Michigan)

The Grand Rapids City Welfare Department distributed grocery staples during the Great Depression. In Grand Rapids and other Michigan cities, aid to the unemployed was instituted almost immediately. (Courtesy of Local History Department, Grand Rapids Public Library)

On March 4, 1931, residents in South Haven, Bangor, and Casco sent a truck convoy of food and supplies for the Arkansas Drought Relief program. (Courtesy of *Photographic Memories - South Haven* by Richard Appleyard)

George Washington Carver with Floyd Starr, founder of the Starr Commonwealth School for Boys in Albion. It has grown to be one of the nation's leading institutions providing positive youth development to young people from challenging backgrounds. (Courtesy of State Archives of Michigan)

heavy-handedness in administering the funds. In spite of federal assistance, however, the depression wouldn't lift for years and, some have argued, would only really be ended by World War II. Until that time, municipal leaders and charity workers surely must have tired of the despair they encountered daily, as poverty and unemployment became a way of life for millions.

Despite private charity's inability to have much effect upon the depression, there were some philanthropic bright spots in the 1930s, particularly in Michigan. Depression Era philanthropic activities in the state included the creation of the W.E. Upjohn Unemployment Trustee Corporation, which researches unemployment issues to this day, and the Mott Foundation's first experiments with a community education project that in later years would sweep the nation.

Elsewhere in Michigan, those with a philanthropic spirit did what they could to help the state's workers. At the Kellogg Company in Battle Creek, for example, founder W.K. Kellogg began a million-dollar plant expansion in 1929, doubled his advertising, and switched to a six-hour work day in 1930 so he could hire a fourth shift from among the city's unemployed. In addition, the company was paying 75 cents an hour for a 36-hour work week—one of the best pay rates in the state.

With a similar eye toward helping the average citizen make ends meet, W.E. Upjohn purchased a 1,200-acre site near Kalamazoo, in Richland Township, in 1931. His plan was to turn the land into individual plots that Kalamazoo's jobless population could farm, and he even provided bus transportation to the plots for unemployed factory workers from the city.

Upjohn's plan might have seemed unrealistic; factory workers and farmers didn't necessarily have the same skills. Still, his farm plots were something and they

Among many other philanthropic activities, W.E. Upjohn was instrumental in establishing the Kalamazoo Foundation, one of the largest community foundations in the country. (Courtesy of Pharmacia & Upjohn)

made a dent, however modest, in the needs of the area's unemployed. Upjohn's plan became a reality in 1932, when up to 100 people began working the land.

As the Upjohn Company's 1987 book *A Century of Caring* notes, Upjohn had long believed that the unemployed should not be put "on the dole." Instead, he was convinced that "the best kind of help to be given to the poor was to furnish employment or in some form an opportunity to work and produce something in order that the dollar might not be uselessly consumed."

Philanthropic organizations have often cooperated to achieve their goals. In the 1930s, the Lions Club joined the Salvation Army to raise money to buy Christmas baskets for Grand Rapids' poor. (Courtesy of Local History Department, Grand Rapids Public Library)

Residents like Upjohn continued their quest for new ways to solve the societal problems that stemmed from unemployment. While the Great Depression made it abundantly clear that private, local charity groups could not handle large issues of need all by themselves, the crisis also made clear the fact that the new philanthropic entities—the large foundations—could do much good in addressing national issues.

The growing acceptance of foundations was something of a compromise. Many people rankled at the notion of private foundations (since the days of Andrew Jackson in the 1820s, Americans had been suspicious of "closed corporations"), but apparently disliked federal paternalism even more. As time went by and their resources grew, the foundations would tackle larger and larger issues and make ever-larger grants for important social purposes. In Michigan, as elsewhere, the foundation in all its forms—private, community, and corporate—was about to come of age.

Former President Gerald R. Ford (top row, fourth from left) was among the Eagle Scouts appointed Guards of Honor for Old Fort Mackinac on Mackinac Island in the summer of 1929. (Courtesy of State Archives of Michigan)

Marjorie Merriweather Post

In 1961, the cereal heiress attended dedication ceremonies for a project she helped fund: a new athletic field for Battle Creek schools.
(Courtesy of Hillwood Museum)

Some have called Marjorie Merriweather Post (1887-1973) the grandest grande dame society has known. Her wealth was enormous; her parties unparalleled; her grace, poise, and charm legendary; her husbands many (but fleeting: four marriages, four divorces).

Two things are even more impressive about this woman, who grew up in Battle Creek. One is that although her fortune was inherited, she increased it manyfold herself. The second is that she gave away an extraordinary amount of money—at least as much as she spent to maintain her lavish lifestyle.

The only child of C.W. Post, the man who created the Postum Cereal Company in Battle Creek, Marjorie grew up with the business, knew it inside and out, and was well prepared when she inherited her father's company at age 27. Over a matter of 15 years, she expanded its holdings significantly by developing or buying new products, including Jell-O, Maxwell House Coffee, and Log Cabin Syrup. In 1929, the company undertook several business negotiations that, essentially, resulted in Post acquiring and becoming known as the General Foods Corporation. The move was largely due to a foresighted deal Marjorie made with Clarence Birdseye, a man who held all the patents to an amazing new convenience: frozen food.

Marjorie continued as principal stockholder in General Foods until her death. Not surprisingly, she was one of the wealthiest women in the world in the late 1950s, with a fortune estimated at more than $250 million. She spent money liberally and conspicuously, decorating gorgeous homes in Washington, D.C.; Palm Beach; and the Adirondacks with some of the world's most valuable art treasures and antiquities.

Marjorie lived, unabashedly, the life of a queen. She threw marvelous, sumptuous parties, sometimes aboard her Sea Cloud, the world's largest privately owned sailing yacht, which could seat 400 guests. One time she even hired Ringling Brothers, Barnum and Bailey to stage their circus at Mar-A-Lago, her Palm Beach home—one night for her guests and two nights for charity.

Interestingly, Marjorie's parties always started early and ended promptly at 11 p.m. She turned in early so as to be fresh for the next day's work: spending hours at her desk writing checks to deserving organizations, including the National Symphony Orchestra in Washington, D.C.; Boy Scouts of America; National Cultural Center (which became the John F. Kennedy Center for the Performing Arts); Salvation Army; and Red Cross, to name her most frequent beneficiaries.

At least a few of those checks made their way back to Battle Creek. In 1961, Marjorie joined with the Post Division of General Foods in building the C.W. Post Athletic Field. The facility was used by all the schools in Battle Creek and was considered the finest in the state. She wrote a $150,000 check for the project and, perhaps more impressively, sat through the entire dedication ceremony (a football game) in the drizzle.

Marjorie also contributed generously to the Lakeview General Hospital building fund, bailed out the Battle Creek Symphony in an especially tight budget year, and made individual gifts to many past Post employees. Upon hearing of her death, one Battle Creek resident remembered, "When she visited Battle Creek … she was very gracious and sincerely interested in the people."

956 RED FEATHER GOAL $35,895,

GIVE

World War II, the Postwar Boom,

and the Emergence of the Foundations

5

These Deerlick School students collected 193,000 pounds of scrap metal for a countywide scrap drive contest during World War II. Twenty-five students gathered an average of 7,720 pounds per person and captured first prize—a $50 war bond. (Courtesy of *Photographic Memories - South Haven* by Richard Appleyard)

(Chapter overleaf photo courtesy of Clarke Historical Library, Central Michigan University)

Chapter Five

World War II,

the Postwar Boom,

and the Emergence of the Foundations

1940-1959

*T*he civic-mindedness that propelled Michigan's benevolent efforts from the state's early history did not wither to dust during the Great Depression of the 1930s, nor could Adolph Hitler make citizens of the Great Lakes State less generous. As World War II raged on, the state's and nation's charitable groups rose to the challenge. Numerous agencies and volunteers worked tirelessly on war preparedness efforts, social welfare projects, and patriotic activities on the home front. In Grand Rapids, for instance, the Council of Social Agencies provided aid to men who were being drafted, as well as to their families. Volunteers across the state organized community sewing and canning centers, air raid drills, war bond drives, paper and metal salvaging drives, and the ubiquitous victory gardens. When air raid fever swept the nation, volunteers banded together to prepare for the possibility of Nazi and Japanese assaults. In Grand Rapids, housewives volunteered to organize home fire-combating units, while the city's funeral directors established an emergency ambulance service that could be called into duty if Michigan were attacked. (One can only wonder what the response might have been among the injured had they been carted off in hearses.)

In fact, as the war effort unfolded, philanthropy here was showing signs of the vitality that would lie ahead: at least two dozen new private foundations sprang into existence in Michigan between 1940 and 1945, and the few foundations that had previously existed in the state—mostly large organizations—redoubled their philanthropic efforts. The Kalamazoo Foundation, for example, awarded grants in such areas as medical research, the arts, and community social and economic welfare; the Kresge Foundation continued its tradition of financial support to the Methodist Children's

Traffic was rerouted when collections for Kalamazoo Central High School's scrap metal drive filled the school lawn and spilled into the street. (Courtesy of Western Michigan University Archives and Regional History Collections)

In 1942, the Hayes Body Corporation, in cooperation with the War Department and the makers of Camel cigarettes, sponsored a cigarette sale in Grand Rapids. Civilians paid $1.50 to purchase 17 packs of cigarettes that would be distributed to troops overseas. (Courtesy of Local History Department, Grand Rapids Public Library)

Home Society of Detroit, as well as to education and medical research; and the Ford Foundation remained largely a local institution, making grants to such organizations as the Detroit Symphony, the Edison Institute, and Henry Ford Hospital.

The foundation stalwarts were also moving in new directions. The Kellogg Foundation, for instance, began phasing out its Michigan Community Health Project; by 1948, funding for the program ended, and the participating health departments were turning to taxpayers for support instead. Kellogg began to transform itself from an operating to a grantmaking foundation, in the process expanding its scope to national and even international arenas. The Ford Foundation slowly began transforming itself into a national foundation by making larger grants to such organizations as the American Red Cross in Washington, D.C.; the Roscoe B. Jackson Memorial Laboratory in Maine; and the Museum of Modern Art in New York.

The Mott Foundation was changing, too, but for reasons directly related to the war. As the auto industry shifted gears to accommodate the military build-up, Michigan rapidly became known as the "Arsenal of Democracy" (a phrase apparently coined by *Life* magazine). The intensified focus on manufacturing created an urgent need for additional skilled workers—the military needed armaments *now*. To help fill the gap quickly, Mott expanded the community education movement it had founded in Flint in the late 1930s—a movement that saw Flint schools used by children during the day and by adult community residents at night. The Foundation's wartime efforts included adding classes in industrial and technical skills for the area's laborers, an expansion of focus indicative of a growing trend toward vocational education in the community, and the subsequent popularity of community colleges.

In 1943, the Spirit of South High was flown to the Kent County Airport for its christening. The B-17 bomber was paid for with $375,000 raised by Grand Rapids' South High School students. (Courtesy of Local History Department, Grand Rapids Public Library)

The Kearney brothers of Grand Rapids say goodbye to their dog Pepper, one of 10,000 canines shipped to the government's "Dogs for Defense" training program during World War II. The dogs were trained for locating wounded soldiers and enemy snipers, transporting equipment carts, and carrying dispatches through battle lines. (Courtesy of Local History Department, Grand Rapids Public Library)

Flint, however, was only one of several Michigan cities in which the war literally was a matter of big business. The state's many manufacturing plants, particularly those in the auto industry, won a great number of defense contracts. Even before the United States' official involvement in the war began on December 7, 1941, some auto companies had been working to produce armaments. Chrysler, for example, had been preparing a mammoth tank arsenal in the Detroit suburb of Warren since mid-1940.

As the United States entered the war, Michigan defense manufacturing kicked into high gear. Ford made Jeeps and bombers; the Nash-Kelvinator Corporation manufactured aircraft engines and propellers; Studebaker produced aircraft engines; Hudson built a naval ordnance plant; and GM churned out munitions of all kinds—cannons, aircraft machine guns, engines, and ammunition. All told, GM would dedicate 120 plants to war production.

The Ford Motor Company undertook one of the largest defense projects in the country, turning out more than 8,500 B-24 bombers in the 2.76 million-square-foot Willow Run bomber plant. It was a controversial undertaking: the 16,000 people who lived in the area before the war weren't prepared for the arrival of more than 30,000 people who moved there for jobs at the factory. The government's plans to build housing for the new workers met with resistance from local residents, who feared the centers would become dilapidated ghost towns after the war. But other factors were at work, too: class and racial prejudice.

Many of those who flocked to Michigan and Willow Run for defense jobs were poor Southerners and African-Americans. Despite the state's history of benevolence, charity, and goodwill, prejudice and racism remained a problem. What happened at Willow Run pointed out the gaps that existed in the state's willingness to help those in need: local residents were unwilling to construct adequate housing, sewage treatment, plumbing, education, or recreation facilities for the newcomers. One book about the era offers the following quote from a Willow Run resident: "Everybody knew everybody else and all were happy and contented. Then came that bomber plant and this influx of riffraff, mostly Southerners. … You can't be sure of these people."

The "riffraff" were forced to live in dreadful conditions. They crammed into basements, garages, and even cars. Entire families lived in trailers parked in front yards—while the tiny houses behind were filled with sometimes more than a dozen workers and their families. And yet, there was no dramatic outcry from the state's

The end of an era: The last B-24 bomber is made at Ford's Willow Run plant in 1945. Signing his autograph is Henry Ford II, grandson of the company founder, who assumed control of Ford Motor Company during World War II. (Courtesy of Detroit Public Library National Automotive History Collection)

The Red Cross, always lending a hand, here with news from home. (Courtesy of Western Michigan University Archives and Regional History Collections)

Members of the Four Leaf Clover Club of Grand Rapids' True Light Baptist Church prepare bags of food for needy families in 1943.
(Courtesy of Local History Department, Grand Rapids Public Library)

major philanthropic quarters. Perhaps the war itself had already seized the collective charitable eye. Or perhaps the economic distress of the 1930s left budgets too tight to be of much help. In any case, even as one government official was terming Willow Run living conditions "the worst mess in the United States," Michigan philanthropy was, for the most part, occupied elsewhere.

As more and more African-Americans and Southern whites moved north for defense jobs, race relations deteriorated to one of the state's all-time lows. Prejudice that prevented African-Americans from living anywhere but in already-overcrowded slums made wartime housing a critical problem, particularly in Detroit. Tensions reached the breaking point late in the summer of 1943, when a two-day riot left 34 people dead—25 of them African-Americans, 17 of whom had been killed by police. (No whites were killed by police.)

Religious prejudice also reared its head. In the face of the extermination of millions of Jewish people in Europe, one could reasonably have expected Americans to rally to their aid, but anti-Semitism actually grew during the war years—as indicated by public opinion polls about the perceived character flaws of Jewish people. Anti-Semitic newsletters and information sheets popped up around the country, with a few loud fanatics sounding warnings about a Jewish conspiracy. In Chicago, a group called the Gentile Co-operative Association was formed to halt the imagined threat of Jewish "power," and, on the eastern seaboard, synagogues were desecrated and Jewish-run businesses vandalized.

The prejudice that instigated these events plays a role in Michigan philanthropy. As we've previously

Always attentive to needs—large and small—within the Flint community, the Mott Foundation has long funded such projects as the Supplementary Breakfast Program at Roosevelt School.
(Courtesy of Charles Stewart Mott Foundation)

Leelanau Township Foundation

For more than 50 years, the Leelanau Township Foundation has been assisting public and charitable institutions close to home—those located within the cherry- and tourist-rich township perched on the tip of Michigan's little finger.

This community foundation was organized in 1945 by Francis H. Haserot, owner of the Northport Cherry Factory, in memory of his friend and business associate G. Marston Dame, who was killed in a car-train collision at Suttons Bay in 1939. Haserot gave $35,000 in stocks and bonds to establish the organization. Over the years, residents of the township have added their own donations and memorials until, in 1995, the community foundation's financial portfolio topped $1.5 million—quite an achievement in a jurisdiction of fewer than 2,000 people.

Understandably, the organization's focus is local. In a recent year, it supported—among other programs—an area day-care center, the Northport Chamber of Commerce Music in the Park program, construction of a pavilion in Northport's Marina Park, the Northport Sportsman's Club pond dredging, Leelanau Township Baseball, Natural Helpers 4-H Program, automation for the Leelanau Township library, and several school and scholarship programs.

Over the years, significant funds have been awarded for developing the waterfront, with improvements such as the G. Marston Dame Marina, public beaches, and Haserot Park, on the site of the Northport Cherry Factory. Improvements at Northport's ski hill and village pond were also supported, and by far the largest award recipient has been Leelanau Memorial Hospital.

Today, the community foundation has a general endowment fund, a youth endowment fund, and five scholarship funds, including a Native American scholarship fund. A successful participant in the Michigan Community Foundations' Youth Project (administered by the Council of Michigan Foundations and funded by the W.K. Kellogg Foundation), the organization pulls together more than 30 young people to act as its Youth Advisory Council, whose goal is to improve youth-oriented programs in the community.

It's likely that these young volunteers, like their counterparts on the community foundation trustees' disbursement committee, allocate funds with special care: their decisions directly affect their family, friends, neighbors, and co-workers.

A recent annual report for the Leelanau Township Foundation shows its disbursement volunteers take their responsibility seriously. It quotes Aristotle: "To give away money is an easy matter and in any man's power. But to decide to whom to give it and how large and when and for what purpose and how is neither in every man's power nor an easy matter. Hence it is that such excellence is rare, praiseworthy, and noble."

Northport Lighthouse renovation funded by the Leelanau Township Foundation. (Photos courtesy of Leelanau Township Foundation and Cherry Marketing Institute)

indicated, early white-run benevolent societies and charities across Michigan generally did not provide aid to African-Americans. The neglect prompted African-Americans to form their own charities. Similarly, subtle and sometimes not-so-subtle prejudice toward the state's Jewish population resulted mainly in the neglect of Jewish people in need. (If one were to give the state's charities the benefit of the doubt, the best that could fairly be said is that Michigan's majority consciousness displayed a lack of awareness of the needs of those who were "different.")

Jewish immigrants who came to the United States and Michigan in large numbers in the twentieth century, mostly from eastern Europe, quickly devised their own charitable safety nets. For example, Detroit's Jewish population—which had risen from 35,000 in 1915 to 85,000 by 1940—worked to consolidate and strengthen community organizations. By 1926, Detroit's Jewish community had myriad philanthropic organizations, including the Jewish Community Council, the Jewish Community Center, the Jewish Home for the Aged, the Jewish House of Shelter, and Sinai Hospital and Shiffman Clinic, to name a few. After World War II and its accompanying anti-Semitic sentiment, charities for Jewish causes grew in large numbers. In Michigan, for instance, a fair number of the private foundations established during the 1940s and '50s either specified Jewish charities as their sole beneficiaries, or displayed a particular interest in Jewish groups and causes.

Detroit-area children assemble to board a bus bound for the Green Pastures Camp near Jackson in 1952. The Detroit Urban League established the camp in 1931, when existing summer camps accepted only white children. (Courtesy of Bentley Historical Library University of Michigan)

Money Pours Into Michigan

After the war ended and soldiers returned home, the economy soared. Jobs related to the defense industry had made many people flush with cash—cash that was burning a hole in the collective U.S. pocket since, during the war, many of the

For many decades, fund drives for building projects have been organized by community-based charity groups across the state. (Courtesy of Willard Library Local History Collection)

Helen Jackson Claytor became the first African-American to lead a YWCA branch when she was elected president of the Grand Rapids YWCA in 1949. Elected to the YWCA's national board of directors in 1946, she served two terms as its president, from 1967 to 1973. During her presidency at the national level, Claytor played a leading role in drafting the organization's mission statement, which calls for the "elimination of racism wherever it exists and by any means necessary." (Courtesy of Local History Department, Grand Rapids Public Library)

most desired consumer goods were difficult to find. Pent-up consumer demand for all kinds of products, not to mention the simple satisfaction of spending one's hard-earned cash, led to one of the greatest economic booms in U.S. history.

This prosperity brought a flood of capital into the state, since many of the much-sought products were made in Michigan: cars, chemicals, refrigerators, furniture, pharmaceuticals, baby food—even a newfangled item called Kitty Litter. In Michigan and across the country, the outpouring of cash helped subsidize an avalanche of new and growing philanthropic activity. Among the more conspicuous developments was the growth of private foundations. Although not uncommon before World War II—Carnegie and Rockefeller had set the pace after the turn of the century, and Kellogg, Ford, Kresge, Mott, and Dow followed quickly on their heels in Michigan—no more than a couple dozen private foundations were established in Michigan before 1939. Between 1940 and 1959, the state became home to no fewer than 100 foundations of every type.

The W.K. Kellogg Foundation staff worked under the directive to "help people help themselves" in the areas of youth, agriculture, health, and education. Here, around 1950, they gathered in front of Foundation headquarters in Battle Creek.
(Courtesy of W.K. Kellogg Foundation)

The sudden acceleration of foundation formation is not surprising, given the combination of a soaring economy, an increase in taxes (largely to help pay for war debt and the rebuilding of Europe), and a somewhat more conservative political atmosphere across the land. Private charities simply made sense. However, foundations were—and largely remain—a distinctly American phenomenon. Postwar Europe was not interested in wholesale private philanthropy. Of course, the United States escaped World War II in far better shape than most of the other countries involved. While death tolls in Europe and Asia were almost surreal—more than 35 million dead, including about 6 million Jewish people—U.S. casualties were estimated at fewer than 300,000. In addition, the war had devastated overseas economic infrastructures in ways Americans could only imagine.

A visit to Mott Camp, funded by the Mott Foundation, enriched the lives of many Flint-area youth. (Courtesy of Charles Stewart Mott Foundation)

A splendid philanthropic tradition enriches the small city of Midland, located a few miles inland from Saginaw. This bounty comes to the community thanks to the legacy of one man, one company, and one brilliant idea. The man was Herbert Henry Dow. The company, of course, is Dow Chemical Company. And the idea was, well, more than worth its salt.

Dow came to Midland in 1890, after the lumber barons had leveled endless acres of white pine in Michigan's "palm," and he discovered brine in the earth beneath their mills. Left behind by prehistoric seas, the brine was pumped to the surface and evaporated to yield its treasure: millions of barrels of salt—enough to supply half the nation at that time.

What brought the young scientist to town, however, was not the salt itself but his interest in extracting bromine from the salty water. While the product wasn't new (a plant for bromine extraction had existed in Midland for many years), Dow's process was. He had devised a way to extract the chemical with electricity instead of evaporation, a less expensive and therefore more profitable venture.

Dow built his company upon that one secret. After a few years of struggling with too little money, grumpy investors, and makeshift production facilities in a rustic building on Main Street, Dow began to turn a profit. He was helped along by a group of loyal and talented managers and a virtually endless supply of raw material: his first plants sat atop a sea of brine rich not only in bromides but in calcium, magnesium, and sodium chlorides. The company soon diversified into other products and

Herbert Henry Dow

eventually helped establish an American chemical industry that freed the nation from dependence on foreign chemical producers.

In 1936, Herbert's widow Grace established The Herbert H. and Grace A. Dow Foundation in memory of her husband, who died in 1930. Since that time, the Foundation has granted well over $200 million to programs and projects in the Midland area and in Michigan. Included are annual $1 million gifts to the Dow Gardens (visited by more than 300,000 each year) and the Midland Center for the Arts. The community also has benefited from generous gifts to the Midland Community Center and downtown development activities. Higher education is another Dow Foundation priority. In recent years, the organization has given major grants in the areas of science and technology education to many institutions, including Delta College, Michigan Technological University, Hillsdale College, and Kalamazoo College.

For many years, this foundation was run by Herbert Henry Dow II, grandson of the company founder. Under his direction, it grew to become one of the largest foundations in Michigan.

As impressive as the record of The Herbert H. and Grace A. Dow Foundation has been, it is far from the only philanthropic benefit visited upon Midland by the Dow Chemical Company. Over the years, other Dow family members and nonfamily shareholders have established a remarkable 20 foundations in this small town. Midland, unlike Carthage, has only prospered from having its fields sown with salt.

To spark interest in the sciences in young minds, the Midland Public Schools Science Resources Center was funded by a grant from The Herbert H. and Grace A. Dow Foundation. This hands-on science program for elementary school students was developed by the National Academy of Sciences and the Smithsonian Institution and was customized by local teachers. (Photos courtesy of The Herbert H. and Grace A. Dow Foundation)

Anna and Jesse Besser

(Photo courtesy of Besser Museum)

Alpena's Jesse Besser (1882-1970) was an engineering genius who found gold in the cement business, revolutionized an industry, and earned his hometown's everlasting gratitude. His devotion to education, religion, and charity leaves its mark on northern Michigan to this day.

Besser, a gentlemanly, soft-spoken man, went to work at his father's factory when he was barely out of school. Besser Manufacturing Company (later Besser Company) built and sold machines that formed concrete blocks—back then, the new construction material that would build industrialized America. Aided by the simple, interminable patience and perfectionism for which he became known, the young Besser redesigned the machines again and again, until they could "turn out more concrete lumber, in a given period, than the largest sawmill can produce in wooden lumber," as he said in 1926. Six decades later, the company was building and selling machinery that could form 26,000 blocks in an eight-hour day.

Besser's wife, Anna, worked by his side at the family company, opening mail, writing checks, and making sure the office ran smoothly. Together, she and Jesse founded the Besser Foundation in 1944 and the Jesse Besser Fund in 1960. Their aim was, in Jesse's words, "to help institutions to help themselves." Early on, both funds made grants out of capital when Jesse felt a worthwhile purpose would be served.

Besser's generosity was wide-ranging: the two funds have supported youth organizations, hospitals, schools, and government programs across the state. Most of all, the man was an ardent believer in the power of his Almighty God. To the architect building the new Alpena Congregational Church (a project Besser made possible), he directed: "Make the [chancel] window say something. That way, if the sermon is dull, the congregation can look at the window and at least receive something from attending the service." Besser funds built the First Presbyterian Church of Alpena, as well.

Education was another of Besser's passions. Reportedly, he had enrolled in classes at the Alpena Business College even before he graduated from high school. Of study, he wrote, "Each hour means just that much enlargement of one's life." Michigan colleges (Adrian, Albion, Alma, Madonna, Michigan Christian, Olivet, and Siena Heights) and universities (Central Michigan, Michigan Technological, and Oakland) have received substantial gifts, as has the Michigan Department of Conservation, Michigan Boy Scouts, and Starr Commonwealth School in Albion.

But the residents of Alpena have the most reasons to thank their concrete king. His funds built many facilities for Alpena Community College and for public and private schools in the area. They have also long supported the Jesse Besser Museum and a host of local social service agencies, and provided seed money and matching grants for new health and education programs for local residents. The Besser Foundation also has generously supported the development of the Community Foundation of Northeastern Michigan, which serves Alpena and surrounding counties.

Over the years, Besser received many prestigious awards and honors, but gestures of thanks made by the citizens of his hometown touched him most deeply. In 1954 and again in 1962, Alpena threw gala parties to celebrate Besser's 72nd and 80th birthdays. In 1964, the citizenry presented special equipment for the planetarium in the new Besser Museum, purchased by the townspeople in his honor. Like the cement that made him wealthy, Besser's generosity helped build things of strength and enduring value.

Some U.S. philanthropic organizations—including Michigan's Ford Foundation and W.K. Kellogg Foundation—would help with rebuilding efforts overseas. The Kellogg Foundation broadened its programming in the 1940s to include agriculture at a time when western Europe was rebuilding farming and food production; ultimately, the Foundation sponsored a variety of agricultural programs in the United Kingdom and western Europe in the '40s and '50s, including leadership development and the purchase of new equipment and supplies for agricultural research.

New Foundations Flourish

The beauty of the economic boom was that its sheer size allowed for a diverse and sweeping philanthropy. Suddenly there were foundations with interests across the board: art, cultural activities, the environment, industry, politics, health, human services, youth, aging, medical research, higher education, secondary education, Catholic charities, Jewish charities, Protestant charities, Armenian religious charities, bricks-and-mortar projects, any projects except bricks-and-mortar projects, charitable causes only in the Detroit area, charitable causes outside the Detroit area, projects that focus on specific religions, and projects that specifically have nothing to do with religion.

Fundraising in the name of care for the sick was often successful, as demonstrated in this view of the dedication of the Southwest Michigan Tuberculosis Sanatorium in Kalamazoo. (Courtesy of State Archives of Michigan)

As you might guess, the new foundations tended to reflect the lives and interests of their founders. For example, the Elsa U. Pardee Foundation, created in Midland in 1944 after Elsa Pardee was afflicted with cancer, has long focused its grantmaking on medical and cancer research, while the Besser Foundation, created in Alpena in 1944 by Jesse H. Besser, fully supports the Jesse Besser Museum, a local historical and art museum, in addition to other projects.

A tendency toward focusing on issues in one's own backyard was apparent in the development of many new community foundations in such places as Berrien

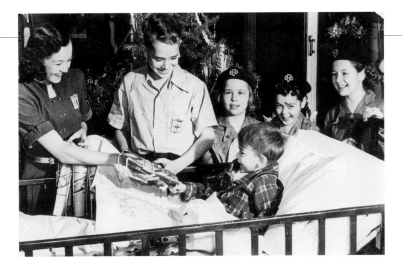

Local Red Cross and Girl Scout organizations work together to bring Christmas joy to young hospital patients, circa 1955. (Courtesy of Western Michigan University Archives and Regional History Collections)

Michigan 4-H Foundation

Shortly after the turn of the century, a program with an enduring four-leaf clover symbol was organized to teach farming principles and living skills to youngsters in rural areas. Today, it is one of the most successful and popular positive youth development programs in rural, suburban, and even urban communities across the United States. It is, of course, 4-H.

In Michigan, 4-H—a United States Department of Agriculture program with the fourfold aim of improving the "head, heart, hands and health"— is particularly popular. Every year, and in every one of the state's 83 counties, more than 200,000 youth join Michigan 4-H youth programs. Headquartered at Michigan State University since 1914, the program is administered through the MSU Extension Service, a relationship that allows 4-H to benefit from the expertise of MSU faculty and staff, who help develop 4-H programs in such areas as career exploration, agricultural sciences, the arts, computer technology, outdoor adventure, and international understanding.

The heart of 4-H—indeed, its mission—is cooperation and collaboration to build strong, healthy youth. In county 4-H offices, paid staff work with local groups and 30,000 adult and teen volunteer leaders to coordinate activities. Valuable as it is, all that peoplepower must be supported with money: 4-H programs are funded by county government, by local donations, and, in many cases, by the Michigan 4-H Foundation.

Established in 1952 and located in East Lansing, this public foundation invites charitable gifts and grants from anyone interested in its mission. Over the years, it has established several significant endowments and launched fundraising campaigns that draw support from thousands of businesses, foundations, individuals, and organizations.

"Which came first, the chicken or the egg?" The youth development activities of Michigan 4-H proved so successful that, in 1952, a foundation was formed to channel citizen donations to the program. Many young people have been well served through the decades. (Courtesy of Michigan 4-H Foundation)

One of the 4-H Foundation's ongoing activities is supporting Kettunen Center in northwest Michigan. Built in 1961 entirely from donated funds, this conference center is situated on 160 acres near Tustin, south of Cadillac. It is a modern training facility for 4-H volunteer leaders and is rented as a meeting site for other groups. More than 2,000 school children visit its surrounding trails, forests, and wetlands on day and overnight programs each year. In 1997, the Foundation successfully concluded a campaign to raise $3.8 million to expand the facilities and services of Kettunen Center, including the Russell and Ruth Mawby Learning Center and a new two-story residential wing.

A very few examples of Michigan 4-H Foundation support illustrate the tremendous variety in this state's 4-H activities:

- Benzie County 4-H Community Garden Project, in which adjudicated youth work with adult mentors to grow nearly 700 pounds of produce to help feed elderly residents.
- Generation of Promise/Toward a Greater Metro Detroit, an advanced leadership skills program for Detroit and area teens, which brings students together with business, government, and media managers for a year of educational activities.
- Michigan 4-H Children's Garden at MSU, which attracts 150,000 visitors each season and has become the national prototype for public gardens that cater to young people.
- Training for 4-H Horseback Riding for Handicappers instructors.
- Hands-On Science Training Program in Muskegon County, which engages elementary school children, particularly minority children, with scientists and their work in chemistry, computers, and robotics.
- Computer-driven "Living Books" educational program in English and Spanish developed in Lenawee County.
- Careers Unlimited Institute, a career exploration experience for youth at MSU.

Although 4-H is a national organization, the success of its activities in Michigan is not surprising. Agriculture, community spirit, and the wise use of natural resources (including such resources as young people) have been fundamental to the state's character since its earliest days. If one could take a picture of Michigan's philanthropic spirit, it would probably look a lot like 4-H.

County, Port Huron, Holland, and Jackson. The organizations were created specifically to provide grants close to home.

> **66 ...the corporate foundations were quintessentially Michiganian. 99**

In a similar vein, the new corporate and company-sponsored foundations that burst onto the scene in the 1940s and '50s typically focused much of their programming on the company's home community, employees and their families, or some special interest with which the company was affiliated. For example, the Gerber Companies Foundation, created in 1952, provides grants to programs that address children's health, education, and welfare; human service and education programs in Fremont and Newaygo counties; and children of company employees (who have a chance to receive college scholarships). Similarly, the La-Z-Boy Foundation in Monroe, which was established in 1953, focuses much of its annual grantmaking in Monroe County, providing support to the county United Way, the Salvation Army of Monroe, the YMCA of Monroe, the American Red Cross in Monroe, and the Community Foundation of Monroe.

The new corporate and company-sponsored foundations were nothing if not good neighbors. The Masco Corporate Foundation in Taylor, created in 1952, focuses on arts and education in Michigan and the Detroit area, while the Louis and Helen Padnos Foundation in Holland, created in 1959 by the Louis Padnos Iron & Metal Company, focuses largely, but not exclusively, on activities and organizations in Holland and Michigan. The list goes on—Steelcase, Whirlpool, Chrysler, and the corporate programs of Ford and Kellogg. If Michigan businesses were raking in the profits of an economic bonanza (and paying the accompanying taxes), they also were sharing the wealth close to home.

One could argue that the new surge in corporate giving was made in self-interest, a way of securing a stable community environment and a healthy, eager-to-work labor force—key requirements for steady profits. However, effecting civic improvement and the individual's ability to achieve personal independence through work had been important objectives of their charity right from the start. In this way, the corporate foundations were quintessentially Michiganian.

The postwar economic boom was not without problems for the state's businesses, however. After accumulating a variety of grievances during the forced

In the mid-1940s, the Harold Upjohn School was able to acquire large-print texts and dictaphone equipment for disabled students, thanks to funding from the Kalamazoo Foundation.
(Courtesy of Kalamazoo Foundation)

employment of the war years (workers literally could not quit a job without approval from the war board), Michigan's labor force moved steadily toward unionization after the war, eventually gaining the right to have a payroll "check-off" for union dues. The labor movement also knew conflict, with confrontations, politics, and contentious strikes.

The Birth of "United Way" Fundraising

Interestingly, two adversaries in the labor movement, Walter Reuther and Henry Ford II, contributed to the arrival of the United Fund movement (which later would be known as the United Way). With Reuther's interest in social issues that affected workers, and Ford's efforts to create the United Health and Welfare Fund of the State of Michigan in 1947, the stage was set for organized community fundraising. Actually, the concept wasn't new—charities had been soliciting funds in the workplace and cooperating in fund drives for years. One major element that was different this time, however, was the move to ban from the workplace those charities that didn't participate in the cooperative effort. Such was Ford's plan, and labor supported the idea. Unified fundraising freed workers from a barrage of donation requests and gave them input into the charity's budgets. One book on the subject recounts the following comment from a labor leader of the era: "Our shop stewards were becoming panhandlers. . . . This had to stop. The United Funds solved the problem with their simple payroll checkoffs. Furthermore, they invited labor into positions of leadership. This was important to us."

The path to a United Fund—united in more than name only—would not be easily traveled. There were numerous disagreements; many organizations, particularly some

Citizens line up to contribute to the March of Dimes campaign in Lansing, circa 1950. (Courtesy of State Archives of Michigan)

of the large and successful health charities, thought they could do better on their own; and many people had difficulties understanding the mechanics of a movement that included different types of individual and cooperative charities, from specific health funds to former community chests.

As a result of the work, however, Michigan philanthropy influenced united fundraising at the national level. According to one publication, the state's United Health and Welfare Fund was "the first state organization to establish and campaign for quotas of both state and national health and welfare agencies." Detroit's and Michigan's move toward formal United Funds thus ignited "the fire that swept the nation in the United Fund development of the 1950s." It is worth noting that another young auto executive worked closely with Ford to lift united giving off the ground. His name was George Romney, and more will be said of him later.

Michigan philanthropy continued to change and grow in other quarters throughout the postwar decades. Hospitals, libraries, universities, school districts, the arts, and local communities were among the beneficiaries. The Kalamazoo Foundation continued the legacy started by W.E. Upjohn when it donated $500,000 toward construction of the Kalamazoo Institute of Arts in 1959. The Kresge Foundation, expanding on its interests in education and medicine, funded the creation of the Kresge Eye Institute in 1948 to provide ophthamological research, education, and better care for indigent eye patients. The Kellogg Foundation began programming in Latin America in 1942, after the U.S. government asked the Foundation to help improve hemispheric relations. Other examples abound. Suffice it to say that the state's older foundations were not being overshadowed by the newcomers.

Education remained a popular cause for Michigan philanthropy in the 1950s. Virtually all of the major foundations in Michigan, and a substantial number of the smaller ones, made grants to colleges, universities, school districts, or individual schools. While some foundations leaned toward grants for private education, others appeared to be partial to public education, and still others showed no clear preference. S.S. Kresge, for instance, had a personal fondness for small, private liberal arts

A large grant from the Kresge Foundation established the Kresge Eye Institute in 1948. The Foundation has supported the Institute on a continual basis for the past half century. (Courtesy of Kresge Foundation)

The Mesick County Health Department Immunization Program, c. 1950, likely saved many children from serious illness or death. (Courtesy of W.K. Kellogg Foundation)

colleges, but his foundation issued millions to both public and private institutions, including Harvard, Massachusetts Institute of Technology, Northwestern, Wayne State, and the University of Michigan.

Education remained one of the Mott Foundation's strongest areas of interest through the 1940s and '50s. In fact, the Foundation and the Flint Board of Education were so closely linked at the time that Frank Manley held the titles of both executive director of the Foundation and associate superintendent of the board of education. The Foundation had no paid staff, relying instead on the school district's staff and board of education to administer grants and programs. Mott also provided generous support for the community education movement in Flint, essentially an effort to broaden the use of local schools as community resources. In time, Mott would support the nationwide expansion of this program.

The Kellogg Foundation expanded its educational programming in the 1950s to support a movement that was taking hold across the state and nation: the growth of community colleges. Kellogg provided grants for the creation and expansion of community colleges throughout the country, with the goal of transforming them from vocational-education establishments into more versatile institutions providing adult continuing education.

It made sense for Kellogg to support community colleges. In the late 1940s, the Foundation had concentrated on expanding medical education at a grassroots level by providing grants for national nursing associations to develop educational and service programs. The nature of that program all but required the easily accessible education offered by community colleges.

Charles Stewart Mott was a great believer in the potential of community colleges, and even donated some of the acreage around his own home for use as the site of Flint Junior College (now known as Mott Community College) and the University of Michigan's Flint campus. He also provided millions for construction of campus buildings. "I used to look out my window and see six cows. Now I see 7,000 students. That's a good exchange," he once told a Detroit newspaper reporter. If Mott were accused of being a tad thrifty on occasion, it wasn't in relation to Flint. "I'd rather save a little here and there, and give it to Flint, than squander it," he told the reporter.

Thriftiness, though, generally wasn't a flaw of Michigan's 1950s-era

Thanks to the foresight of Michigan philanthropists, community colleges across the country open new careers to millions of students each year. (Courtesy of W.K. Kellogg Foundation)

Rose and Robert Skillman

Usually "abrasive" is considered a pejorative term, but not so when one looks at the origins of Detroit's Skillman Foundation. Long before the invention of Post-it brand sticky notes, the Minnesota Mining and Manufacturing Company (3M) found great success with another product uniquely its own—waterproof sandpaper. Credit for this development goes to Robert Skillman, 3M's sales representative for the eastern United States. He convinced Frank Okie, the sandpaper's inventor, to come on board with the St. Paul, Minnesota, company. Skillman's foresight resulted not only in tremendous growth and profits for the company, but ultimately in significant philanthropic activity hundreds of miles to the east, in Metropolitan Detroit.

In 1929, after two decades spent introducing 3M's products in the United States and Europe, Skillman decided he'd had enough of Minnesota winters. He asked to be relieved of his active duties (by that time, he had been named vice president and director of the company) and moved with his wife, Rose, to Bloomfield Hills, Michigan, and Winter Park, Florida. His retirement was relatively short-lived, however. In 1939, 3M decided to open an adhesive plant in Detroit. The company asked Skillman to return and negotiate the purchase of the Studebaker plant on Piquette Street. He assisted with the coordination of the new project until his death in 1945.

Rose Skillman survived her husband by nearly 40 years, continuing to reside in both Bloomfield Hills and Florida. But she considered the Motor City her true home, and 15 years after Robert's death established the Skillman Foundation to serve the interests of children, youth, and families in Detroit.

From the beginning, trustees believed the Foundation's resources should be devoted to programs and services that prevent human problems and maximize human potential. In a recent year, grant payments totaling more than $17 million went to programs that support the Foundation's three major long-term initiatives—parenting, school development, and youth sports and recreation—as well as to more than 100 other projects in Wayne, Oakland, and Macomb counties. They include before- and after-school programs, and programs in art, music, educational enrichment, and youth development.

This focus was important to Rose Skillman, who served as the Foundation's president, then honorary chairperson, and finally trustee before her death in 1983. She was a quiet woman who never sought publicity for her charitable works. Now the legacy of Rose and Robert, and waterproof sandpaper, is the strong, ongoing support for underprivileged residents of southeast Michigan.

Harold Brooks

(Photo courtesy of Lawrence Brooks Hughes)

Although people across the state know of Marshall, the small city famous for its nineteenth-century architecture, fewer have probably heard of a truss salesman named Harold C. Brooks. Long-time Marshall residents, however, can tell you that Brooks (1885-1978) should get much of the credit for the city's architectural identity.

Brooks, who championed efforts to save the town's distinctive old buildings long before "historic preservation" came into vogue, is largely responsible for the fact that Marshall is the nation's largest "small urban" National Historic Landmark District. Before he earned a national reputation as an historic preservationist, however, Brooks was busy turning his father's Marshall-based business, the Brooks Rupture Appliance Company, into a booming international enterprise. The young man's introduction of advertising and mail-order sales (both revolutionary concepts at the time) sent profits soaring.

One of Brooks' earliest interests in the community was to beautify its green spaces. In the 1920s, he paid for a landscape architect to come to town for two years and advise residents on gardens and plantings, and he even offered prizes for the best garden, best lawn, and best-kept home in the community.

A more fanciful contribution to Marshall is Brooks' most famous. On a business trip to Europe, the "Temple of Love" in Marie Antoinette's garden at Versailles caught his imagination. It became the model for Marshall's beloved Circle Fountain. (One notable difference is that the Marshall fountain is not topped with a nude statue of Aphrodite.) Of chaste Greek Doric design, it was constructed for the city's centennial celebration in 1930. This was no mere water-spouter: Brooks' masterpiece featured more than 90 light and water patterns in an 11-minute cycle. The Circle Fountain was fully restored in 1976 and remains a symbol of the city.

Among the businessman's less visible contributions were donations of land for Marshall's first airport and VFW hall, and funds to cover most of the costs of converting an old livery stable into the town hall. He is also remembered for saving a grand and quirky 1860 landmark, the Honolulu House, from the wrecker's ball.

Brooks was more than a little determined that there would be no crackerbox structures in town. When he didn't like the nondescript blueprints for the new post office, he cut a deal with the U.S. Postal Service, offering to pay for the architect and building materials if the feds would use the Greek Revival lines he loved. The phone company, too, learned that architectural character was a serious issue with this man who owned the land on which the giant utility wanted to build. Brooks agreed to sell only after he was granted design approval.

Marshall's residents would tell you that this caretaker of buildings took care of people, too. Brooks enjoyed watching children skate on the free ice rink he built in 1926. If he spotted a youngster who wasn't warmly dressed, he would send the child downtown to buy warmer clothes with instructions to charge the coat or mittens to his account. In addition, many fine local students might never have gone on to college without Brooks' help. As one local history book notes, "Much of the good things that Brooks did for individuals in the community will never be known."

foundations and charities. Times were good, and the state's philanthropic organizations made use of the prosperity admirably: the large number of Michigan hospitals, schools, libraries, and community facilities that bear 1950s dates on their cornerstones is the visible evidence of that era's philanthropic generosity.

Clouds on Charity's Horizon

By the end of the 1950s, however, the charmed decade of Michigan's foundation community was drawing to a close. So, too, was the country's decade of domestic bliss. The countercultural explosion of the 1960s loomed on the horizon, and a number of domestic hotspots were about to erupt—in fact, the long-suppressed issue of civil rights was already bubbling. Furthermore, we were about to become involved in yet another bloody and socially divisive war. In addition to the impending unrest on the social front, philanthropy was about to tackle some major issues of its own, and would have to tangle with Congress in the process.

Actually, politicians already had started hinting at what lay ahead. As early as 1950, some in Congress suggested that foundations with holdings in only one company should lose their tax-exempt status. The Ford Foundation, which in the mid-1950s held as much as 90 percent of the Ford Motor Company's stock, was a natural target of criticism. Congress investigated the Ford Foundation on several occasions, most pointedly during the 1950s McCarthy era, when grants made abroad were viewed with suspicion by those dedicated to rooting out communist plots. As one book on the Ford Foundation notes, a 1951 *Chicago Tribune* headline reported, "Leftist Slant Begins to Show in Ford Trust." About the same time, leaflets were distributed in New York City with the following warning: "DO YOU OWN A FORD, MERCURY OR LINCOLN? If you do . . . then you are unwittingly giving support to the Communist cause thru Ford Company profits being spent by the leftist-leaning Ford Foundation."

Conspiracy theories notwithstanding, the Ford Motor Company, and the Foundation by association, was again doing well. (Ford had slipped into third place

County supervisors from the Grand Traverse area participated in a conference, c. 1950, to explore the advantages of joining resources to approach the area's health problems.
(Courtesy of W.K. Kellogg Foundation)

Education has always been an important focus of Michigan philanthropy.
(Courtesy of State Archives of Michigan)

among the Big Three automakers, and profits had been sagging until Henry Ford II took the helm and brought the company back into the number two slot. Company profits soared.) In 1950 alone, the Foundation received more than $87 million in company dividends and found itself unequipped to distribute the windfall. Despite major contributions to Ford Hospital, the Edison Institute, and local arts groups, the Foundation could not spend money fast enough.

Although a 1949 study commissioned by the Ford Foundation to plan its own future had outlined a dramatically new and larger Foundation, complications delayed implementation of the grand plan. In 1951, its new leader, Paul Hoffman, moved the Foundation—by then one of the world's largest—out of Michigan to Pasadena, California, with an office in New York City. Two years later, the Foundation established its headquarters in mid-town Manhattan. Although the Ford Foundation has left the state, the Ford family continues to make its philanthropic mark here. The Benson and Edith Ford Fund, the Eleanor and Edsel Ford Fund, the Walter and Josephine Ford Fund, the William and Martha Ford Fund, the Henry Ford II Fund, and the Ford Motor Company Fund all are based in Michigan and make grants in the arts, health, education, community development, and human services. And these are only the most conspicuous examples of Ford family philanthropy. The Ford Foundation itself remains an active member of the Council of Michigan Foundations, of which more will be said later.

Ultimately, the Ford Foundation would loosen its ties to the man who named it. In 1956, the Foundation put its first block of Ford Motor Company stock on the market. The sell-off continued as Ford—a company that didn't even make its earnings public until the early 1950s—became a publicly traded stock. By the end of the 1960s, the government was closely scrutinizing such transactions, and when the coming tax and nonprofit battle concluded in Washington, D.C., the Tax Reform Act of 1969 would regulate the ways in which private charities do business. As we shall see, the fallout was immediate and profound.

In the postwar years, the Kellogg Foundation supported a distinctive program in Plainwell and other small, rural communities to exchange outdated library books for new ones. (Courtesy of W.K. Kellogg Foundation)

Reform, Reaction,

and the Turbulent Sixties

6

66 **... The melancholy and distressing point** *is that, under the banner of reform and public benefit, a wise and valuable tradition has been consciously and seriously curtailed."*

—from a Kresge Foundation annual report, on the subject of the Tax Reform Act of 1969.

Chapter Six

Reform, Reaction, and the Turbulent Sixties 1960-1979

*I*f, as cynics like to say, every silver lining has a cloud, then the 1960s qualify as a thunderhead compared with the relative calm of the 1950s. Granted, American folklore has transformed both decades into caricatures of themselves; still, the contrast between the two eras is vivid: while the '50s produced *Gigi,* Pat Boone, and the Hula Hoop, the '60s gave us *Midnight Cowboy,* Jimi Hendrix, and LSD. Certainly, there were exceptions to the antithetical stereotypes of domestic bliss and ragged discord. Nonetheless, a clear social pattern emerged in the '60s: one of turnabout, protest, and change.

The new climate—which essentially declared open season on tradition and the existing social order—did not bode well for philanthropy in general, and private foundations in particular. Michigan philanthropy had done well in the '50s, both from an increase in the value of assets as the economy soared, and from donations, because the public had more disposable income. Also, as we've seen, new foundations—private, community, and corporate— were established at a rapid clip, increasing the number of social and charitable needs that could be addressed and putting foundations into the forefront of U.S. philanthropy. Given such a climate of prosperity, radical, '60s-style change was certain to rock the philanthropic boat.

This isn't to suggest that philanthropy in the 1950s was a case study in perfection and that any change at all was undesirable and unwarranted. Quite the contrary. In retrospect, hints of complacency were as evident in the philanthropic sector as in the rest of the nation. While

(Chapter overleaf photo courtesy of State Archives of Michigan)

The 1967 race riots in Detroit caused more than $100 million in property damage and spurred "white flight" from the city. (Courtesy of State Archives of Michigan)

the United States spent much of the '50s taking satisfaction in the American way and shunning most anything that displayed the slightest evidence of being "un-American," the nation spent much of the '60s dealing with a host of issues that had been created or exacerbated by the preceding years of neglect: teacher shortages, falling educational standards and student test scores, critically tense race relations, and cracks in the veneer of U.S. technological superiority. One can easily make a case that, had the United States not been quite so contented in the '50s, these and other issues would not have reached such a critical state in the decade that followed.

In Detroit, for instance, only 3 percent of the housing built in the 1950s was open to African-Americans; this, despite the fact that the city's African-American population doubled between 1940 and 1950, and reached more than 480,000 by 1960. In 1967, tensions over inadequate housing, police brutality, and other issues of discrimination erupted in a bloody riot that left at least 43 dead, and caused millions in property damage. The riot fueled the flight of white residents and business owners to the suburbs.

In a similar vein of inattention, the United States failed to notice, until Sputnik 1 was launched in 1957, that the Soviet Union was doing the nitty-gritty research required to create a space program. The resulting U.S. scramble to overtake Soviet space technology would bring educational improvements across the country.

Large companies supported the concept of coordinated fundraising because it would limit the number of times their employees would be approached for donations. Here, the United Fund Drive is supported by Clark Equipment Company, circa 1960. (Courtesy of Willard Library Local History Collection)

Although its current incarnation came alive in the 1960s, Detroit's Young Woman's Home Association (YWHA), as it's known today, evolved from the Working Woman's Home, which opened its doors on Jefferson Avenue in 1877. The home must have looked like heaven to young women alone in the city. Many were farm girls who had moved north from the southern states or west from Canada for the jobs Detroit offered in abundance. Most of the newcomers had very little money and no families nearby to protect them from the city's dangers.

To come to their rescue, a group of socially promi-nent citizens, led by Mrs. John F. Bagley, founded the Working Woman's Home. Accommodations there were much sought, and, in 1887, the Association's board pur-chased land at the corner of Clifford and Adams to build a new home that would house 70 women.

Even with the expansion, the home often had a waiting list, probably because it was both well-managed and well-maintained. "May I say, too, that the home was always spotless. We kept the home up, doing rooms over, bathrooms over, etc.," wrote then-board member and historian for the Association Marjorie C. Jewell in 1983. A manager resided on the property to solve problems and enforce the house rules. (Residents had an 11 p.m. curfew and were allowed to meet guests only in the parlor.)

Now 88, current board member Alice Johnston lived at the home after she relocated from Windsor in 1932. She was one of the "Nickel Immigrants," folks so named because they'd paid the five-cent fare to cross the river by ferry to take up resi-dence in Detroit. Johnston volunteered for the house chairman position soon after she arrived. For her half of a double room and two meals daily, she paid $6.50 per week.

Young Woman's Home Association

From its first years, residents paid for their room and board ($2 a week early on). The home also was supported by private donations and, much later, fundraisers such as the annual Geranium Tea and Bridge Party. Jewell remembers the teas fondly: "We all worked enthusiastically on this project and had a wonderful time doing it, knowing there would be new linens, rugs, and lamps to freshen the rooms."

Eventually, however, even shiny new furnishings couldn't attract the more adven-turesome young women of the early 1960s. They were venturing out to rent their own apartments, where there were no rules limiting the entertainment of guests to the parlor. Rooms at the YWHA were going empty, and the Association was losing money. Reading the writing on the wall, the board sold the home in 1963 for $90,000. (It has since been razed.) The proceeds from the sale became the principal for an endowment fund that continues to operate in Detroit today: the current board of the Young Woman's Home Association makes grants to a broad range of projects that benefit women and children in Michigan.

The group's long history is important to its members, evident in sentiments expressed by Jewell: "After a meeting at which we have given money away, I feel like 'Lady Bountiful.' We couldn't do it separately but oh! what a great feeling to think we can do it as a group. We all feel this is a sacred trust that has been handed down through the years."

Similarly, philanthropy across the United States, and in Michigan, could not boast of a superfluity of forward thinking in the 1950s. Throughout the decade, Michigan philanthropic organizations were admirably involved in traditional areas of charity: tending to the sick, elderly, and young, for example, and funding various endeavors related to education.

But as one historian wrote in 1962, "Philanthropy on the whole has avoided controversial issues, the very issues, perhaps, that offer the greatest challenge and that point to the greatest need." Not until the 1960s did Michigan philanthropy significantly add to those necessary and more traditional efforts by expanding into such areas as civil rights and neighborhood redevelopment.

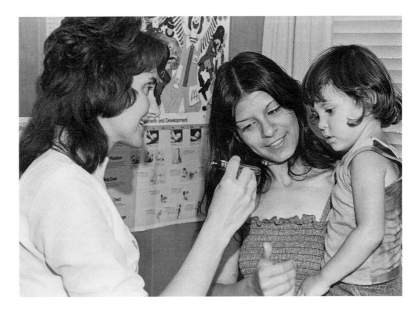

Early in 1967, for instance, the Grand Rapids Foundation funded a one-year program to help ease tensions between the community and the police department. (The program had been spurred by a request from a pastor at the city's Fountain Street Church who wanted to improve relations between police and Hispanic and African-American residents.) Depending upon one's point of view, the resulting program was either too little, too late, or a display of foresight that helped the city avoid much of the strife experienced by Detroit and several other cities. Although Grand Rapids was among the cities in which racial rioting broke out in 1967, the unrest was mild compared to what happened around the country.

For more than two decades, New Detroit has supported the Community Health and Social Services Center in Detroit's Latino community. (Courtesy of Council of Michigan Foundations)

Philanthropy Takes on Issues of the Times

If Michigan philanthropists were reluctant when it came to programming in more controversial areas in the 1950s, they were also willing to adapt and change in the 1960s. Across the state, many philanthropic organizations rapidly expanded their focus to keep pace with the social issues of the day. The Kellogg Foundation, for example, launched a multi-million dollar grantmaking program for historically black colleges in 1968 and funded programs throughout the '60s and '70s to develop leadership within community colleges. (To be fair, Kellogg had been laying the groundwork for its community college grantmaking since the

Living at the
YOUNG WOMAN'S CLUB
YOUNG WOMAN'S CLUB
...is congenial—and it's comfortable, convenient, and inexpensive

IN THE HEART OF DOWNTOWN DETROIT

In 1952, the Young Woman's Home Association celebrated its 75th Anniversary. The organization continues its philanthropic activities today. (Courtesy of Young Woman's Home Association)

1950s.) Later, Kellogg would fund the United Way of America to undertake a nationwide Hispanic Leadership Development Program.

Throughout the 1960s, the Mott Foundation supported research and programming that addressed various issues of urban renewal and urban life. Mott also took its community education program national and began a 10-year program that offered educational leadership internships to graduate and doctoral students from around the country. Significantly, the Mott Foundation also began capping its funding to the Flint public school district in the 1960s and, in the 1970s, would announce plans to phase it out completely. In 1963, C.S. Mott's right-hand man at the Foundation, Frank Manley, left the post he had concurrently held in the Flint school district, and the Mott Foundation broadened its scope to include the rest of the country on a much larger scale.

The Grand Rapids Foundation, as already noted, committed itself to a variety of new social programming in the 1960s. In 1967 and 1968, the Foundation would be particularly ambitious in the area of urban affairs, awarding more than $150,000 for such inner-city projects as day-care centers and teenage neighborhood patrols; helping to subsidize the Grand Rapids Urban League's Housing and Related Projects Program; making grants of more than $150,000 for new urban housing projects; contributing to a new, city-run program that focused on inner-city housing repair; and making a grant to Grand Valley State College (now University) to establish an Urban Studies Institute.

In 1960, the Grand Rapids Foundation issued its largest gift ever—$50,000— to start Grand Valley State College. Over the years, the Foundation has awarded millions in continued support for Grand Valley State University. (Courtesy of Local History Department, Grand Rapids Public Library)

Across the state, it seemed, the 1960s were a time of revitalized philanthropy. While the '50s brought more money and an increased number of philanthropic organizations, the '60s brought an expanded philanthropic vision. For example, Detroit's McGregor Fund helped establish New Detroit, a coalition of business, government, and nonprofit sector leaders that sought to rebuild the city in the wake of the 1967 riot; the Kresge Foundation expanded its traditional focus on bricks-and-mortar projects for existing university and medical institutions, to provide grants for job training, legal aid, and inner-city education in the Detroit area; and

Though Motown Records moved its headquarters from downtown Detroit to Los Angeles in 1972, Esther Gordy Edwards, senior vice president and corporate secretary, insists, "Motown didn't leave Detroit. We've constantly been here. We'll always be here!" Edwards is the sister of Berry Gordy, Jr., the famous songwriter who founded the Motown Record Company in the 1960s.

Edwards worked for the company 30 years, from the very beginning until it was sold. Early on, she managed the budding careers of Motown's recording artists, including Diana Ross and Stevie Wonder. When Motown headquarters moved west, Edwards did not follow. Luckily for the Motor City, she stayed in Detroit to fulfill her corporate management responsibilities and maintained a Motown office there.

It was Edwards who convinced Berry Gordy that Motown heritage deserved to be preserved and made accessible to tourists eager to visit the place known as "Hitsville, USA." Since 1985, music lovers have enjoyed an up-close look at memorabilia and the famous Motown Studio A, in the original building at 2648 West Grand Boulevard in Detroit.

Just down the street, another former Motown building is home to the Gordy Foundation. Edwards was instrumental in forming this family foundation in 1968. Thanks to a $100,000 gift from brother Berry Gordy and donations from other sources over the years, the Foundation has helped hundreds of inner-city youth attend Wayne State University, Interlochen Center for the Arts, the University of California at Los Angeles, and many other institutions.

Berry Gordy's siblings were instrumental in building his record business. Their raw materials were unity and a first-hand knowledge of basic business principles— principles instilled by their hardworking parents, who ran, among other things, plastering and grocery businesses. "We grew up from day one being in business," Edwards said in a 1986 newspaper interview. She recalled that in her family, each of the eight Gordy children started working as soon as they could walk and talk. "My dad and mother felt that there were no limits in business—that you could build it and soar as high as you wanted, based on what you put into it," she said.

The Gordy Foundation awarded its first grants in 1969 to nine students from Detroit high schools. None of them had intended to pursue higher education, but all nine graduated from college, and several earned Ph.Ds. Then and now, a high grade point average does not determine whether a Gordy Foundation scholarship will be awarded; the people who receive them must have talent, potential, and determination.

The Foundation's beneficiaries aren't so different from the young artists Motown made famous decades ago. In a 1981 newspaper interview, Edwards said: "Most of the Motown acts were just kids who walked in off the street. Most of them were from one-parent homes and all of them were poor. But to Berry Gordy it didn't matter about your economic status or where you came from. He looked to young people with three things: They had to have talent. They had to want to be a star. And they had to have character."

("The Supremes" photo courtesy of State Archives of Michigan)

the Michigan Council for the Arts was created in 1966, accepting gifts, contributions, and bequests for the purpose of furthering cultural objectives and programs.

The Douglass Community Association, a neighborhood center serving the north side of Kalamazoo, has received funds from the Kalamazoo Foundation for a number of years. (Courtesy of Kalamazoo Foundation)

In addition to these efforts undertaken by established philanthropy, citizens' groups and nonprofit organizations either sprang up to focus on specific new issues or gained new momentum. This was the era that brought prominence to such organizations as the National Association for the Advancement of Colored People (NAACP), the National Organization of Women (NOW), the Southern Christian Leadership Conference (SCLC), and the Congress of Racial Equality (CORE), as well as to numerous organizations that focused on the concerns of Asian-Americans, Latinos, and Native Americans.

Many such organizations were active in Michigan. *The Encyclopedia of African-American Culture & History* notes a 1961 incident in which the Ann Arbor Fair Housing Association picketed a housing development called Pittsfield Village for six months because it refused to sell to an interracial couple. (A city housing ordinance was passed there in 1962.) CORE activists began demonstrations in Grand Rapids in 1963 to open rental housing to African-Americans, while the same year, the Reverend Martin Luther King, Jr. led a Walk for Freedom in Detroit that attracted 125,000 people.

Despite the abundance of new and more adventurous programs, there is room to contend—and some critics have—that existing foundations were not being especially dynamic or innovative at all. Instead, the criticism runs, foundations did not tackle new areas until the terrain was made safer by government actions such as the Civil Rights Act of 1964, the Peace Corps, President John Kennedy's commitment to the space race and educational changes, President Lyndon Johnson's Great Society, and so on.

To take such criticism at face value, however, is to ignore the social and political pressures private philanthropy was facing at the time. It also is to overlook the fact that foundations were created by specific people, at specific points in time, with specific personal interests that may or may not have been particularly germane to the social ills that would develop 20, 30, or 40 years hence. Criticizing an organization founded by one businessman in the 1920s for not anticipating the social problems of the 1960s or casting aside the founder's long-standing personal interests—whatever they may have been—seems shortsighted. Michigan philanthropists, like philanthropists across the country, likely did the best they could under difficult circumstances.

Society's view of private philanthropy—what it should and shouldn't be doing, and how well it was doing it   was decidedly mixed. Depending on one's point of view, in the 1960s foundations were either too conservative or too liberal; too bigoted or too meddlesome in civil rights; tax shelters for the privileged wealthy or warehouses of intellectual radicalism.

Imagine the average philanthropist's dilemma. Should one play it safe and donate only to traditional and, no doubt, worthy charities, such as health organizations and prestigious colleges and universities (thereby ruffling the feathers of almost no one)? Or should one also become involved in the social issues of the day by, for example, donating funds to rebuild decaying urban areas (thereby earning the enmity of traditionalists everywhere)?

Our imaginary dilemma is not far-fetched. As the book *The Big Foundations* explains, "Southern conservative politicians, led by George Wallace, were furious about grants for black voter registration and school desegregation, and northern conservatives were equally upset by foundation activism in the ghettos." As the book notes, a host of other interest groups held grudges against foundations, as well: state universities, for example, thought Ivy League schools were getting more than their fair share of grants; the AFL-CIO saw foundations as tax havens for wealthy industrialists. Those who opposed the war in Vietnam were suspicious of Ford Foundation President McGeorge Bundy, who was a prominent spokesperson for philan-thropy and who, as assistant for national security affairs on the staffs of both President Kennedy and President Johnson, played a major role in the escalation of the Vietnam War.

In 1975, the Grand Rapids Foundation gave $10,000 to the Freedom Flight Task Force, a group that aided Vietnamese refugees resettling in the city. (Courtesy of *Grand Rapids Press*)

As immigrants poured into the United States, many ethnic communities created schools, churches, and charity groups to meet the many needs of their members.
(Courtesy of State Archives of Michigan)

Politically speaking, foundations could scarcely move an inch in any direction—left or right—without stepping into hot water.

Given such a touchy political landscape, we should marvel not at how slowly foundations changed in the 1960s, but that they changed at all. Actually, the fact that so many of them recognized political land mines and decided to go into controversial programming areas on both sides of the political divide serves as testament to the severity of the 1960s upheaval. Apparently, many philanthropists decided that to do nothing new was to invite social chaos, even though it was going to cost them later, literally and figuratively.

Tax Reform Rocks Philanthropy Nationwide

It would not be accurate, however, to suggest that foundation support of such noble causes as civil rights was the sole reason for the political attack private philanthropy was about to face. Despite its increasing willingness to adapt to the 1960s, and risk political disfavor, philanthropy still had problems. As the decade got under way, foundations were particularly vulnerable in the areas of accountability and public relations. For example: According to the 1970 book *Foundations Under Fire*, few of the 15 foundations with assets over $50 million, and not any of the 10 largest family foundations, bothered to release a financial report in 1965. In that year, according to the editor of the *Foundation News*, only 212 foundations issued public reports, and fewer than 120 did so regularly—this, at a time when the country was home to more than 10,000 private foundations. As Harold C. Coffman, author of *American Foundations: A Study of Their Role in the Child Welfare Movement*, said, "Many foundations feel that their activities are private, and that they do not have a responsibility of reporting them to the public."

America's postwar transportation boom begat the mobile home, and the mobile home, in turn, begat one of west Michigan's leading charitable foundations.

The foundation was established by Edward J. Frey, (1910-1988), heir to Union Bank and Trust (an institution founded in Grand Rapids by his father in 1918), who accumulated considerable wealth not only in banking but also as founder of a new breed of insurance company. In the 1940s, as he granted new installment loans for mobile home purchases, he realized he'd feel more comfortable if his customers owned physical damage insurance on their properties. Other lenders shared his concern. In 1952, he launched the highly successful Foremost Insurance Company, which specialized in mobile home and recreational vehicle insurance.

Frances and Edward Frey

Successes in business allowed Frey and his wife, Frances, to make significant donations within their community. They helped establish the Grand Rapids chapter of Junior Achievement and Grand Valley State College (now University), and generously supported community initiatives in the arts, economic development, education, and family health care. They firmly believed in sharing resources and in using money as a means to get things done.

In 1974, Ed and Frances established the Frey Foundation to carry on their charitable interests. They made substantial bequests to the Foundation at the time of their deaths in the late 1980s. Today, the organization remains a family foundation, with four Frey children among its current trustees.

The Foundation's focus is five-fold: enhancing the lives of children and families, protecting the environment, nurturing community arts, encouraging civic progress, and strengthening philanthropy. In a recent two-year span, the Foundation made grants totaling more than $10 million to more than 200 organizations, channeling most of its resources along the west side of Michigan's Lower Peninsula, with most emphasis in Greater Grand Rapids, and in Charlevoix and Emmet counties.

The breadth of the Foundation's interest is illustrated in recent large gifts, including funds given to Grand Valley State University for development of an international trade center, school of business, and graduate library; to the Grand Action Foundation for construction of a new entertainment and sports arena in downtown Grand Rapids; and to the Child and Family Resource Council for evaluation of the Kent County Healthy Start home visit and family support program. The Frey Foundation has also been a staunch supporter of the development and expansion of community foundations serving Charlevoix and Harbor Springs.

(Photo courtesy of Frey Foundation)

Max Fisher

Called an "introverted, quiet, determined, and resolute American" by a reviewer of his biography, Max Fisher has led a rags-to-riches life that has hugely benefited the Jewish communities of Detroit, the United States, and the world.

The son of a man who arrived in the United States as a penniless Eastern European immigrant, Fisher spent his early years in Salem, Ohio, and attended Ohio State University on a football scholarship. After graduation, he moved to Detroit, where he joined the oil business that his father had built. The younger Fisher soon introduced innovative oil-refining processes and formed, with a few investors, Aurora Oil Company in 1933. When Aurora, with its chain of nearly 700 Speedway 79 gas stations, was sold to Marathon Oil Company in 1959, Fisher, who was just 50 years old, became a wealthy man. He engaged in other business activities thereafter and was successful in all of them.

Increasingly, however, Fisher's passion became philanthropy. Not that his interest in charitable giving was new: his parents had instilled a sense of responsibility for helping those in need, especially Jewish people. When his weekly paycheck totaled just $15, Fisher pledged a third of his income to Detroit's united Jewish charitable fund. As Fisher's finances improved each year, so did his contributions. By 1981, he was donating half of his more-than-considerable income to various charitable causes. To an interviewer, he said he "always felt a great obligation to the community because of the great success of Aurora. You can't take without giving something back."

Fisher's interest in philanthropy was spurred by a visit to Israel in 1954. As a member of the inaugural United Jewish Appeal (UJA) study mission, he saw first-hand how American donations were being used there, and was shocked at the way many Israelis were forced to live. By the mid-1960s, Fisher held the most prestigious position in American Jewish philanthropy: general chairman of UJA, which brought together various fundraising bodies and advocated for overseas needs. Under his direction, UJA revolutionized fundraising and pulled in many of the Jewish faith who had never given before. Fisher was involved in other national Jewish philanthropic organizations as well, including the United Israel Appeal and the American Jewish Joint Distribution Committee.

In 1955, Fisher and his wife created the Max and Marjorie Fisher Foundation to assist community, state, and national causes they believed in. Among the many organizations supported by the Fishers' generosity are the Kennedy Center for the Performing Arts, Cranbrook Schools in Bloomfield Hills, Lovelight Foundation, Family AIDS Foundation, Michigan Opera Theater, Library of Congress, and Detroit Zoological Society.

In 1957, Fisher was appointed chairman of the Jewish Welfare Federation in Detroit and served as the first Jewish president and chairman of the United Foundation of Detroit (forerunner of the United Way). Under his direction, the 1961 campaign raised a record $19.5 million for projects in the city.

For his philanthropic work at all levels, Fisher received the United Way of America's top volunteer honor, the Alexis de Tocqueville Award, in 1994. It joined scores of prestigious awards and honorary degrees, many of which had come Fisher's way for work central to Detroit's economic life: in 1970, he and Henry Ford II founded Detroit Renaissance, the project that revitalized the downtown riverfront with the Renaissance Center. Fisher also was a founding member and chairman of New Detroit, Inc., which created jobs and raised funds for low-cost housing after the 1967 race riots.

Fisher's philanthropic and business activities brought him great influence on the national scene. He has been a valued adviser to governors, congressmen, senators, secretaries of state, and presidents, including Nixon, Ford, Reagan, and Bush. When Israeli Prime Minister Menachem Begin presented Fisher to President Jimmy Carter in 1979, he summed up Fisher's accomplishments in his introduction, calling this Detroit resident "the most important member of your country's Jewish community."

Besides lacking an air of openness, a fair number of foundations lacked a corresponding sense of accountability. For example, some philanthropists, reasoning that their foundations were private institutions, posited that they need not answer to anyone about their choices in grantmaking. With private philanthropy so uneven in its sense of accountability to the public, it's not surprising that some organizations misused their nonprofit status.

While flagrant disobedience of the laws governing nonprofit institutions was not endemic in Michigan or anywhere else in the nation, the few instances it did occur did not spread goodwill among the taxpaying public. And 1960s antifoundation crusader Wright Patman, a Democratic congressman from Texas, would do his best to ensure that such abuses found their way to the glaring bulb of public scrutiny. At a time of brewing taxpayer revolt, news that some (no matter how few) nonprofit organizations were using tax-sheltered dollars to control commercial businesses, earn a tidy profit for themselves and their donors, or evade taxes with no discernible intent of benefiting the public, only fanned the flames. (The cause of tax-sheltered charitable institutions was not advanced, either, when Patman revealed in the mid-'60s that a few foundations were serving as conduits for CIA money.)

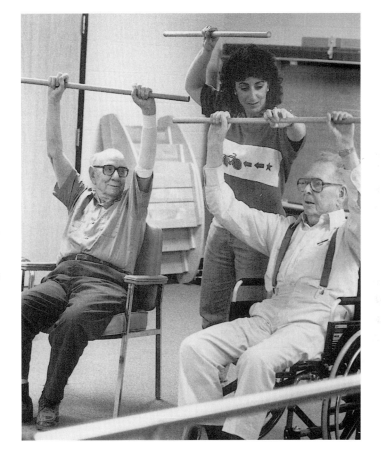

The United Jewish Foundation supports fitness classes for older adults, among many other programs. (Courtesy of Jewish Federation of Metropolitian Detroit)

If philanthropy wasn't perfect, however, neither was it suffering from the epidemic of criminal tax evasion and frivolous programming that some in Congress were about to suggest. But given the spirit of the age, it's less than surprising—from the safe distance of several decades, of course—that private philanthropy came under fire as intensely as it was about to. Today, the words "congressional inquiry" and "tax reform" can generate considerable trepidation. At the time, however, philanthropists were caught relatively unprepared. Or perhaps their past experiences with congressional inquiries had provided a false sense of security. (Even cronies of the forceful Senator Joseph McCarthy had been unable to seriously threaten the existence of private foundations, despite their best attempts at assailing the Ford Foundation, in particular.)

Whatever the case, when the U.S. House Ways and Means Committee began hearings on the tax status of nonprofit organizations early in 1969, private foundations did not have a united plan of action or self-defense. Patman opened the first hearing on a harsh note that didn't much mellow: "Today, I shall introduce a bill to end a gross inequity which this country and its citizens can no longer afford: the tax-exempt status of the so-called privately controlled charitable foundations, and their propensity for domination of business and accumulation of wealth.

"Put most bluntly, philanthropy—one of mankind's more noble instincts—has been perverted into a vehicle for institutionalized, deliberate evasion of fiscal and moral responsibility to the nation."

Unfortunately for philanthropy, Patman's combative tone would linger throughout the first round of hearings. Many of those who testified from private foundations later said they felt they had been treated either as hostile witnesses or ignored. Still others privately expressed worry that some of the foundation testimony had sounded arrogant and condescending, feeding critics' perception of foundations as elitist institutions that lacked accountability. In short, all signs were pointing to a dark cloud on the horizon.

The full extent of the bad news was learned a few months later, when the Ways and Means Committee outlined its tentative plans for legislating nonprofit philanthropic groups. Although no one who had been paying attention could have expected a congressional love letter, the tenor of the proposed legislation surprised more than a few. Among the proposals were excise taxes on foundation income, the prohibition of fellowships and scholarships to individuals, and stringent asset-distribution requirements that would make it difficult, if not impossible, for foundations to grow. (Some even professed satisfaction that the distribution requirements, combined with limitations on stock ownership, would, over time, erode foundation assets.)

The fact that foundations were held in such generally low regard in the House as to warrant severe restrictions must have been eye-opening for any philanthropist who still thought invoking the word "charity" was enough to establish oneself as honorable and good. As the events in Congress demonstrated, foundations had a fair amount of work to do if they were going to be considered even trustworthy by many legislators.

Foundation leaders set about doing that work almost immediately after the House proposal was unveiled. Before the U.S. Senate conducted its own hearings on the legislation

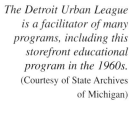

The Detroit Urban League is a facilitator of many programs, including this storefront educational program in the 1960s.
(Courtesy of State Archives of Michigan)

At age 94, Charles Stewart Mott was one of the Michigan philanthropists who testified at Senate tax reform hearings in 1969. He cautioned legislators not to "burn down the barn to kill a few rats."
(Courtesy of Charles Stewart Mott Foundation)

later in 1969, representatives from numerous foundations met to organize their efforts and present a coordinated, more constructive message.

Michigan philanthropists were among those who participated, and Mott Foundation founder and chairman Charles Stewart Mott was not to be left out, even at the age of 94. Testifying before the Senate committee in October of 1969 in a firm, sure voice, Mott cautioned senators not to "burn down the barn to kill a few rats."

"If some foundations do a poor job, regulate them—but do not penalize the foundations clearly operated for the public advantage," Mott told Senators. "The foundation functions as government's equivalent of industry's research-and-development department."

Mott outlined many of the specific programs the Mott Foundation had supported, such as health centers, health exams, and community education, and analyzed and critiqued the proposed legislation point by point:

"If spending foundation income for acceptable purposes is good, then a 7.5 percent tax on that income is not logical.... Proposed prohibition of all dealings between foundations and donors [the so-called 'self-dealing' portion of the legislation] could create unreasonable paperwork problems.... Proposed distribution of annual income or 6 percent of the fair market value of investment assets within 12 months could be unduly restrictive and detrimental.... The proposed stock-ownership limitation seems to us the most unfair, unworkable, and destructive of proposed changes."

Fetzer Institute

The Fetzer Institute in Kalamazoo funds research that explores the role of energy in health and healing. Here, John E. Fetzer is with former Egyptian First Lady Jehan Sadat at the Institute's Helping Heal the Whole Person and the Whole World conference in 1988. (Courtesy of Fetzer Institute Archives, John E. Fetzer Collection)

Arriving in Kalamazoo in the 1930s with not much more than a second-hand car, some radio equipment, and $156, John E. Fetzer, (1901-1991), soon went to work creating a broadcasting empire. He operated southwest Michigan's first radio station, WKZO, and soon branched out with radio and television stations in other cities and states. Ultimately, his fortune would be worth $200 million, thanks to the 1983 sale of his Detroit Tigers baseball team and 1985 divestiture of his vast broadcasting holdings. Most of his wealth was converted, well before his death, to an endowment for the Fetzer Foundation, which he had created in 1962. The Foundation was later renamed the Fetzer Institute.

"If there was going to be some innovative engineering done on my estate, then I was the guy who was going to do it," Fetzer explained, at age 87. He had an unusual mission in mind for his philanthropic enterprise: it would fund the search for that unknown phenomenon that would balance the physical, emotional, mental, and spiritual sides of human existence. In particular, he was interested in exploring what he termed "energy medicine"—harnessing the body's electrical energy to drive personal and global healing.

A hundred years ago, according to Fetzer, the medical profession narrow-mindedly embraced a theory of treatment that focused on chemistry (drugs), leaving untapped the science of physics (energy) in the pursuit of health and healing. Feeling that healing-by-the-mind should complement, not supersede, traditional medical practice, Fetzer called it "an additional arm of medicine that belongs in the doctor's inventory of skills."

The Fetzer Institute supports research and education exploring the relationship of the physical, mental, emotional, and spiritual dimensions of life. Past projects have included modern applications of ancient Tibetan meditative and religious healing rituals (Harvard); production of the five-part Public Broadcasting System series, "Healing and the Mind with Bill Moyers"; and pilot research studies to understand how religiousness and spirituality may be useful to address in the treatment of physical disability and an important component of health for the aging population. "I think that one of our main contributions will be to give some of these researchers, regarded as black sheep by their peers in many instances, some legitimacy, some standing," Fetzer said. He recognized that this field of inquiry is not widely applied in the medical profession. "What we want to do," he summarized, "is get physics back into medicine where it has belonged all along. ...I think that we can truly make a difference in the provision of health care."

John E. Fetzer died in 1991, four years after moving his Institute to a new 57,000-square-foot headquarters in Oshtemo Township, west of Kalamazoo. A stunning, triangular building, it is constructed of black, gray, and white granite to represent balance in physical, mental, and spiritual existence. Inside, a waterfall suggests cleansing and purification, and several giant natural crystals represent perfect order, harmony, and enlightenment.

Skepticism is the price that all funders must pay when they dare to support innovators in any field. For instance, many thought the Guggenheim Foundation foolish when it underwrote the pioneering rocketry works of Robert Goddard during the 1920s, but 30 years later the new National Aeronautics and Space Administration was thankful that it had. Perhaps in time, Fetzer's vision "to be part of a very serious attempt to find out a lot of things that have been unknown" will prove that it was his critics who were shortsighted.

Unlike the testimony presented earlier to the House Ways and Means Committee, the support aired on behalf of private foundations before the Senate Finance Committee was relatively well-orchestrated. Executives and lawyers from various foundations garnered support from leaders in business, education, civil rights organizations, and research centers, who appealed to individual legislators on the foundations' behalf. The result was not only a more unified front, which many believe encouraged the Senate to temper its legislation, but also an increased public awareness of the social benefits derived from foundations.

The best efforts of foundation leaders did much to improve the outcome of the legislation. Congress ultimately did pass the Tax Reform Act of 1969, albeit without some of the more restrictive elements that had been proposed. For instance, the excise tax was reduced from 7.5 percent to 4 percent, the prohibition against individual grants and fellowships was withdrawn, and Senator Albert Gore Sr.'s amendment that all foundations lose their tax-exempt status after 40 years was removed.

Although the consensus almost 30 years later is that the Tax Reform Act did not hit foundations as hard as it might have, and indeed produced some beneficial reforms, parts of the bill were worrisome to foundations at the time. Not the least of their concerns was a provision that prohibited any grant that would affect the public's political views—a tricky proposition since anything, even an educational program, can be argued to have an effect on politics.

The new law also held "grantmaking" foundations accountable for any grant that is misused, and gave "operating" foundations the more favorable tax status. (Operating foundations are those that generate and spend most or all income for their own activities, such as medical research or the operation of a research institute; grantmaking, or private, foundations are those that generally are established through a donation by an individual or group of individuals and spend only income from the original endowment, and include what we think of as the traditional foundations, such as Kellogg, Mott, and Kresge.) In addition, the Internal Revenue Service was granted new ways to penalize nonprofit organizations it considered to be in violation of the law.

Opponents of the Tax Reform Act claimed these provisions effectively discouraged people from donating to, or establishing, foundations. Donations to hospitals and libraries, for

The Community Foundation for Southeastern Michigan was the first foundation in the state to meet the W.K. Kellogg Foundation's $1 million challenge grant for the Michigan Community Foundations Youth Project. Pictured here in 1989, from left, are Joseph L. Hudson, chairman, Community Foundation of Southeastern Michigan; Richard Austin, Michigan Secretary of State; and Russell G. Mawby, former chairman and chief executive officer, W.K. Kellogg Foundation. (Courtesy of Council of Michigan Foundations)

example, now provided the better tax write-off, and on top of that, running a private foundation suddenly meant the possibility of increased skirmishes with the IRS.

Unfortunately, we will never know the precise number of foundations that were not established because would-be founders were discouraged by the Tax Reform Act. The 1969 law did, indeed, appear to have that effect; in Michigan, the creation of new foundations slowed considerably. While more than 65 new foundations were established in Michigan between 1959 and 1969 (which itself represented a bit of a slowdown from the feverish pace of the 1950s), fewer than 40 new foundations came into existence in Michigan between 1969 and 1979. The rate of new foundation formation did recover somewhat after 1972. (Philanthropists waited a few years to see what type of working relationship the IRS had in mind, and foundation executives pressed, often successfully, for clarification and modification of the Act's more vague and restrictive provisions.)

Besides a slowdown in new foundation growth, the post-1969 years also witnessed the demise of several private Michigan foundations. Between 1971 and 1974, more than 50 foundations began or completed the process of closing down. Although it's difficult to ascertain accurate reasons for the closures—some may have been due to the death of founders, or dissipating interest in the original mission—we can safely assume that at least some were due to the paperwork demands imposed by the Tax Reform Act and the uncertainty over future relationships with the IRS and Congress.

One complicating aspect of the Tax Reform Act that proved unsettling to foundations in terms of paperwork, sound fiscal management, and the ability to comply was a provision that limited the amount of stock a foundation could own in any one business. The new regulation sounded simple enough: No foundation may own more than 20 percent of any one company's stock. Foundations that did had 10 years to divest their excess holdings. (The Ford Foundation, which had once owned as much as 90 percent of Ford Motor Company stock, was fortunate that it had started divesting back in the 1950s.)

The stock limitation, however, was a bit more complicated than it appeared. Many foundations had been created through a single, or family, donation of stock in one company. For those foundations, divesting of significant amounts of their holdings in a limited time period could spell serious financial losses—losses that ultimately came directly out of the funds available for philanthropic grants. In addition, maintaining a tally of one's stock holdings in any company was relatively straightforward if only the foundation's assets were considered. The law, however, also appeared to require that stock held by foundation board

Guadalupe Vargas became a leader in Grand Rapids' Mexican-American community soon after she arrived in the city from Texas in 1941. She helped establish the Chapel of our Lady of Guadalupe, which offered religious services in Spanish, and visited migrant worker camps, bringing food, clothing, and religious classes to those in need. Vargas' daughter, Virginia Moralez, carries on that charitable tradition today.
(Courtesy of Local History Department, Grand Rapids Public Library)

members, officers, and children and grandchildren of the original donor be included in the 20 percent limitation. Tallying the stock holdings of these people was another matter altogether.

Some Michigan foundations were among those adversely affected by the stock limitations. The Kellogg Foundation, for example, owned about 51 percent of the Kellogg Company's common stock when the new law took effect. Educational efforts led by Foundation chief executive officer Russell G. Mawby convinced Congress to "grandfather in" existing foundations so that they could hold 35 percent of the common shares of a publicly traded company. Kellogg duly sold down to 35 percent in the early 1980s.

Also of concern to Michigan foundations was the law's payout requirement that a set percentage of assets must be spent each year. (The law essentially required foundations to spend a certain amount, and if their investment portfolio didn't yield that amount in income, they had to make up the difference by selling assets.) Opponents of the provision pointed out that the law was so complex as to be unworkable, that it made it difficult for foundations to grow (and increase philanthropic grantmaking), and that it required them to seek out more high-risk and (they hoped) high-return investments if they wanted to protect their assets. Kellogg Foundation executives were among those who actively worked to have the payout requirement eased, which it was (from 6 percent of net asset value to 5 percent) in 1981.

Foundations also were able to obtain a reduction in the excise tax that was levied against all income—from 4 to 2 percent. Included in the Act with the rationale that it was a fee to pay for the required government scrutiny of nonprofit institutions, the excise tax was in fact little more than a penalty or surcharge. It was not specifically earmarked for the IRS budget, and instead went directly into the country's general coffers. Also, it was estimated that the excise tax would generate at least twice as much money as any tax accounting procedures would have cost.

State Foundations Form Council

Clearly, as a result of the Tax Reform Act, foundations became more active in their own defense. At the very least, they began to collaborate with one another to stay apprised of action in Congress, discuss ramifications of the Tax Reform Act, and articulate goals for future grantmaking.

The Council of Michigan Foundations' annual conferences provide an arena for sharing a broad range of philanthropic perspectives. Here, movie star Paul Newman visits the event to discuss his successful food conglomerate, which donates all profits to charity. (Courtesy of John Lacko)

In Michigan, that spirit of collaboration and self-awareness led to the creation, in 1972, of the Council of Michigan Foundations. The organization actually grew out of a "get-acquainted" luncheon that took place in the Detroit area in 1970. Hosted by Bill Baldwin, the Kresge Foundation president, the luncheon included a relatively small group of representatives from such institutions as the Kellogg Foundation, the Dow Foundation, and the Kalamazoo Foundation. Not surprisingly, the main topic that day was the new tax law. Still, the event laid the groundwork for something more: now a core group of Michigan foundation representatives knew one another. Prior to the 1970 luncheon, "few of us in Michigan knew anyone in the other foundations around our state," said Russell G. Mawby, chairman and chief executive officer of the Kellogg Foundation. "We had many common interests, common grounds, basic goals, but no forum where we could come together and share our experience and our information with each other."

In 1972, another luncheon took place, this time in Battle Creek at the Kellogg Foundation. Those who attended agreed to start planning a formal structure for the organization that eventually would become the Council of Michigan Foundations (CMF), and they scheduled a statewide conference for the next year. The conference drew private philanthropists from around the state, along with such notable speakers as Michigan State University President Cliff Wharton and Congresswoman Martha Griffiths.

With another statewide conference scheduled for 1974, the organization continued moving toward a more concrete structure. Bylaws were drafted, the steering committee was expanded from eight members to 22, and the number of sponsoring institutions grew from just a handful to more than 30. In essence, the Council of Michigan Foundations was officially born, though it would be known as the Conference of Michigan Foundations until 1975. Among the early supporters were such institutions as the W.K. Kellogg Foundation, the Charles Stewart Mott Foundation, the Kresge Foundation, the Hudson-Webber Foundation, the Miller Foundation, the Dyer-Ives Foundation, and the Harry A. and Margaret D. Towsley Foundation. The Council would continue growing, from a few folks who met for lunch one day to the largest regional association of grantmakers in the United States, with a membership (by the late 1990s) of more than 380 foundations and corporate-giving programs of diverse interests and resources.

The furor over the Tax Reform Act of 1969 dissipated after Congress offered clarifications and alterations that made the bill more workable. Michigan foundations began to focus on new issues. In 1976, former Michigan Governor George Romney told attendees at that year's CMF conference that philanthropy's future remained rocky unless it took steps to improve its image. (Romney himself was involved in a number of philanthropic causes, including the National Center for Voluntary Action in Washington, D.C., which he founded in 1972. Later, he would be involved in founding the Points of Light Foundation, and in 1991 bringing under its umbrella the successor organization to the National Center for Voluntary Action, the National VOLUNTEER Center.)

Among the recommendations highlighted at the 1976 CMF conference were increased philanthropic leadership among the private sector, increased development of community foundations, and increased public understanding about philanthropy and volunteerism.

The Michigan Nonprofit Forum (now the Michigan Nonprofit Association) was founded in 1990 to unite the educational, health care, human service, arts and culture, and religious organizations that comprise Michigan's nonprofit sector. Pictured are then Kellogg Foundation Chairman and Chief Executive Officer Russell G. Mawby; John Lore, president, Sisters of St. Joseph Health System; Governor George Romney; and Michigan Secretary of State Richard Austin. (Courtesy of Council of Michigan Foundations)

Michigan foundations recognized both that the real work was over, and that the real work would now begin.

In short order, CMF members put together a public information program to communicate with public policymakers, and began publishing the organization's periodical, *The Michigan Scene*, on a regular basis. Led by CMF Executive Director Dorothy Johnson, who became president of the organization in 1985, the Council also launched an aggressive program to disseminate information to the public and began tackling many of the new issues of the day. CMF annual conferences included presentations on such topics as disintegration of the family and criminal justice.

There was one other significant fallout from the Tax Reform Act of 1969: some philanthropic organizations in Michigan examined the law and their institutional structure and

A meeting of three giants of Michigan philanthropy, circa 1965: (from left) Flint's Charles Stewart Mott, Governor George Romney, and Alpena's Jesse Besser. (Courtesy of Besser Museum)

decided it was time to reorganize. Among them was the Fremont Foundation, which in 1971 split into the Fremont Area Foundation and Newaygo County Community Services (NCCS). While NCCS continued to provide the direct services originally administered by the Fremont Foundation (and has, in fact, expanded its community programming), the Fremont Area Foundation was established as a community foundation. The new foundation combined the assets of the Fremont Foundation and several other private foundations (including some bearing the Gerber name), and now awards grants—including major funding to NCCS—aimed at improving the quality of life throughout Newaygo County. In essence, the original institution split into an operating foundation (NCCS) and a grantmaking foundation (the Fremont Area Foundation). As the new tax bill treated the two types of institutions differently, it made sense for foundations to make clear which type of organization they were.

Much of the story of Michigan philanthropy in the 1970s is a tale of response and adaptation to the Tax Reform Act of 1969. Still, the state's philanthropic leaders were not so preoccupied with tax concerns as to neglect

George Romney (left), then chief executive officer of American Motors Corporation, talks with students during a school inspection conducted by the Detroit School Needs Committee in 1961. (Courtesy of State Archives of Michigan)

the social needs of the era. The 1970s brought a rash of new social issues and corresponding philanthropic programming. Environmentalism and new energy sources were among the areas that attracted increased support. The Mott Foundation, for instance, would begin supporting The Nature Conservancy in 1973 and, by the 1980s, the Council of Michigan Foundations would begin discussing the issue of alternative energy sources.

As the '70s progressed, the number of new, private foundations being established in Michigan would increase again, and corporate foundations would see a growth spurt. (By 1979, U.S. foundation giving was exceeded by corporate giving for the first time since records were kept.) But the growth in corporate giving was only a hint of what was to come. After the

Dorothy A. Johnson has built the Council of Michigan Foundations into the nation's largest regional association of grantmakers, with over 380 foundation and corporate giving program members. Here she is shown talking with David Hunting Sr. from the Steelcase Foundation. (Courtesy of Council of Michigan Foundations)

The year 1969 proved to be an auspicious one for Grand Rapids. It was at that time that Jay Van Andel and Rich DeVos, each with his wife, set up private foundations in their shared hometown. Only a decade old, their direct sales business, Amway, was already taking off. The founders decided it was time to establish a formal mechanism to share a portion of their growing fortunes with their neighbors in Grand Rapids, throughout Michigan, and around the world.

Both foundations were and are strongly committed to supporting Christian ministry and outreach, as well as a host of Grand Rapids-area causes. The Richard and Helen DeVos Foundation gives significant sums to faith-based causes such as Calvin College, the Grand Rapids Christian Schools, and the Salvation Army; to education, including Grand Valley State University and Northwood University; to the arts, including the Grand Rapids Art Museum, DeVos Hall performing arts auditorium, the Grand Rapids Symphony, and Frederik Meijer Gardens; and to many other local organizations, including the United Way, Grand Rapids' Butterworth Hospital, John Ball Zoo, and the Western Michigan Boy Scouts.

Rich DeVos and Jay Van Andel

The Jay and Betty Van Andel Foundation also gives generously to local hospitals, churches, cultural, arts, and educational facilities—to the tune of $9 million distributed to 120 organizations in a recent year. The Foundation also provided lead funding for several projects in downtown Grand Rapids, including the Van Andel Museum Center, the Van Andel Arena, and most recently, the Van Andel Institute for Education and Medical Research. In close association with Michigan State University, the Institute will engage in research that focuses on connections between nutrition and human genetics.

Jay and Betty Van Andel expect the Institute to become one of the most notable medical research facilities in the world. In announcing its formation, they issued the following statement: "It is our hope and prayer that the resources with which God has blessed our lives may through prudent stewardship be used for the benefit of mankind and the improvement of the human condition through medical research and education."

That's quite a legacy from a young man whose earliest days in business were spent selling vitamins person-to-person. With a supply of Nutrilite supplements and a distinctive plan for helping others establish businesses of their own, DeVos and Van Andel founded Amway in 1959. Today, it is one of the world's largest direct-selling companies. Through 2.5 million independent distributorships worldwide, Amway Corporation sold $6.3 billion worth of soap, cosmetics, vitamins, and household products in a recent year. The privately held company is experiencing runaway growth. It posted record sales for 11 consecutive years and has tripled sales since 1990. Both DeVos and Van Andel are billionaires many times over.

The two men have thought a lot about the importance of philanthropy, and how their business success gives them the opportunity to make a difference. In his recent book, **Compassionate Capitalism**, DeVos writes: "Becoming a compassionate capitalist begins with the decision that you can make a difference. We don't have to solve the world's problems by ourselves. But we must believe in ourselves enough to be convinced that we can do something."

(Photo courtesy of
Amway Corporation)

A philanthropic leader in her own right, Lenore Romney addresses the 1996 Grantmakers/Grantseekers Seminar held in Lansing, jointly sponsored by the Council of Michigan Foundations and the Michigan Nonprofit Association. Romney is flanked by Rick Cole, chairman of the board of the Michigan Nonprofit Association, and William C. Richardson, president and chief executive officer of the W.K. Kellogg Foundation. (Courtesy of Council of Michigan Foundations)

recession of 1981-82, the nation's economy would take off once again, allowing for a new rush of corporate giving and the formation of new foundations.

The latest philanthropic efforts would come at an opportune time when the nation was facing a host of challenges—gangs, drug wars, cocaine addiction, homelessness, violence among youth, and the specter of AIDS. Simultaneously, the federal government would begin cutting back funds for many long-standing social programs, and the phrase "a thousand points of light" would enter the national lexicon. With the charitable pendulum swinging back toward the private sector, the 1980s arrived at our doorstep.

A 1980s 4-H drug-abuse-prevention program demonstrates that the organization's focus extends far beyond its original programs in farming and animal husbandry. (Courtesy of Michigan 4-H Foundation)

Epilogue

The 1980s and Beyond

"The man who dies thus rich dies disgraced."

—*Andrew Carnegie, 1880s*

"He who dies with the most toys wins."

—*Malcolm Forbes, 1980s*

We end almost where we began: with Charles Dickens. Because if ever there was a jumble of contradictions—a best of times and a worst of times—the United States of the 1980s surely qualifies. In the early years of that decade the economy of the nation—and especially Michigan—was in the doldrums. Recovery began in 1983, but even as the economy was sailing to new heights, making consumerism and displays of wealth something of a national credo, crack cocaine was devastating inner cities, AIDS was killing thousands, and homeless people were appearing on the streets.

Perhaps a more accurate view of the decade would be one that encompasses all of those things and still includes the efforts of dedicated philanthropists. In Michigan, as elsewhere in the country, they put in long hours looking for ways to meet both new and more familiar social needs. The 1980s were a time of bolstered traditional philanthropy, as soaring share values on Wall Street (notwithstanding the brief crash of 1987) increased the portfolios of endowed organizations. It also was a time of dynamic new programs, as philanthropists tried to tackle a host of problems that intensified in that era, such as crime and violence among youth; poor, single-family households; AIDS; and a relentless deindustrialization that was leaving thousands unemployed and still others working for less money.

Among the new programs was the Michigan Emergency Cash Flow Loan Fund, created by the Council of Michigan Foundations in 1983 and administered by the Michigan League for Human Services (MLHS) to help nonprofit organizations facing short-term cash flow shortages. Deindustrialization, which had caused factories and businesses to close or to cut their payrolls, led to

Thanks in part to support from the Kalamazoo Foundation, a young harpist performs at the Black Arts Festival, sponsored by the Black Arts and Cultural Center in Kalamazoo.
(Courtesy of Kalamazoo Foundation)

Ed Lowe (1920-1995) thought "entrepreneur" was the gutsiest, fanciest title a person could have. His own inventiveness sparked what is now an $800 million-a-year industry—cat-box filler—and, in some years, his business acumen netted him nearly 40 percent of that industry's retail sales.

Lowe grew up in Cass County, in southwest Michigan. He established his company in Cassopolis in 1947 at age 27 after making an amazing discovery: the clay he had been bagging and delivering to gas stations to soak up spilled motor oil did a cleaner, better job of absorbing cat waste than the ashes or sawdust most people used. In no time, he had christened the clay "Kitty Litter" and was peddling it at pet stores and cat shows.

A down-to-earth, folksy soul who seldom carried cash or wore a necktie, Lowe once called himself "just an old country boy bumbling along." Bumbling? Hardly. One of this multimillionaire's favorite sayings (from Percy Ross) was, "He who gives while he lives, also knows where it goes." In 1985, Lowe established the Edward Lowe Foundation on 3,000 acres near his hometown of Cassopolis, then headquarters of Kitty Litter Industries. The philanthropist had well-defined goals for this project: his foundation would help entrepreneurs succeed and compete in the world market. Lowe feared the United States was losing its manufacturing edge and believed entrepreneurship offered the country's best chance to win it back.

Edward Lowe Foundation

In 1988, Lowe announced several projects that would be housed in a new Business Opportunity Center on his farm. A venture capital business, partnership program, school for business training (the American Academy of Entrepreneurs), and advanced teleconferencing facilities would all support entrepreneurial growth. As part of this initiative, Lowe selectively gave $1 million grants to new manufacturing ventures.

In 1993, Lowe's foundation began operating the new Cass County Business Center, an incubator service that would support small businesses—manufacturers in particular—during their first critical years of operation. He also donated funds to an entrepreneurship program at Michigan State and Western Michigan universities, and reported spending more than $2 million informing policymakers to make success easier for the small, independent business owner.

He had many outside interests. One of his best-known projects was an attempt in the 1970s to turn the run-down Cass County town of Jones into "Everybody's Home Town"—a historical tourist attraction. He invested significant time and money in restoring many of the downtown buildings, but abandoned the project after three years. Lowe also built a golf course that used pickle barrels for the holes, and he wrote books of poetry and prose, including an autobiography, **The Man Who Discovered the Golden Cat.**

Golden, indeed. Lowe sold his business in 1990 for an undisclosed sum and, a year later, gave $21 million to his Foundation. A deferred gift of another $27 million, including his Cassopolis farm, went to the Edward Lowe Foundation when its founder died in 1995. These funds continue to generate grants and training for American entrepreneurs.

(Photo courtesy of Edward Lowe Foundation)

Michigan Women's Foundation

In 1986, the Michigan Women's Foundation was founded to support efforts that improve economic well-being for women and girls. Here, MWF representatives receive a grant from the Metro Health Foundation. (Courtesy of Michigan Women's Foundation)

Since the state's early days, women have played an active and vital role in philanthropy: raising funds; tending to the sick, young, elderly, and poverty-stricken; and working as volunteers on the front lines of charity, while men largely did the administrative work and controlled the philanthropic purse strings.

Today, of course, things are different. Women are increasingly occupying administrative and board positions at the state's charitable, nonprofit institutions, making many of the top-level decisions about programs and financing.

A most logical extension of women's expanded role in philanthropy is the Michigan Women's Foundation. Founded in 1986 by a group of Michigan women who were active in politics, business, law, and other professions, the Foundation's primary goal is to serve the needs of women and girls, particularly in areas that contribute to a female's economic well-being. (The Michigan Women's Commission had reported in 1990 that more than 50 percent of all female-headed households with children were living at or below the poverty level, and that two out of three poor adults were women.) Former Michigan First Lady Helen W. Milliken and state legislator Lana Pollack were among the women involved in the organization.

Since its inception, the Foundation has provided about a million dollars in grants to more than 100 organizations such as domestic violence shelters, Girl Scout councils, women's economic development organizations, and YWCAs. It has funded such programs as business development, job training, new educational opportunities, substance-abuse counseling, recreational projects, and other efforts that seek to empower women and girls.

Supported by individual donors and various institutions across the state—including the Ford Motor Company, Chrysler Corporation Fund, General Motors Foundation, Blue Cross and Blue Shield Foundation, W.K. Kellogg Foundation, and the Michigan Department of Public Health, among others—the Foundation also is working to address obstacles that set women up for failure at an early age, as well as health issues that impede women's and girls' economic welfare. The organization noted in a 1990 report, for example, that "60 percent of elementary school girls and 67 percent of boys surveyed described themselves as 'happy the way I am.' ...The gender gap increases from 7 points to 17 points by high school—only 29 percent of high school girls say they are happy with themselves, as compared with 46 percent of high school boys."

Clearly, much work remains to be done to improve women's lives—and, by extension, the lives of their families. The Michigan Women's Foundation is one of the many philanthropic organizations that recognize the direct correlation between women's welfare and Michigan's future. As a 1993 Foundation report said, "Partnerships among funders and service providers designed to assure that women and girls can walk with confidence through the doors that are open to them—and can open others that still remain closed—can do much to help our state make use of the full capacities of its citizens."

financial shortfalls for numerous smaller nonprofit agencies around the state. The deficits came just as the services those agencies offered were most needed: health care, job training, career development, family counseling, drug abuse counseling, economic development, and AIDS testing, to name just a few. MLHS, which is supported by local United Way agencies through the United Way of Michigan, received capital for the emergency loan program from the Kellogg Foundation and the Skillman Foundation.

A Council of Michigan Foundations Legislator's Seminar works to educate public officials on issues that affect foundations. (Courtesy of Council of Michigan Foundations)

Another new program in the 1980s also was aimed at aiding and pulling together nonprofit organizations, much as the Council of Michigan Foundations had pulled together foundations back in the 1970s. The Michigan Nonprofit Forum, founded in 1988 with leadership impetus from the Council of Michigan Foundations and the Kellogg Foundation, began to serve as an information clearinghouse for nonprofits, working with policymakers, the public, and news media to promote public understanding of the nonprofit sector and how it functions. Creation of the organization was supremely logical: by 1988, Michigan had more than 40,000 nonprofit organizations, most of which had only volunteer staff. Not surprisingly, included in the Forum's mission was a commitment to promote volunteerism. Toward this goal, the organization worked closely with that tireless champion of volunteerism, former Governor George Romney. Later, the Forum evolved into a trade association for all Michigan nonprofit organizations and, accordingly, changed its name to the Michigan Nonprofit Association.

In contrast with the narcissism and self-indulgence of the times, volunteerism was staging a comeback, at least in terms of public relations sound bites. President Ronald Reagan had called upon the private sector, and especially the nonprofit sector's spirit of volunteerism, to help pick up the slack when the rate of growth in social welfare programs slowed early in the 1980s. President George Bush further shone the spotlight on America's philanthropic spirit when he referred to it as "a thousand points of light" later in the decade.

The Cheff Center, near Augusta, provides therapeutic riding experiences for handicapped children. Over the years, the Center has benefited from the generous support of many foundations. Here, former Kellogg Foundation Chief Executive Officer Russell G. Mawby (right) assists a young rider. (Courtesy of W.K. Kellogg Foundation)

The private and nonprofit sectors, however, could not handle the load of responsibility that the federal government was handing them. By 1982, the nation's unemployment rate was nearly 11 percent—and more than 20 percent among African-Americans. Areas of the country that had relied on manufacturing, such as Michigan, were particularly hard hit. The Big Three automakers—Chrysler, General Motors, and Ford—already had been having business difficulties because of increased foreign competition in the late 1970s. When the recession

of the early 1980s hit, Chrysler lost more than $1.5 billion in a single year; General Motors, $763 million; Ford, $1.5 billion. The recession and the loss of market share to foreign competitors caused staggering job losses in the auto industry. Between 1979 and 1991, the Big Three would slash their payrolls from more than 480,000 employees to fewer than 300,000. Michigan, because of its reliance (or dependence) on the auto industry, suffered more than most states: in 1982, the state's unemployment rate reached 17 percent.

New Philanthropy in Michigan

Despite the hard economic times and the budget cuts, many Americans began helping those in need. In Michigan, several new philanthropic organizations were established, everything from community food banks and local Habitat for Humanity organizations to corporate and special interest foundations. While the state had fewer than 500 foundations in 1972, it had more than 900 by 1988, including such new public charities as the Michigan Women's Foundation and the Michigan Native American Foundation.

Corporate giving increased as well. The Amway Environmental Foundation, the Dow Corning Foundation, the MichCon Foundation, the Standard Products Company Charitable Foundation, the Upjohn Company Foundation, and the Domino's Foundation are just a few of the organizations that emerged as corporate/company-sponsored institutions or as independent institutions created through corporate gifts in the 1980s. The wave of increased corporate giving, incidentally, was one that would continue well into the '90s.

Continuing a trend that began in the mid-1970s, community foundations also blossomed. The Community Foundation for Southeastern Michigan, for example, was founded in 1984 by a number of Motor City community leaders to serve seven Michigan counties, primarily around the Detroit area. Other community foundations that sprang to life in the '80s included the Bay Area Community Foundation, the Saginaw Community Foundation, and the Four County Foundation, which serves portions of Macomb, Oakland, Lapeer, and St. Clair counties. In numerous instances, the organizations (including the Battle Creek Community Foundation) were aided with grants and donations from corporations, and from corporate and private foundations.

To further expand and assist the state's relatively new network of community foundations, and to invest in the future, several members of the Council of Michigan Foundations created a challenge-grant program called the Michigan Community Foundations' Youth Project (MCFYP) in 1988. The project was aimed at helping community foundations build their endowment funds, ensuring that every donor in the state had access to community foundation resources for establishing new endowments, and involving youth in philanthropy and volunteerism. MCFYP would continue throughout the 1990s, with more than $59 million for the matching and technical assistance grants provided by the Kellogg Foundation, and $600,000 in technical assistance funds supplied by the Mott Foundation. As a result, by 1997, more than

Summer camps are one of the many programs for youth funded by the United Jewish Charities. (Courtesy of Jewish Federation of Metropolitian Detroit)

50 new community foundations and geo-graphic component funds (funds established within a large community foundation to ben-efit areas too small to support a freestanding community foundation) were established, more than $117 million was endowed in community foundation permanent funds, and more than 5,000 young people were trained in philanthropic giving.

Despite the challenges encountered in the 1980s, the decade did begin with some good news that would help foundations in their future work: in 1981, Congress voted to reduce the payout requirements outlined in the Tax Reform Act of 1969. After 1981, foundations had to spend only the equivalent of at least 5 percent of net asset value, something most could do without spending all of their investment income. In addition, they no longer were required to spend all net investment income. (Previously, the law had required that they spend at least 6 percent of their assets, or all net income, whichever was greater.) As a result of the change in the payout requirement, the chipping away at foundation assets largely ended, and foundations became better able to build up assets to increase future program payouts and thus meet future needs. Finally, foundations could worry more about their philanthropic activities, and less about government-required paperwork and short-term expenditures.

"I literally danced a jig when I heard," said William S. White, president of the Mott Foundation and then CMF chairman. "Under the old Tax Act we had to give away our income. Now, if we invested wisely we could keep pace with inflation."

White, by the way, also was a proponent of more venturesome foundation program-ming. In 1982, during Mott Appreciation Week in Flint, White told the local newspaper that he believed U.S. foundations should use their resources to try new things and experiment for the future. Echoing the comments of founder C.S. Mott, White said he thought that foundation grant-making should be used as a type of risk capital—"government's equivalent of industry's research-and-development department," as C.S. Mott himself put it back in 1969.

Certainly, Michigan foundations have been willing to encounter the "risk" in risk capital grant-making. Not all programs have been dazzling suc-cess stories, and the 1980s saw more than a few disappointments. For instance, although the Mott Foundation led the nation into community

The W.K. Kellogg Foundation is involved in many cross-cutting programs including leadership, community development, information systems/technology and capitalizing on diversity. (Courtesy of W.K. Kellogg Foundation)

A reading program is an important activity of the Hispanic American Council in Kalamazoo, which has received support from the Kalamazoo Foundation. (Courtesy of Kalamazoo Foundation)

education, Foundation officials candidly admitted that some Mott-sponsored community education centers around the country were less than exemplary in the 1980s. On the other hand, had it not been for Mott's willingness to take a chance on community education in the first place, the concept might never have become a staple of education in the United States. As one Mott executive told the *Flint Journal* in 1982: "To be innovative, you have to expect some bombs. You have to be willing to risk failure.... You need people with imagination. Any foundation worth its salt is a bit flaky."

While we can't testify to the flakiness of Michigan philanthropists, it is apparent that they're a plucky lot. Despite harsher tax laws, fluctuating economic cycles, and an overwhelming number of social needs, Michigan philanthropy continues to grow. Between 1988 and 1996, for example, the number of foundations in Michigan grew from around 900 to nearly 1,300—at least 115 of those between 1994 and 1996 alone.

Clearly, our state's philanthropic heart is beating soundly, and making the future a little less scary. It is heartening to know that across the state, philanthropists from all walks of life—representing all religious beliefs, ethnic groups, socioeconomic brackets, political persuasions, lifestyles, interests, and ages—are working to make Michigan a better place to live. The strength of that activity and commitment bodes well for Michigan philanthropy in the twenty-first century. Michigan's philanthropists of years past have built a splendid legacy for current and future Michiganians. No one owns our state's philanthropic resources; those who administer them are only stewards for those who can benefit from them. This is as it should be, for in the words of Abigail Scott Duniway, "The debt that each generation owes to its past, it must pay to the future."

Youth Leadership Camp, sponsored by the Council of Michigan Foundations, trains young philanthropists who will serve on the Youth Advisory Councils of Michigan's community foundations. (Courtesy of Council of Michigan Foundations)

Then Kellogg Foundation Chief Executive Officer Russell G. Mawby testifying before the Oversight Subcommittee of the House Ways and Means Committee in June of 1983 on the subject of excess business holdings (the amount of stock in a publicly-held company that a private foundation is allowed to own). Congressional oversight is an ongoing fact of life for Michigan philanthropy. (Courtesy of Council of Michigan Foundations)

Dr. John Porter knows first-hand how much the state's philanthropic resources can do for education. Porter, an Albion College and Michigan State University graduate, ascended to the position of state superintendent of public instruction in 1969, rescued Eastern Michigan University from extinction in the 1980s, bailed out the Detroit Public Schools as its superintendent from 1989 to 1991, and then went to work as director of the Urban Education Alliance, Inc. (UEA) in Ann Arbor.

Along the way, he's helped thousands of students across Michigan achieve academic success, and he's done it by making good use of the state's abundant philanthropic giving. For example, in Detroit, Porter used people power, foundation support, and the assets of the Ford Motor Company to save the public school system from collapsing under a $160 million debt. "Private money was very, very critical to our success," he said in a 1995 magazine article.

John Porter

Charitable donations also support Porter's current work with the Urban Education Alliance in Ann Arbor. The organization was established in 1983 at Eastern Michigan University in response to concerns expressed by superintendents of the five urban "GM districts": Detroit, Pontiac, Lansing, Saginaw, and Flint. They recognized that the needs of their students were not being met.

UEA stepped in to develop and implement programs at the local school district level designed to help at-risk students succeed. Today, UEA programs continue to focus on increasing reading readiness through preschool and kindergarten; helping students with learning skills during elementary and middle school; and teaching life-role competency skills in high school. The organization is supported by several Michigan corporate foundations, including those associated with Consumers Energy, Chrysler, Ford, and Ameritech.

"[Foundations] should be in the leveraging business..."

Porter believes foundation investments should leverage change, not finance it. He notes that while a single foundation may not have the funds to accomplish a task, a collaborative effort by education, the private sector, and government can achieve success. "[Foundations] should be in the leveraging business, attracting other sources of support for tackling a problem or an issue," he says. "Being identified as a lone party committed to solving a problem is a delicate situation in which to be placed."

"Foundations can't run the schools," he continues. "But what they can do is leverage funds to help schools invent ways to solve problems. To me that's the major principle of good philanthropy."

Porter spends time on the other side of the charitable checkbook as a Charles Stewart Mott Foundation trustee. In this role, he participates in project site visitations and approves funding proposals in the foundation's main program areas: the environment, civil society, poverty, and Flint-area projects.

"I guess I see philanthropy the way that C.S. Mott, one of its pioneers, did some 70 years ago," Porter says. "He knew that philanthropy allows people 'to dream the dream.' That's what it's been, it is, and what it ought to continue to be."

During his two decades with the Detroit Tigers, Hall-of-Famer Al Kaline never was paid more than $100,000 per year. During his second year in the major leagues, Michigan native Derek Jeter was earning more than $500,000 per year as a New York Yankee.

Clearly, today's professional athletes are well-equipped to create a philanthropic legacy. And they're doing just that, although the legacy often has as much to do with a player's community-mindedness as it does the size of his or her contract. Fortunately for us, in an era of highly paid, superstar athletes, Michigan is home to a number of big earners who also happen to be big on generosity and civic pride.

For example, Jeter, a Kalamazoo native, created the Turn 2 Foundation in 1997 to assist programs that work with kids who are at risk of drug and alcohol abuse. But Jeter's low-key personality, graciousness, and accessibility in the face of superstardom have made him as popular back home as any monetary donations. He's been welcomed back with a Derek Jeter Day at Kalamazoo Central High School, and business leaders and corporate sponsors lined up to attend the kickoff for his foundation.

"The support for the foundation is just great," Jeter told the **Kalamazoo Gazette.** *"I wanted to give back to the community and this is a great way to do it."*

Similarly, Detroit Pistons forward Grant Hill takes time out to organize summer camps for youngsters and has established a fund at the Community Foundation for Southeastern Michigan. Former Pistons superstar Isiah Thomas has also been involved in a variety of philanthropic activities over the years, long before his retirement in 1994. Thomas, who earned an undergraduate degree in criminal justice during the off-season, makes no bones about the fact that he wants to use his celebrity status to help improve society. When he was pursuing his degree, he told **U.S. News & World Report:** *"I wanted to be a lawyer because I thought that the platform for social change would come through law and politics. Once I got to the NBA, I could see that the celebrity aspect gave you an instant credibility."*

Thomas, like other Michigan professional athletes, has supported his philosophy with action. He was co-chair (along with Detroit Mayor Coleman Young) of No Crime Day in Detroit in 1987, an event that featured a citywide march and scholarships for at-risk youth. He's also given numerous anti-drug and motivational talks to Michigan young people; co-chaired (along with his wife, Lynn) a celebrity auction in Royal Oak to help raise funds for the fight against AIDS and HIV; donated funds to pay for student scholarships in Detroit; and once even donated his $300,000 paycheck from an All-Star game to help rescue the Detroit Public Schools' athletic program.

Apparently, neither Jeter, nor Hill, nor Thomas is the person critics have in mind when they accuse professional athletics of fostering a new breed of belligerent, self-centered superstars by handing out million-dollar paychecks. In Michigan, at least, the increased number of highly paid athletes is simultaneously increasing the number of athletes who are involved with philanthropic causes. Whether that fact is more a reflection on the individuals involved or the Great Lakes State itself is hard to say. Either way, the people of Michigan win.

Appendices

Bibliography

"American Women in Civic Work," *The Woman Citizen*. (February 14, 1920): 874-875.

Aminoff, Helen. "The First Jews in Ann Arbor," *Michigan Jewish History*. 23 (Winter 1983): 3-14.

Amway Corporation. *Biographical Sketches of Richard DeVos and Jay Van Andel*. Grand Rapids: Amway Corporation, n.d.

Andrews, F. Emerson. *Foundations: Twenty Viewpoints*. New York: Russell Sage Foundation, 1965.

Arnove, Robert P., ed. *Philanthropy and Cultural Imperialism*. Bloomington: Indiana University Press, 1982.

Bald, F. Clever. *Michigan in Four Centuries*. New York: Harper, 1954.

Bales, Clarine, Youth Foundation of America. Interview, 12 February 1997.

Barnard, Harry. *Independent Man: The Life of Senator James Couzens*. New York: Scribner, 1958.

Barnes, Al. *Vinegar Pie and Other Tales of the Grand Traverse Region*. Detroit: Wayne State University Press, 1958.

Barnes, Gilbert H. *The Antislavery Impulse*. New York: Harbinger, 1933.

Bates, George. "By-Gones of Detroit: Joseph Campau and the Early French," *Michigan Pioneer Collections*. 40 vols. Lansing: Robert Smith & Co., 1894. vol. 22: 336, 373.

Baxter, Albert. *History of the City of Grand Rapids, Michigan*. Grand Rapids: Munsell & Co., 1891.

Bazell, Robert. "Tax-Exempt Litigation: IRS Curbs Draw Widespread Opposition," *Science*. 170 (November 13, 1970): 716-717.

Berg, Barbara. *The Remembered Gate: Origins of American Feminism*. New York: Oxford, 1978.

Berner, Robert. "S.S. Kresge," *Dictionary of American Biography*. New York: Scribners, 1977.

Besser, Jesse, Foundation. *Annual Report*. Alpena: Jesse Besser Foundation, 1995.

————. *A Jesse Besser Centennial Commemoration*. Alpena: Besser Foundation/Besser Fund, Inc., 1982.

"Big Reason for Motown's Great Success, A," *Detroit Free Press*. 12 February 1970, n.p.

Bingay, Malcolm W. *Detroit is My Hometown*. New York: Bobbs-Merrill, 1946.

Black Women in America. 1992 edition, s.v. "Sojourner Truth," by Nell Irvin Painter.

Blackburn, George, ed. *The Diary of Captain Ralph Ely of the Eighth Michigan Infantry*. Mount Pleasant: Central Michigan University, 1965.

"Blacks Who Give Something Back," *Ebony*. 45 (March 1990): 64-69.

Blair, Karen. *The History of American Women's Voluntary Organizations 1810-1960*. Boston: Hall, 1989.

"Blind Visionary Honored," *Grand Rapids*. 29 (November 1993): 11.

Bolkosky, Sidney. "A Review of *Quiet Diplomat: A Biography of Max Fisher*." *Michigan Jewish History*. 33 (Winter 1992): 10-11.

Bolt, Christine. *The Women's Movement in the United States and Britain from 1790 to the 1920s*. Amherst: University of Massachusetts, 1993.

Bondi, Victor, ed. *American Decades 1970-1979*. Detroit: Gale Research, 1995.

Boorstin, Daniel J. *The Decline of Radicalism*. New York: Random, 1969.

Brandt, E.N., Rollin M. Gerstacker Foundation. Interview, 3 April 1997.

Brandt, E.N. and Brennan, Barbara S. *The Papers of Herbert H. Dow*. Midland: Post Street Archives, 1990.

Bremner, Robert. *American Philanthropy*. Chicago: University of Chicago, 1960.

————. *From the Depths*. New York: New York Press, 1972.

————. *The Public Good: Philanthropy and Welfare in the Civil War Era*. New York: Knopf, 1980.

Brockett, L.P. *Woman's Work in the Civil War*. Philadelphia: Zeigler, McCurdy, & Co., 1967.

Brown, Alan, Houdek, John and Yzenbaard, John. *Michigan Perspectives, People, Events and Issues*. Dubuque: Kendall/Hunt Publishing Co., 1974.

Brown, Paul, Youth Foundation of America. Interview, 12 February 1997.

Bryson, Bill. *Made in America*. London: Reed International Books, 1994.

Bureau of the Census. U.S. Department of Commerce. *1990 Census of Population and Housing Characteristics for the Congressional District of the 103rd Congress of Michigan*. Washington, D.C.: Superintendent of Documents, 1992.

Burton, C.M. "Detroit in the Year 1832," *Michigan Pioneer Collections*. 40 vols. Lansing: Robert Smith Printing, 1900. vol. 28: 168-170.

Busby, Joseph. "Recollections of Pioneer Life in Michigan," *Michigan Pioneer Collections*. 40 vols.

Busby, Joseph. "Recollections of Pioneer Life in Michigan," *Michigan Pioneer Collections*. 40 vols. Lansing: Wynkoop, 1908. vol. 9: 122.

"Businesses Asked to Sponsor No Crime Day Scholarships," *Michigan Chronicle*. 21 November 1987.

"By Our Deeds," *The Flint Journal*. 13 June 1982, p. 1-35.

Byran, Ford R. *Henry's Lieutenants*. Detroit: Wayne State University Press, 1993.

Caddy, Frank. *A Home for Our Heritage: The Building and Growth of Greenfield Village and Henry Ford Museum 1929-1979*. Dearborn: Henry Ford Museum Press, 1980.

Campbell, Murray. *Herbert Dow, Pioneer in Creative Chemistry*. New York: Appleton-Century, 1951.

Carlisle, Robert. *A Century of Caring*. Elmsford, N.Y.: The Benjamin Co., 1987.

Carson, Gerald. "Kellogg, W.K.," *Dictionary of American Biography. supplement 5*. New York: Scribners, 1977.

Carter, L.J. "Foundations and the Tax Bill: Threat to the Private Sector?" *Science*. 166 (December 5, 1969): 1245-1248.

Carver, Richard. *A History of Marshall*. Virginia Beach, VA: Donning, 1993.

Carwardine, Richard. *Transatlantic Revivalism*. Westport: Greenwood Press, 1978.

"Cass Business Incubator is Latest Lowe Endeavor," *Kalamazoo Gazette*. 5 October 1995, p. A-1.

Catton, Bruce. *Michigan: A History*. New York: Norton, 1976.

Celebrity Register. 1973 edition. s.v. "Marjorie M. Post."

Center for Urban Educational Improvements. "Education is the Best Defense of Democracy," Ann Arbor: n.p., n.d.

Chafe, William. "Flint and the Great Depression," *Michigan History*. 53 (Fall 1969): 225-239.

Charles, Searle F. *Minister of Relief, Harry Hopkins and the Depression*. Westport: Greenwood Press, 1963.

Cherin, Elizabeth, Fremont Area Foundation. Interview, 11 February 1997.

"City Poor, The," *Grand Rapids Evening Press*. 13 November 1894, p. 1.

Clifton, James. *The Potawatomi*. New York: Chelsea, 1987.

Clifton, James, Cornell, George and McClurken, James. *People of the Three Fires*. Grand Rapids: Grand Rapids Intertribal Council, 1986.

Cole, Maurice F. *Voices from the Wilderness*. Ann Arbor: Edwards Brothers, 1961.

Commission on Private Philanthropy and Public Needs. *Giving in America*. Washington: Commission on Private Philanthropy and Public Needs, 1975.

"Community Cookie Jar, The." *Encore Magazine*. 11 (September/October 1983): 4-21, 41-42.

Community Foundation for Southeastern Michigan. *Community Foundation Report*. Detroit: Community Foundation for Southeastern Michigan, vol. 7, no. 1 & 2; vol. 8, no. 1 & 2, n.d.

————. *1996 Yearbook*. Detroit: Community Foundation for Southeastern Michigan, n.d.

Community Surveys, Inc. *Community Chest*. Toronto: University of Toronto Press, 1957.

"Congress and Tax Status of Foundations," *Congressional Digest*. 48 (May 1969): 130-160.

Consumers Energy. "Consumers Energy Walking Hand-in-Hand," brochure. Jackson: Consumers Energy, 1997.

"Conversations: Esther Edwards Keeping Motown Home Fire Burning," *Detroit Free Press*. November 2, 1986.

Cott, Nancy F. *The Bonds of Womanhood*. New Haven: Yale University Press, 1977.

Council of Michigan Foundations. *Council of Michigan Foundations 20th Annual Conference Review*. Unpublished video script. Grand Haven: Council of Michigan Foundations, 1992.

————. *An Opportunity to Make A Difference: Michigan Community Foundations' Youth Project*. Grand Haven: Council of Michigan Foundations, n.d.

————. *Get into Action, Growing Community Foundations, Empowering Youth*. Grand Haven: Council of Michigan Foundations, n.d.

————. *Michigan Foundation Directory*. Grand Haven: Council of Michigan Foundations, 1975.

————. *1996 Survey of Michigan Foundation Philanthropy*. Grand Haven: Council of Michigan Foundations, 1996.

Crathern, Alice T. *In Detroit ... Courage Was the Fashion*. Detroit: Wayne State University, 1953.

Cuninggim, Merrimon. *Private Money and Public Service*. New York: McGraw-Hill, 1972.

Curti, Merle and Nash, Roderick. *Philanthropy in the Shaping of American Higher Education*. New Brunswick: Rutgers, 1965.

Dalton, Richard F. *The Life and Legacy of Charles J. Strosacker*. Midland: Northwood University Press, 1995.

Davis, Allen F. *Spearheads for Reform: Social Settlements*. New York: Oxford University Press, 1967.

150

Davis, David B., ed. *Ante-Bellum Reform*. New York: Harper, 1967.

"Detroit Nearly Five Decades Ago," *Michigan Pioneer Collections*. 40 vols. Lansing: Wynkoop, 1908. vol. 10: 103.

DeVos, Rich. *Compassionate Capitalism*. New York: Dutton, 1993.

DeVos, Richard and Helen, Foundation. Letter describing the foundation and its programs. 21 April 1997.

Dillon, Merton. "Elizabeth Chandler and the Spread of Anti-Slavery Sentiment to Michigan," *Michigan History*. 39 (December 1955): 481-494.

Doan, Herbert D., Herbert H. and Grace A. Dow Foundation. Interview, 3 April 1997.

Dow, Herbert H. and Grace A., Foundation. *Annual Report*. Midland: Herbert H. and Grace A. Dow Foundation, 1975, 1995.

"Dow, Herbert Henry II, August 6, 1927-January 26, 1996," memorial service biography, 1996.

Draeger, Carey. "Use It All, Wear It All," *Michigan History*. 78 (September/October 1994): 39-41.

Drake, Thomas E. *Quakers and Slavery in America*. New Haven: Yale Press, 1950.

Dummond, Dwight. *AntiSlavery. The Crusade for Freedom in America*. New York: Norton, 1961.

Dunbar, Willis. *Kalamazoo and How it Grew ... and Grew*. Kalamazoo: Western Michigan University, 1969.

—————. *The Michigan Record in Higher Education*. Detroit: Wayne State University, 1963.

—————. *Michigan Through the Centuries*. New York: Lewis Historical Publishing, 1955.

Dunbar, Willis and May, George. *Michigan: A History of the Wolverine State*. Grand Rapids: Eerdman Publishing, 1980.

Duranceau, James, Louis G. Kaufman Endowment Fund. Interview, 4 & 11 February 1997.

Eastern Michigan University. *1979-1989, A Decade of Advancement: The Presidency of Dr. John W. Porter*. Ypsilanti: Eastern Michigan University, n.d.

Eckert, Kathryn B. *Buildings of Michigan*. New York: Oxford, 1993.

"Ed Lowe Did OK for a Country Boy," *Kalamazoo Gazette*. 6 October 1995, P. A-8.

Edwards, Esther Gordy, Gordy Foundation. Interview, 4 and 27 February 1997.

Elliott, Frank N. *When the Railroad was King*. Lansing: Michigan Historical Commission, 1965.

Elliot, Richard C. "Captain Alpheus White, of Detroit During the Thirties," *Michigan Pioneer Collections*. 40 vols. Lansing: Robert Smith Printing, 1896. vol. 26: 269-270.

Ellis, Helen H. *Guide to the Material in Detroit Newspapers 1861-1866*. Lansing: Michigan Civil War Centennial Observance Commission, 1965.

Ellis, Susan and Noyes, Katherine. *By the People: A History of Americans as Volunteers*. San Francisco: Jossey-Bass, 1990.

Encyclopedia Judaica. 1971 ed. s.v. "Detroit," "Fisher, Max" and "Michigan."

Encyclopedia of African-American Culture and History. 1996 ed., s.v. "Civil Rights and the Law" by Donald G. Nieman. "Civil Rights Movement" by Robert Weisbrot. "Detroit" by Wilbur Rich. "Detroit Riots of 1943 and 1967" by Gayle Tate. "McCoy, Elijah" by Allison Miller. "Michigan" by Marcia Sawyer. "Philanthropy and Foundations" by Emmett Carson. "Sojourner Truth" by Margaret Washington.

Farley, Christopher. "Sugar Hill," *Essence*. 7 (November 1995): 80-82, 144-145.

Farmer, Silas. *History of Detroit and Wayne County and Early Michigan*. Silas Farmer & Co., 1890.

Ferry, W. Hawkins. *Buildings of Detroit: A History*. Detroit: Wayne State University Press, 1980.

Fetzer, John E. *The Founder's Statement*. Kalamazoo: John E. Fetzer Institute, 29 September 1989.

—————. *John E. Fetzer Foundation Preamble*. Kalamazoo: John E. Fetzer Institute, 1973.

—————. *The Men From Wengen and America's Agony*. Kalamazoo: John E. Fetzer Foundation, 1971.

—————. *One Man's Family: A History and Genealogy of the Fetzer Family*. Ann Arbor: Ann Arbor Press, 1964.

—————. "A Talk with John Fetzer. transcribed exerpts from a personal interview with three Fetzer Foundation employees." Kalamazoo: Fetzer Institute, 29 August 1986.

Fetzer, John E., Foundation. *Articles of Incorporation*. Kalamazoo: John E. Fetzer Foundation, 1962.

—————. *John E. Fetzer Foundation Agreement*. Kalamazoo: John E. Fetzer Foundation, 1954.

Fetzer. John E., Institute. *Advances, The Journal of Mind-Body Health*. Kalamazoo: John E. Fetzer Institute, 1991 and Winter 1997.

—————. *Dreams are Necessary for Fulfillment*. Kalamazoo: John E. Fetzer Institute, n.d.

—————. *The Institute Report*. Kalamazoo: John E. Fetzer Institute, 1995.

————. *Seasons, A Center for Renewal.* Kalamazoo: John E. Fetzer Institute, n.d.

————. *A Visual Dialog. A Tour of the Fetzer Institute.* Kalamazoo: John E. Fetzer Institute, 1995.

Finney, Charles G. *Lectures on Revivals of Religion.* Cambridge: Belknap, 1960.

Fisch, Edith L., Freed, Doris J. and Schachter, Esther. *Charities and Charitable Foundations.* Pomona: Lond Publications, 1974.

Fisher, Max M. Interview, 16 March 1997.

Fitzpatrick, Ellen. *Endless Crusade.* Oxford: Oxford University Press, 1990.

Flax, Steven. "When Do You Build Character," *Forbes.* 128 (September 14, 1981): 64-67.

Ford, Henry. *My Life and Work.* Garden City: Garden City Publishing, 1922.

"Ford, Henry, II," *Current Biography,* Yearbook 1978. New York: Wilson, 1978.

Forgue, Dennis and Simek, James. *The N.M. Kaufman Collection.* Chicago: Rare Coin Company of America, 1978.

Foundation Center. *Foundation Directory.* New York: Columbia University Press, 1996.

Fox, Daniel. *Engines of Culture.* Madison: State Historical Society of Wisconsin, 1963.

Freeman, David and The Council on Foundations. *The Handbook on Private Foundations, Revised Edition.* New York: The Foundation Center, 1991.

Fremont Area Foundation. *The Fremont Area Foundation,* brochure. Fremont: Fremont Area Foundation, n.d.

————. *The Fremont Area Foundation 1995 Report to the Community, Woven Together.* Fremont: Fremont Area Foundation, 1995.

————. *The Steward.* Fremont: Fremont Area Foundation, November and December 1996.

Fuller, George N., ed. *Michigan, A Centennial History of The State and Its People.* Chicago: Levi Publishing Co., 1939.

"Gentleman Slam Dunker," *Time.* 145 (February 13, 1995): 78.

"George Romney Dies at 88," *New York Times.* 27 July 1995.

"Gerstacker, A Conversation with Carl and Esther," Video hosted by Philip P. Mason. Grand Haven: Council of Michigan Foundations, n.d.

Gerstacker, Rollin M., Foundation. *Annual Reports.* Midland: Rollin M. Gerstacker Foundation, 1971-1973, 1978-1996.

Gilbo, Patrick. *The American Red Cross: The First Century.* New York: Harper-Row, 1981.

Ginzberg, Lori D. *Women and the Work of Benevolence.* New Haven: Yale, 1990.

Giradin, J.A. "Life and Times of Rev. Gabriel Richard," *Michigan Pioneer Collections.* 40 vols. Lansing: Robert Smith Printing, 1900. vol. 1: 481-494.

Golden, Peter. *Quiet Diplomat. A Biography of Max M. Fisher.* New York: Cornwall Books, 1992.

Goodykoontz, Collin B. *Home Missions on the American Frontier.* Caldwell, Idaho: Caxton, 1939.

"Grant Hill," *Parade.* 6 April 1997, p. 2.

Greenleaf, William. *From These Beginnings.* Detroit: Wayne State University, 1964.

Gregory, Ross. "Living on the Edge," *Michigan History.* 75 (November/December 1991): 8-17.

Griffon, Clifford S. *Their Brothers' Keepers.* New Brunswick: Rutgers University Press, 1960.

Grimwood, Scott, John E. Fetzer Institute. Interview, 7 February 1997.

Hammond, John L. *The Politics of Benevolence.* Norwood: Ablex, 1979.

Harley, Rachel and MacDowell, Betty. *Michigan Women Firsts and Founders.* Lansing: Michigan Women's Studies Association, 1993.

Harms, Richard. "Bissell House," *Grand Rapids.* 29 (November 1993): 31.

————. "Paid in Scrip," *Michigan History.* 76 (January/February 1991): 37-43.

————. "Welfare Health Care," *Grand Rapids.* 30 (June 1992): 47.

Harris, Fran. *Focus: Michigan Women 1701-1977.* Lansing: Michigan Coordinating Committee for the National Commission of the Observance of Women's Year, 1977.

Henry, Christopher. *Forever Free: From the Emancipation Proclamation to the Civil Rights Act of 1875.* New York: Chelsea, 1995.

Henshaw, Sarah. *Our Branch and Its Tributaries: Being a History of the Work of the Northwestern Sanitary Commission and its Auxilaries during the War of the Rebellion.* Chicago: Sewell, 1868.

"Her Generosity Helped Hundreds [Rose Skillman]," *Detroit Free Press.* 1 May 1983, p. F-7.

Hodgkinson, Virginia. *Nonprofit Almanac, 1992-1993. Dimensions of the Independent Sector.* San Francisco: Jossey-Bass, 1992.

Holli, Melvin G. *Reform in Detroit.* New York: Oxford University Press, 1969.

Holmes, Betty, Young Woman's Home Association. Interview, 25 February 1997.

"Home Away From Home, A," *Detroit News.* 8 June 1958, p. C-3.

"Home for Women is 50 Years Old," *Detroit News.* 19 April 1927, n.p.

"Home Index, The," Michigan Housing Authority. 1 (November 1928).

Horowitz, Helen L. *Culture and the City.* Lexington: University Press of Kentucky, 1976.

Hudson-Webber Foundation. *Annual Report.* Detroit: Hudson-Webber Foundation, 1996.

Ierley, Merritt. *With Charity for All.* New York: Praeger, 1984.

Independent Sector. *Giving and Volunteering 1992.* Washington, D.C.: Independent Sector, 1992.

"Isiah Thomas Calls It Quits," *Jet.* 86 (May 30, 1994): 48.

"Isiah Thomas Scores in Front Office as Vice President of NBA Toronto Raptors," "Toronto, Thomas Team Up," *Detroit Free Press.* 25 May 1994, n.p.

James, Herman S. "Crime in the Making," position paper. Michigan Housing Association, 1928.

Jennings, Frank G. "Tax Reform and the Foundations," *Saturday Review.* 52 (October 18, 1969): 32.

Jewell, Marjorie. *Time Certainly Flies: A History of the Young Woman's Home Association.* Detroit: Young Woman's Home Association, 1983.

Jewish Federation of Metropolitan Detroit. *Annual Report.* Detroit: Jewish Federation of Metropolitan Detroit, 1996.

"John Fetzer ... 20-20 Visionary, Veteran Broadcaster with a Crystal-Clear Perspective of the Future," *Encore Magazine.* 15 (March 1988): 9-27, 74.

"John Porter," *Encore Magazine.* 23 (November 1995): 40-45.

Johnson, Dorothy, Council of Michigan Foundations. Interview, 20 March 1997.

Johnston, Alice, Young Woman's Home Association. Interview, 25 February 1997.

"Jones Cleaned Out, Sale Grosses $400,000," *Kalamazoo Gazette.* 27 June 1977, p. A-3.

Kaminer, Wendy. *Women Volunteering.* New York: Anchor, 1984.

Katz, Irving I. *The Beth El Story with a History of Jews in Michigan Before 1850.* Detroit: Wayne State University Press, 1955.

———. *The Jewish Soldier from Michigan in the Civil War.* Detroit: Wayne State University Press, 1962.

Katzman, David. "Ann Arbor: Depression City," *Michigan History.* 50 (December 1966): 306-317.

"Kaufman Auditorium Rededication Weekend," program for rededication ceremony, 19 September 1993.

"Kaufman Coin Collection at First National Bank One of Finest in America," *The Mining Journal.* 22 January 1964, n.p.

Kaufman Endowment Fund. Scholarship award certificate text, Marquette, n.d.

"Kaufman, Funeral of L.G." *Marquette Journal.* 14 March 1942, n.p.

"Kaufman, L.G." Unpublished manuscript, December 11, 1928.

"Kaufman Played Major Role as 'Builder' of First National Bank," *The Mining Journal.* 22 January 1964, n.p.

Kedzie, Robert C. *The Cholera in Kalamazoo.* Kalamazoo: Kalamazoo Public Museum, 1961.

Kellogg, W.K., Foundation. *Annual Report.* Battle Creek: W.K. Kellogg Foundation, 1970.

———. *W.K. Kellogg Foundation: The First Eleven Years. 1930-1941.* Battle Creek: W.K. Kellogg Foundation, 1942.

———. *W.K. Kellogg Foundation: The First Fifty Years.* Battle Creek: W.K. Kellogg Foundation, 1980.

———. *W.K. Kellogg Foundation: The First Twenty-Five Years.* Battle Creek: W.K. Kellogg Foundation, 1956.

"Kid Helps Kids, The," *Kalamazoo Gazette.* 8 February 1997, p. A-1, A-2.

Kirkland, Edward C. *Dream and Thought in the Business Community 1860-1900.* Ithaca: Cornell University Press, 1956.

"Kitty Glitter; Cassopolis' Lowe Inventor of Cat Litter, Wants to Boost New Businesses," *Kalamazoo Gazette.* 23 October 1988, p. F-1.

"'Kitty Litter's Founder, Cassopolis' Ed Lowe Dies at Age 75," *Kalamazoo Gazette.* 5 October 1995, p. A-1.

"Kitty Litter Sold to Investor Group, Former Gen Foods CEO New Chair," *Kalamazoo Gazette.* 6 November 1990, p. A-6.

Korn, Claire. *Yesterday Through Tomorrow: Michigan State Parks.* East Lansing: Michigan State University Press, 1989.

Kresge Foundation. *Annual Report.* Detroit: Kresge Foundation, 1968, 1971-72, 1993-95.

————. *The First Fifty Year Report 1924-1974.* Detroit: Kresge Foundation, 1974.

————. *The First Thirty Years: A Report on the Activities of the Kresge Foundation 1924-1953.* Detroit: Kresge Foundation, 1953.

Kresge, Stanley S. *The S.S. Kresge Story.* Racine, WI: Western Publishing Co., 1979.

Krut, Joshua D. "Safe But Not Secure," *Michigan Jewish History.* 36 (Winter 1995-96): 9-22.

Kuhns, Frederick I. *The Operations of the American Home Missionary Society in the Old Northwest 1826-1861.* Chicago, 1947.

Landon, Fred. "Extracts from the Diary of William C. King, A Detroit Carpenter in 1832," *Michigan History.* 19 (Winter 1935): 68-70.

Lankton, Larry. "Autos to Armaments," *Michigan History.* 75 (November/December 1991): 42-49.

Lasky, Victor. *Never Complain. Never Explain. The Story of Henry Ford II.* New York: Marek, 1981.

Layman, Richard, ed. *American Decades. 1960-1969.* Detroit: Gale Research, 1995.

Laymen, Robert. "The Alpena Jewish Community," *Michigan Jewish History.* 26 (Winter 1985): 4-12.

Layton, Daphne N. *Philanthropy and Volunteerism: An Annotated Bibliography.* New York: Foundation Center, 1987.

Leelanau Township Foundation. *Annual Report. Celebrating 50 Years 1945-1995.* Leelenau: Leelenau Township Foundation, 1995.

"Leelanau Township Foundation," *Northport Point Cottage Owner's Association Newsletter,* n.d.

"Legend of Big Rock Valley, The," A video on Edward Lowe and the Lowe Foundation hosted by Philip P. Mason. Council of Michigan Foundations, n.d.

Lewis, Ferris. *Michigan Yesterday and Today.* Hillsdale, MI: Hillsdale Educational Press, 1980.

"L.G. Kaufman's Success," *New York Herald.* n.d., n.p.

"Louis G. Kaufman Dies in Florida; President of Banks Many Years," *Daily Marquette Journal.* 11 March 1942, p. 1.

"Louis G. Kaufman Honored by Marquette," *Marquette Journal,* 15 October 1927, n.p.

"Lowe and Behold; Kitty Litter Creator to Boost Entrepreneurs," *Kalamazoo Gazette.* 20 December 1988, p. B-10.

Lupica, Mike. "Amazing Grace," *Esquire.* 123 (February 1995): 60-61.

"Luxury-Loving Lady Bountiful," *Battle Creek Enquirer.* 11 March 1973, p. D-1, D-2.

Lydens, Z.Z. *The Story of Grand Rapids.* Grand Rapids: Kregel Publications, 1966.

Lyon-Jenness, Cheryl. "They Hoed the Corn," *Michigan History.* 78 (July/August 1994): 34-40.

Macdonald, Dwight. *The Ford Foundation.* New York: Reynal, 1956.

Magat, Richard. *The Agile Servant.* New York: Foundation Center, 1989.

Manassah, Sallie, Thomas, David and Wallington, James. *Lansing: Capital, Campus and Cars.* East Lansing: Contemporary Image Advance, 1986.

"Marjorie Merriweather Post Dies," *Battle Creek Enquirer.* 19 September 1973, p. A-1, B-1.

Martin, John B. *Call It North Country.* Detroit: Wayne State University Press, 1986.

Marx, Gary E., Hunter, Deborah D. and Johnson, Carol D. "Increasing Student Achievement, An Urban District's Search for Success," *Urban Education.* 31 (January 1997): 529-544.

Massie, Larry and Schmitt, Peter. *Battle Creek. The Place Behind the Product.* Northridge, CA: Windsor Publications, 1984.

Mawby, Russell, W.K. Kellogg Foundation. Interview, 27 February 1997.

May, George S. *Michigan: An Illustrated History of the Great Lakes State.* Northridge, CA: Windsor Publications, 1987.

McCarthy, Kathleen D., ed. *Lady Bountiful Revisited.* New Brunswick: Rutgers University, 1990.

McGeehan, Albert H., ed. *My Country and Cross; The Civil War Letters of John Anthony Wilterdink.* Dallas: Taylor Publishing, 1982.

McGraw, Dan. "Driving Hard to the Hoop," *U.S. News and World Report.* 119 (December 11, 1995): 73-79.

McGregor Fund. *Annual Report.* Detroit: McGregor Fund, 1996.

McHenry, Sharon. "Riot of 1943," *Michigan History.* 77 (May/June 1993): 34-39.

McLoughlin, William G. *Revivals, Awakenings, and Reform.* Chicago: University of Chicago Press, 1978.

Meyer, Katharine, ed. *Detroit Architecture AIA Guide.* Detroit: Wayne State University Press, 1980.

Michigan 4-H Foundation. *Annual Report.* Lansing: Michigan 4-H Foundation, 1995 and 1996.

————. "Invest in the Power of 4-H," brochure. Lansing: Michigan 4-H Foundation, n.d.

————. *Vantage*. Newsletter. 18 (Winter 1997).

Michigan Women's Foundation. *About the Michigan Women's Foundation*. Lansing: Michigan Women's Foundation, 1997.

————. "The History and Structure of the Michigan Women's Foundation." Lansing: Michigan Women's Foundation, n.d.

————. Informational Brochure. Lansing: Michigan Women's Foundation, 1996.

————. *Investing in Michigan Women*. Lansing: Michigan Women's Foundation, 1993.

————. Minutes, Board of Trustees, 23 March 1987.

"Motown Lady, Esther Gordy Edwards—Midwife to the Sound," *Detroit News*. 22 February 1981, n.p.

"Motown Museum is Worth Saving and Improving," *Detroit Free Press*. 5 January 1992, n.p.

"Mott, Charles Stewart," *Current Biography*. New York: Wilson, 1970: 296-298; 1974: 378-379.

Mott, Charles Stewart. "Story of What a Foundation Did," *U.S. News and World Report*. 67 (October 20, 1969): 101.

Mott, Charles Stewart, Foundation. *America's Tattered Tapestry*. Flint: Charles Stewart Mott Foundation, 1995.

————. *Annual Report*. Flint: Charles Stewart Mott Foundation, 1991.

————. *Community Education: Partnerships for Tomorrow*. Flint: Charles Stewart Mott Foundation, 1982.

————. *Mott Exchange*. Flint: Charles Stewart Mott Foundation, 1986-1995.

————. *Rediscovering Hopefulness: People and Communities Change Their Destiny*. Flint: Charles Stewart Mott Foundation, 1992.

————. *Small Steps Toward Big Dreams: Enterprise Development Programs for the Disadvantaged*. Flint: Charles Stewart Mott Foundation, 1994.

Motz, Marilyn F. *True Sisterhood: Michigan Women and Their Kin 1820-1920*. Albany, NY: State of New York University Press, 1983.

Musser, Necia A. *Home Missionaries on the Michigan Frontier I, II, III*. Ann Arbor: University of Michigan, 1967.

Myers, Walter. Draft video script of interview and background information on Robert and Rose Skillman, n.d.

National Cyclopedia of American Biography. 1916 edition, s.v. "Clara Barton."

National Cyclopedia of American Biography. 1979 edition, s.v. "Charles Stewart Mott" and "Marjorie M. Post."

Nielsen, Waldemar A. *The Big Foundations*. New York: Columbia University, 1972.

————. *The Golden Donors*. New York: Truman Talley Books, 1985.

Noland, Mariam C., Community Foundation for Southeastern Michigan. Interview, 6 February 1997.

Notable American Women 1607-1950. 1971 edition, s.v. "Elizabeth Chandler."

Notable Black American Women. 1992 edition, s.v. "Sojourner Truth," by Nell Painter Irvin and "McCoy, Mary E." by Dewitt Dykes, Jr.

Odendahl, Teresa, ed. *America's Wealthy and the Future of Foundations*. New York: Foundation Center, 1987.

Olson, Gordon. *History of the Grand Rapids Foundation*. Grand Rapids: Grand Rapids Foundation, 1992.

O'Neill, Michael. *The Third America: The Emergence of the Nonprofit Sector in the United States*. San Francisco: Jossey-Bass, 1989.

Ortquist, Richard T. "Unemployment and Relief: Michigan's Response to the Depression During the Hoover Years," *Michigan History*. 57 (Fall 1973): 209-235.

Patterson, Carl. "Tracy W. McGregor-Exemplar." Unpublished manuscript, McGregor Fund, 1995.

Peebles, Robin. "Detroit Black Women's Clubs," *Michigan History*. 70 (January/ February 1986): 48.

Plummer, William and Alexander, Bryan. "Shooting Star," *People*. 43 (January 23, 1995): 74-75.

Porter, John, Urban Education Alliance. Interview, 26 March 1997.

Powell, Horace B. *The Original Has This Signature*. Battle Creek: W.K. Kellogg Foundation, 1956.

Poynter, Nelson, ed. "Tax Law of 1969," *Congressional Quarterly*. Washington, D.C.: Congressional Quarterly, Inc., 1970.

Pray, Carl E. "A Historic Michigan Road," *Michigan History*. 11 (July 1927): 325-341.

Quaife, M.M. and Glazer, Sidney. *Michigan: From Primitive Wilderness to Industrial Commonwealth*. New York: Prentice Hall, 1948.

Quaife, M.M. and White, William, eds. *This Is Detroit*. Detroit: Wayne State University Press, 1951.

Rabinowitz, Alan. *Social Change Philanthropy in America*. Westport, CT: Quorum, 1990.

Reeves, Thomas, ed. *Foundations Under Fire*. Ithaca, N.Y.: Cornell, 1970.

Reiman, Lewis C. *When Pine Was King*. Ann Arbor: Edwards Brothers, 1952.

Renz, Loren and Lawrence, Steven. *Foundation Giving-1992 Edition*. New York: Foundation Center, 1992.

Richards, William C. *Biography of a Fund: The Story of the Children's Fund of Michigan 1929-1954*. Detroit: Children's Fund, 1957.

Richmond, Mary E. *The Long View*. New York: Sage, 1930.

Riecker, Margaret, Harry A. and Margaret D. Towsley Foundation. Interview, 3 April 1997.

"Roberts, Jessie C., Obituary of," n.p., n.d. (from Detroit Public Library).

"Roberts, Thomas Reed, Obituary of," n.p., n.d. (from Detroit Public Library).

Rockaway, Robert. *The Jews of Detroit. From the Beginning 1762-1914*. Detroit: Wayne State University, 1986.

Rogow, Faith. *Gone to Another Meeting*. Tuscaloosa: University of Alabama Press, 1993.

"Romney Dead at 88," *Kalamazoo Gazette*. 26 July 1995, p. A-1.

"Romney, George W." *Current Biography*. New York: Wilson, 1995.

Romney, Lenore. Interview, 22 April 1997.

Rosenberg, Carroll S. *Religion and the Rise of the American City*. Ithaca: Cornell University, 1971.

Rosentreter, Roger. "Huron County," *Michigan History*. 67 (July/August 1983): 10-11.

————. "Leelanau County," *Michigan History*. 69 (September/October 1985): 8-11.

Rotary Charities of Traverse City. *Annual Reports*. Traverse City: Rotary Charities, 1995, 1996.

————. *Chronological Listing of Grant Recipients*. Traverse City: Rotary Charities, 1996.

————. *History*. Traverse City: Rotary Charities, 1997.

————. *Interim Reports*. Traverse City: Rotary Charities, 1979, 1981.

Rothman, Gerald C. *Philanthropists, Therapists and Activists*. Cambridge: Schenkman, 1985.

Rothman, Sheila. *Woman's Proper Place*. New York: Basic Books, 1978.

Rusk, Dean. *The Role of the Foundation in America*. Claremont, CA: Claremont University Collection, 1961.

Sagatoo, Mary A. Henderson Cabay. *Wah Sash Kah Moqua, or Thirty-Three Years Among the Indians*. Caledonia: Bigwater Classics, 1897.

Salmon, Lucy M. "Education in Michigan During the Territorial Period," *Michigan Pioneer Collections*. 40 vols. Lansing: Wynkoop, 1904. vol. 7: 36-51.

Sears, Stephen W., ed. *The Country Cause and Leader; The Civil War Journal of Charles B. Haydon*. New York: Ticknor & Fields, 1993.

Simonds, William A. *Henry Ford and Greenfield Village*. New York: Stokes, 1938.

Skillman Foundation. *Annual Report*. Detroit: Skillman Foundation, 1994.

"Skillman, Rose, Obituary of," *Detroit Free Press*. 1 May 1983. p. D-2.

Smith, Leonard, Skillman Foundation. Interview, 12 February 1997.

Smith, Timothy L. *Revivalism and Social Reform*. New York: Abingdon, 1957.

Spiro, Robert. *History of the Michigan Soldiers' Aid Society, 1861-1865*. Ann Arbor: University of Michigan Press, 1959.

Strosacker, Charles J., Foundation. *Annual Report*. Midland: Charles J. Strosacker Foundation, 1995.

Sward, Keith. *The Legend of Henry Ford*. New York: Rinehart, 1948.

Swartz, Mary Jane. *So I'm Told*. Berrien Springs, MI: Hardscrabble Books, 1990.

Symon, Charles and Symon, Barbara. *U-People*. Gladstone, MI: RonJon Press, 1987.

Thinnes, Tom. "Kalamazoo's Cookie Jar, Part II," *Encore Magazine*. 21 (December 1993): 19-27.

"Thomas is Detroit Athlete of the World," *Michigan Chronicle*. 28 January 1989. p. D-2.

Thornton, Barbara. *Historical Dates of Interest: Young Woman's Home Association*. Detroit: Young Woman's Home Association, 1990.

Tice, Karin E. *Growing Community Foundations: Empowering Youth, Lessons Learned from the Michigan Community Foundations' Youth Project, 1991-1996*. Grand Haven: Council of Michigan Foundations, 1996.

Towsley, Harry A. and Margaret D., Foundation. *Annual Reports*. Ann Arbor: Harry A. and Margaret D. Towsley Foundation, 1974, 1995.

"Tribe Pledges $100,000 to Community Foundation," *L'Anse Sentinel*. 12 February 1997, p. 1.

Troester, Rosalie Riegle, ed. *Historic Women of Michigan*. Lansing: Michigan Women's Studies Association, 1987.

Tyler, Alice F. *Freedom's Ferment*. Minneapolis: University of Minneapolis, 1944.

United Jewish Foundation. *Progress Report*. Detroit: United Jewish Foundation and Jewish Federation of Metropolitan Detroit, 1996.

United States Statutes at Large, Containing the Concurrent Resolutions Enacted During the First Session of the Ninety-First Congress of the United States of America, 1969. vol. 83. Washington, D.C.: Government Printing Office, 1970.

United Way of America. *People and Events: A History of United Way*. Alexandria, VA: United Way of America, 1977.

Urban Education Alliance, The. *Annual Report*. Ann Arbor: The Urban Education Alliance, 1995.

Van Andel, Jay and Betty, Foundation. Letter describing the Foundation and its programs, 21 April 1997.

"Van Andels Endow New Medical and Genetic Research Institute," *Grand Haven Tribune*. 3 July 1996, n.p.

VanBuren, A.D.P. "The Women of Our Pioneer Epoch," *Michigan Pioneer Collections*. 40 vols. Lansing: Wynkoop, 1908. vol. 14: 517-521.

Vision Enrichment Center. *The Story of Our Beginnings*. Grand Rapids: Vision Enrichment Center, 1988.

Walsh, John. "Foundations: Taking Stock After the Tax Reform Bill," *Science*. 167 (March 20, 1970): 1598-1600.

——————. "Foundations Under Fire in Congress," *Science*. 163 (February 28, 1969): 913.

Walters, Ronald G. *American Reformers 1815-1860*. New York: Hill and Wang, 1978.

——————. *The Antislavery Appeal*. Baltimore: John Hopkins University Press, 1976.

Warren, Francis, comp. *Michigan Manual of Freedman's Progress*. Detroit: Freedman's Progress Commission, 1915.

Watson, Frank D. *The Charity Organization Movement in the United States*. New York: Macmillan, 1922.

"We Pay Too Much," *Grand Rapids Evening Press*. 16 February 1895, p. 1.

Weddon, Willah. *Michigan Governors: Their Life Stories*. Lansing: NGO Press, 1994.

Weeks, George. *Stewards of the State*. Detroit: Detroit News, 1987.

Weingarten, Dan. "Family History, Early Families Left Lasting Legacies," Superiorland Sunday, *The Mining Journal*. 17 April 1994, p. 3-4.

Whitaker, Ben. *Foundations. An Anatomy of Philanthropy and Society*. London: Eyre Methuen, 1974.

White, Ronald C. and Hopkins, C. Howard. *The Social Gospel*. Philadelphia: Temple, 1976.

Whitehead, Don. *The Dow Story, The History of the Dow Chemical Co*. New York: McGraw-Hill, 1968.

"Whiting, Dr. J. L.," *Michigan Pioneer Collections*. 40 vols. Lansing: Wynkoop, 1906. vol. 4: 116-117.

Who's Who Among African-Americans. 1996 edition, s.v. "Esther Gordy Edwards" and "John Porter."

"William S. White: President's Values Anchor Mott Foundation," *Flint Journal*. 19 March 1995, n.p.

Williams, Beth. "The Woman Pioneer of the Eighteen Forties," *Michigan History*. 26 (Spring 1942): 215-222.

Wilson, Mark I. *The State of Nonprofit Michigan 1991*. East Lansing: Michigan State University, 1991.

Woodford, Frank B. *Father Abraham's Children*. Detroit: Wayne State University Press, 1961.

Woodford, Frank B. and Hyma, Albert. *Gabriel Richard, Frontier Ambassador*. Detroit: Wayne State University Press, 1958.

Woodford, Frank B. and Mason, Philip P. *Harper of Detroit: The Origin and Growth of a Great Metropolitan Hospital*. Detroit: Wayne State University, 1964.

Woodford, Frank B. and Woodford, Arthur. *All Our Yesterdays: A Brief History of Detroit*. Detroit: Wayne State University, 1969.

Wyllie, Irvin G. *The Self-Made Man in America*. New Brunswick: Rutgers, 1954.

Yates, Dorothy Langdon. *Salt of the Earth, A History of Midland County, Michigan*. Midland: Midland County Historical Society, 1987.

Young Woman's Home Association. *75 Years of Service; Young Woman's Home, Detroit, Michigan*. Detroit: Young Woman's Home Association, 1962.

Additional Photo Bibliography Information

Appleyard, Richard. *Photographic Memories – South Haven*. Jostens Printing and Publishing, 1996.

"George Shiras was Marquette's Most Prominent Citizen," *Mining Journal*. Marquette, August 9, 1966.

May, George S. *Michigan: An Illustrated History of the Great Lakes State*. Windsor Publications, 1987.

——————. *Pictorial History of Michigan, Early Years*. Grand Rapids: William B. Eerdmans Publishing, 1967.

——————. *Pictorial History of Michigan, Later Years*. Grand Rapids: William B. Eerdmans Publishing, 1967.

Olson, Gordon. *Making a Difference: Women Leaders in Grand Rapids History*. Ryerson Gallery Exhibit, Grand Rapids Public Library: Nokomis Foundation, 1997

Qualfe, M.M. *This is Detroit*. Detroit: Wayne University Press, 1951

Index

How to use this index:

Boldface page numbers designate **biographical sketches.** *Italic numbers* refer to *sidebars;* an *italic f* indicates a *figure.*

Names of discussed churches and synagogues, colleges and universities, hospitals, foundations, museums, newspapers, and wars have been collected for listing as subentries under these subjects, *e.g.* wars, specific.

A

abolition movement, 18, 20–22, *39*
  abolitionists, 6, 21, *32, 32f, 39f*
acquired immunune deficiency syndrome. *See* AIDS
Ada, MI, trading post, *16*
Addams, Jane, 58
Adrian, MI, 21, *32, 102*
AFL-CIO, 121
African-Americans
  civil rights groups, 120 (*see also* racial
    discrimination)
  clubs, *52*, 62–63, *67f*, 70
  education, *32*, 117
  health and recreation, 51*f*, 62*f*, 67*f*, 70, 138*f*
  job opportunities, viii*f*, *39*, 64, 96, 141
  leaders, 21*f*, *39*, 62, *63*, 99*f*
aged, *60, 104, 128*
  care for, 28, *59, 63*, 99, 125*f*
agriculture, 70, 85–85*f*, 90–91, 103–*104*, 130*f*
agriculture industry, 34*f*, 45
aid societies
  for Civil War relief work, 33*f*, 35, *36, 36f*
  during economic depressions, 37–38, 50–51, 53
AIDS, *124*, 138, *146*
"Ain't I a Woman" (speech), *39*
aircraft, *76*, 95*f*, 96, 96*f*
Albion, MI, 81, 90*f*, *102*
alcohol consumption, *16*, 18
  destitution from, and rescue missions, *68*, 86*f*
  discouragement of, 20, 20*f*, *63*, 70, 82
Alexis de Tocquerville Award, *124*
Algonquin tribe, settlements, 2*f*
Allegan County, health service, 85
Alma, MI, *8*
almshouses. *See* poorhouses
Alpena, MI, *102*, 103
Alphadelphian Society, 18, 18*f*
American Academy of Entrepreneurs, *139*
American Association of Workers for the Blind, *60*
American Fur Company, outposts, *16*
American Home Missionary Society, 17–18
American Motors Corporation, 134*f*
American Red Cross
  activities, *47f*, 58*f*, 69*f*, 96*f*, 103*f*
  as beneficiary, *92*, 95, 105
Ameritech (firm), foundation, *145*
Amway Corporation, *135*, 142
Ann Arbor, MI, 67*f*, 87, 120, *145*
anti-Semitism, 97
anti-slavery. *See* abolition movement
Apostle to the Indians. *See* Eliot, John
architecture, *109, 128*
Arkansas Drought Relief, 89*f*
army of Michigan residents. *See* Union Army,
  Michigan troops

art galleries, 46, 48, *74*, 95, *135*
arts centers
  John F. Kennedy Center for the Performing
    Arts, *92, 124*
  in Michigan, *101*, 107, *135*, 138*f*
  programs, 94, *109, 119*, 120
Asian-Americans, ix, *59*, 120, 121*f*
Associated Charities, Detroit, 66
Association for the Blind and for Sight
  Conservation, Grand Rapids, *60*
Astor, John Jacob, *16*
asylums, era of, 26, 28
athletes, professional, *146*
Atwater, Mrs. J. D., 22
Augusta, MI, therapeutic riding near, 141*f*
Aunt Laura. *See* Haviland, Laura Smith
Austin, Richard, 129*f*, 133*f*
automobile industry, 64–66*f*, 82
  competition, 111–112, 141–142
  manufacturing, 64*f*, 65*f*, 72–73, *76*, 95–96, *109*
  philanthropists, ix, 65, 73, *83, 88*

B

Bad Axe, MI, fire, *47*
Bagley, Mrs. John F., *116*
Baldwin, Bill, 132
Bangor, MI, donated goods, 89*f*
banking industry, 17, *84, 123*
Baptists in Michigan, 23*f*, 65, 97*f*
Barbour, Levi L., reformer, 41
Barbour, Will, 64, 73
barn raising, as volunteerism, 42*f*
Barrier, Fannie. *See* Williams, Fannie Barrier
Barry County, health service, 85
Bartlett, Caroline. *See* Crane, Caroline Bartlett
Barton, Clara, *47*
Battle Creek, MI, 18, 62, 65
  as beneficiary, 85, *92*
  black history, 21*f*, 22, *39*
  foundations, 21*f*, 100*f*, 142
Battle Creek Sanitarium, 53*f*, *79*
Battle Creek Symphony, 88, *92*
Battle Creek Toasted Corn Flakes Co., 65
Baumfree, Isabella. *See* Truth, Sojourner
Baxter home, Van Buren County, 33*f*
Bay City, MI, *43*, 48, 65, 142
Bellevue, MI, log cabins, 15*f*
benevolent societies. (*See also* charitable
  associations)
  activities, *10*, 14, 25–26
  values, 11–12, 23, 28, 99
Benzie County, garden project, *104*
Berrien County, community foundation, 103, 105
Besser, Anna (Mrs. Jesse), *102*
Besser, Jesse H., *102*, 103, 133*f*
Bible societies, 34
Big Foundations, The (Nielsen), 121
Birdseye, Clarence, *92*
Bissell House, Grand Rapids, 58, 58*f*
Black Arts and Cultural Center, Kalamazoo, 138*f*
blind people. *See* visually-impaired persons
Bliss, Aaron T., 48
Blodgett, Minnie C., 82*f*
Blodgett Clinic for Infant Feeding, 82*f*
Bloomfield Hills, MI, schools, *124*
boats, 46*f*, *76*, 88, *92*

river transports, *8f, 116*
  steamships, *7f*, 8–*10*
Bonifas, Big Bill ("Timber King"), *74f*
Bonifas, Katherine, 48, *74f*
Bonifas Art Center, Escanaba, *74*
booms, economic
  after World War II, 99–100, 103, 105–106,
    136, 138
  at turn of 20th century, 45–46, 48
Boy Scouts of America
  activities, 70, 75*f*, 91*f*
  as beneficiary, viii*f*, *92, 102, 135*
Braille system, development, *60*
Branch County, health service, 85
Branch County Women's Club, 67, 69
bricks-and-mortar projects. *See* construction
  projects
Bridgman, Ansel, missionary, 17–18
Brimley Commercial Club, 88
Brimley State Park, 88
broadcasting industry, *128*
Brook Farm, utopian society, 18
Brooks, Harold C., *110*
Brown City, MI, barn raising, 42*f*
Bruce Crossing, MI, railroads, 50*f*
Brucker, Wilber, belief, 86, 89
Buckley and Douglas Lumber Company,
  Manistee, 46*f*
Buick, David, 73
Buick factories, laborers' housing, 66*f*
Bundy, McGeorge, 121
Burt, Wellington, 48
Bush, George, points of light, 141
businesses, 45. (*See also* corporations; *specific
  names*)
  collapse of, 50–51, 55
  development of, 57*f*, 65, 75, 96
  influence on philanthropy, 40, 66, 82, *139*,
    143–144
  philanthropy by, *16, 19*, 25, 65, 105 (*see also
    specific industries, e.g.,* food products
    industry)
  reform of abusive, *52, 54*, 57
  skills for, 35, 37, 95, *119, 139–140*
  values of, ix, 46, *135*

C

Cabay, Joseph, *43*
Cabay, Mary. *See* Sagatoo, Mary Cabay
Cadillac Square, Detroit, *19*, 55*f*
Calhoun County, health service, 85
Camp Custer, Battle Creek, 67*f*. (*See also* Fort
  Custer)
Camp Fire Girls, relief work by, 70
campaign kickoffs. *See under* fundraising
Campau, Louis, trading post, 23*f*
camps, 67*f*, 70*f*, *74*. (*See also* children's camps)
cancer, research, 103
Carnegie, Andrew, 78, 80
  as pacesetter, 46, 48, 100, *138*
Carver, George Washington, 90*f*
Casco, MI, donated goods, 89*f*
Cass, Lewis, *13*
Cass County Business Center, *139*
Cass Lake, park, *88*
Cassopolis, MI, 22, *139*

Catholepistemiad, *13, 24*
Catholic Female Benevolent Association, *10*
Catholics in Michigan, *9f, 10, 13, 16, 74*
    Jesuits, 2–3, *16*
"Century of Caring, A" (Carlisle), 91
cereal industry. *See under* food products industry
Chandler, Elizabeth Margaret, 21, *32*
charitable associations, 34–35. (*See also e.g.,* aid
    societies; benevolent societies)
    activities, 22–26, 61–64, 70
    beneficiary segregation by, 62, *63,* 99
    impact of Great Depression on, 87, 91
    joint fundraising among, *59,* 66, *68,* 87, 106
    as networks, 21*f,* 21–22, 28
    traditions, 7, 9, 11–12, 44, 117
    values, 12, 58, 99, 105, *116*
charity organization movement
    London model for, 40–42, 44
    as outdated, 50–51, 53, 56–58, 61
Charles Mears State Park, *88*
Charles Stewart Mott Foundation, 80
    beneficiaries of, 81, 97*f,* 118, 134, 142–143
    community education movement, 73*f,* 90, 95, 108
    Council of Michigan Foundations, 132, 134
    officers, 143, *145*
Charlevoix, MI, *123*
Charlevoix County, *123*
Cheff Center, Augusta, 141*f*
Chemical Bank, New York, *84*
chemical industry, 35*f,* 65, *101*
children
    African-American, *32,* 51*f, 63*
    as beneficiaries, *68, 83f, 109, 123*
    as beneficiaries of women's groups, 14, 25–26,
        28, *116, 140*
    care for, *59,* 69, 97*f,* 141*f*
    Christmas aid for, 86*f,* 103*f*
    day nurseries for, 57, *63,* 65
    education of, *13, 16, 101f, 104*
    health care for, *83,* 85*f,* 105, 107*f,* 136*f*
    summer camps for, *59, 83f,* 99*f,* 142*f, 146*
    as volunteers, 70, 94*f*
children's camps, as beneficiaries
    black donors, 99*f, 146*
    Mott Foundation, 81, *83, 83f,* 100*f*
    United Jewish Charities, *59,* 142*f*
Children's Fund of Michigan, *83,* 83*f*
Chippewa Indian Women's Club, 41*f*
Chippewa tribe, 2–3, 41*f, 43*
cholera, *10,* 11, *13*
Christian Commission. *See* U. S. Christian
    Commission
Christian Scientists in Michigan, *52*
Christmas aid, 69, 86*f,* 91*f,* 103*f*
Chrysler Corporation, 96, 105, *140,* 142, *145*
Church of Jesus Christ of Latter-day Saints, 18
churches, 15*f,* 30*f*
    black, *32,* 33*f,* 62*f,* 97*f*
    nondenominational, *52,* 53
churches and synagogues, specific
    African Methodist Episcopal Church, Detroit, 33*f*
    Alpena Congregational Church, *102*
    Beth El Synagogue, Detroit, *59*
    Chapel of our Lady of Guadalupe, Grand
        Rapids, 130*f*
    First Presbyterian Church, Alpena, *102*
    First Unitarian Church, Kalamazoo, *52*
    Fountain Street Church, Grand Rapids, 117
    Holy Trinity Church, Detroit, *10*

People's Church, Kalamazoo, 53
St. Anne de Detroit Church, *10, 13*
St. Anne's Church, Mackinac Island, *16*
St. Luke African Methodist Episcopal Church,
    Grand Rapids, 62*f*
True Light Baptist Church, Grand Rapids, 97*f*
Zion Baptist Church, Cincinnati, *32*
civic projects, 38*f, 68,* 94, *109, 146*
    funded by community foundations, 66, 142
    Upper Peninsula improvements, 35*f,* 46, 48, *74*
civil rights groups, rise of, 120
Clark Equipment Company, 115*f*
Clarke, Rev. C. G., 20
Claytor, Helen Jackson, 99*f*
Cliff Mine, profits, 12*f*
clubs, 58, *60,* 67*f,* 97*f.* (*See also* Detroit, men's
    clubs; women's clubs; *names of specific*
    clubs, e.g., Lions Club)
    national impacts on Michigan, 35
Coffin, Levi, *32*
Coffman, Harold C., 122
Coldwater, MI, Underground Railroad, 22
Cole, Rick, 136*f*
colleges and universities, viii*f, 13, 24,* 57, 121
    admission policies, 27, *59*
    as beneficiaries, 46, *68,* 107
    community colleges, 95, 108, 108*f,* 117
colleges and universities, specific
    Adrian College, *102*
    Agricultural College of Michigan, 37*f*
    Albion College, 81, *102*
    Alma College, 48, *102*
    Alpena Community College, *102*
    California Polytechnic University at Pomona, 81
    Calvin College, *135*
    Central Michigan University, *102*
    Delta College, *101*
    Eastern Michigan University, *145*
    Flint Junior College, 108
    Grand Valley State College, 118, 118*f, 123*
    Grand Valley State University, 118*f, 123, 135*
    Harvard University, 108, *128*
    Hillsdale College, *101*
    Kalamazoo College, 65, *101*
    Madonna College, *102*
    Marquette University, *74*
    Massachusetts Institute of Technology, 108
    Michigan Christian College, *102*
    Michigan State University (MSU). *See main*
        entry
    Michigan Technological University, *101, 102*
    Mott Community College, 108
    Northwestern University, 108
    Northwood University, *135*
    Oakland University, *102*
    Olivet College, *102*
    Sienna Heights College, *102*
    University of California at Los Angeles, *119*
    University of Michigan, *68,* 81, 107–108
    University of Michigan, Flint, 108
    University of Michigania, *13, 24*
    University of Virginia, *68*
    Wayne State University, 108, *119*
    Western Michigan University, *139*
Columbian Exposition, Chicago, 51*f*
communes. *See* utopian societies
communitarian settlements, 9*f,* 18, 18*f*
community chests, 66, 82, 86–87

community education movement
    community colleges, 95, 108, 108*f,* 117
    as foundation risk-capital example, 143–144
    funded by Mott Foundation, 73*f,* 90, 95,
        108, 118
Community Foundation for Southeastern
    Michigan, 66, 129*f,* 142, *146*
community relations, and police, 115, 117
Compassionate Capitalism (DeVos), *135*
Comstock Township, Kalamazoo County, 18
Conference of Michigan Foundations, 132
Congress of Racial Equality (CORE), 120
construction projects, 81*f,* 99*f, 102, 123*
    purposes of, 55, *74, 98,* 107
Consumers Energy, corporate foundation, *145*
CORE (Congress of Racial Equality), 120
corporations, 65, 75, 91, 105, 121. (*See also*
    specific corporate names)
Council of Michigan Foundations
    activities, *98,* 138, 141, 142–143, 144*f*
    history, ix, 112, 132–134, 134*f,* 143
    meetings, 131*f,* 136*f,* 141*f*
Council of Social Agencies, Grand Rapids, 94
Couzens, James, *83f*
Crane, Dr. Augustus Warren, *52*
Crane, Rev. Caroline Bartlett, *52f,* 53, 57, 62
crime, 20, 22, 26, 44, 138
Crozier, Alfred, reformer, 41
currency, *84,* 87*f,* 89
customs, and philanthropy, ix, 50*f*

D

D. H. Day State Park, *88*
Dame, G. Marston, memorial, *98*
Dansville Society of the Red Cross, New York, 47*f*
Daughters of the American Revolution, 67, 67*f*
Day Spring (schooner), 46*f*
deaf persons. *See* hearing-impaired persons
Dearborn, MI, *76*
Deerlick School, scrap collected, 94*f*
deindustrialization, 138, 141–142
depressions, economic, 48, 56
    19th century, 15, 23, 37–38, 50–51, 53
    20th century. *See* Great Depression
Detroit, MI, 11*f,* 55, 58, 120
    as beneficiary, 94–95, *109,* 117*f*
    benevolent societies, 23, 25, 66
    diseases (19th century), 8, *10,* 11
    fires, 6*f, 7, 13,* 56*f*
    housing for special groups, 99, *116,* 117*f*
    impact of economic depressions on, 37–38, 53*f,*
        54–56, 86–87
    Jewish aid organizations, *59,* 99, *124,* 125*f*
    men's clubs, 12, 14, 23, 25, 62, *68*
    in Michigan Territory, 4, 7, *10,* 17*f*
    Pingree Potato Patches, 53*f, 54,* 55–56
    politicians, *54, 83,* 86, *146*
    population growth (post-1850), 22, 55*f, 59*
    population growth (pre-1850), 3, 7, *13,* 22, 99
    riots, 97, 115, 115*f,* 118, *124*
    schools, *13,* 14, *24,* 134*f, 145*
    street sites, 15*f,* 68*f, 109, 116, 119*
    women's clubs, 14, 62–64, 70
Detroit Association of Charities, 40, 41
Detroit Association of Colored Women's Clubs, *63*
Detroit Board of Commerce, 66
Detroit Charity Organization Society, 40
Detroit Colored Women's War Council, *63,* 70

Detroit Community Fund, *68*
Detroit Community Trust, 66
Detroit Community Union, *68*
Detroit Day Nursery, 57
Detroit Opera House, 56*f*
Detroit Pistons (team), *146*
Detroit Renaissance, co-founders, *124*
Detroit Symphony, support, 95
Detroit Tigers (team), *128*
Detroit Zoological Society, *124*
Detroit-Michigan Stove Company, 51*f*
DeVos, Helen (Mrs. Richard), *135*
DeVos, Richard, *135f*
Dexter, MI, temperance societies, 20
direct sales industry, *135*
disabled people. *See* handicapped persons
disaster relief. *See* relief work
diseases. (*See also specific disease names*)
   causes, 22, 45, 57
   fundraising, *68*, 75*f*, 103*f*, 106*f*, *146*
   Michigan's reputation for, *6*, 8, *10*
   prevention, 34–*36*, 65*f*, 107*f*
Disraeli, Benjamin, *50*
Dix, Dorothea, 28
doctors, *10*, 11, 26, *128*
documentation, 40, *52*
Dodge, Horace, 64, 73, *88*
Dodge, John, 64, 73, *88*
Dodge Bros. State Parks, *88*
"Dogs for Defense," 95*f*
donations, 42*f*, 55–57, 75
   appeals for, 53, 66*f*, 82*f*
   land, *16*, *19*, *88*, 108, *109*
   material goods, viii*f*, 3, 33, *36*, 89*f*
   material goods, during wartime, 94*f*, 95*f*
   money, ix, 28, 37, 61*f*, 95*f*
   time, 2, 7, *16*
Douglass Community Association, Kalamazoo, 120*f*
Dow, Grace A. (Mrs. Herbert H.), *101*
Dow, Herbert Henry, 35*f*, 100, *101f*
Dow, Herbert Henry, II, *101*
Dow Chemical Company, 65, *101*
Dow Gardens, *101*
Dowagiac, MI, women's club, 62
downtowns, renewal of, *123*, *124*, *139*
drug abuse, 136*f*, 138
Dunbar, Willis, 18, 28
Duniway, Abigail Scott, 144
Dwight, Ed, sculptor, 21*f*

E

Eagle River, MI, mining profits, 12*f*
Eagle Scouts, activities, 91*f*
East Saginaw, MI, sewage facilities, 45
Eaton County, 26, 85
Eaton Rapids, MI, women's club, 62
economic cycles. *See* booms, economic; depressions, economic
Eddy, Arthur, 48
Edison, Thomas, laboratory, 77
Edison Institute, *76*, 77, 77*f*, 95, 112
Edsel B. Ford Institute for Medical Research, 75*f*
education, viii*f*, 7, 9. (*See also* public education)
   for children, *83*
   curricula, 24, 57, *101f*
   funding for, *74*, 80, 111*f*, *135*
   institutions for. *See* colleges and universities; schools

non-school programs for, *52*, 58–*60*, *68f*, 70*f*, *104*. (*See also* community education movement)
non-school sites for, 35, 37, 126*f*
scholarships, 85, *98*, 103, *109*
in science and technology, *101*, *104*, 115
for special groups, 118, *128*, 141*f*, 143*f*
Edwards, Esther Gordy, *119*
Eliot, John, *43*
Ely, Ralph, *8*
emigrants to Michigan, *13*
   from the Northeast, 7*f*, 9, 15
   from Ohio, 9, *68f*, *124*
   from Pennsylvania, *19*, 50*f*
   from the South, *63*, 64, 96–97, *116*, 130*f*
Emmet County, *123*
Empire State Building, New York City, *84*
employment, *60*, 81
   clearinghouse offices for, viii*f*, 25, *39*, 59
   discrimination in, *59*, 64
   increased opportunities for, 90, 96, 105–106, 118
   of women, 21, *52*, 57*f*
Encyclopedia of African-American Culture & History, 120
endowments, 48, 138
   from asset sales, *116*, *128*
   by foundations, 81, *84*, 98
energy, gift of, 33–34
entrepreneurs. *See* businesses; *specific persons*
epidemics, *10*, 11, *32*, 45, 57
epilepsy, *68*
Erie Canal, impact, 8–9
Escanaba, MI, 48, *74*
Europeans in Michigan. *See* immigrants to Michigan

F

fairs, 11*f*, *36*, 51*f*
families, 50*f*
   as foundation beneficiaries, *109*, *123*, *124*
   indigent, aid to, 86–87, 97*f*
   soldier's, aid to, *63*, 70, 94
Farmington, MI, circuit rider, 17–18
Fetzer, John E., *128*
Fetzer Institute, *128*
filthy conditions. *See* sanitation, improvements in
fire fighters, 7, 41*f*, 70
fires, 6*f*, 7, *13*, *47*
First National Bank, Marquette, *84*
Fisher, Max, *124f*
Fisher Body (firm), women workers, 57*f*
Flint, MI, 2, 87, 143
   beneficiary of Mott Foundation, 95, 97*f*, 100*f*, 108
   industries in, 65, 66*f*, 96, *145*
food banks, 87*f*, 89*f*, 142
food conservation, 55–56, *63*, 69–70
food drives, 53
   as relief work, viii*f*, 8, *13*, 67
food products industry, ix, 105, 131*f*
   cereals, 65, *79*, *92*
Forbes, Malcolm, on wealth, *138*
Ford, Benson, 112
Ford, Edith (Mrs. Benson), 112
Ford, Edsel B., 75*f*, 80, *88*, 112
Ford, Eleanor (Mrs. Edsel), *88*, 112
Ford, Gerald R., as Eagle Scout, 91*f*

Ford, Henry, *76f*
   automobile innovator, 64*f*, 64–65, 65*f*, 73
   memorials, *76*, 77, 77*f*, 95
   philanthropy of, ix, 75, 77, 80, 106
Ford, Henry, II, 96*f*, 111–112, *124*
Ford, Josephine (Mrs. Walter), 112
Ford, Martha (Mrs. William), 112
Ford, Walter, 112
Ford, William, 112
Ford family, 75, 77, 112
Ford Foundation, *76*, 121, 125
   activities, 95, 103, *145*
   evolution, 80, 95, 112
   Ford Motor Company stock, 112, 130
   tax reform and, 77, 111, 112
Ford Motor Company
   as business, 83*f*, 86, 96, 96*f*, 142
   philanthropy of, 105, 112, *140*, *145*
   stock ownership in, 112, 130
   tax reform and, 77, 111
Foremost Insurance Company, *123*
Fort Custer, 70*f*. (*See also* Camp Custer)
foundation types
   community, 66, 80*f*–81, *98*, 103, 105. (*See also main entries for specific cities and counties*)
   corporate, 105, 134, 136, 142, *145*
   family, 66, *101*, *119*, *123*. (*See also under foundations, specific names of family subentries*)
   private, 65–66, 80, 122, 125, *135*
   private, growth in number, 75, 77, 94, 100, 130
foundations
   evolution of, 7, 65, 95, 122, 125
   government regulation of, 130–131, 143, 144*f*
   grantmaking role, ix, 95, 134*f*, 143–144
   grantmaking *vs.* operating, 129, 134
   growth in number as public charities, 142, 144
   interests of, 103, 105, 120–121. (*See also specific interests, e.g., youth*)
   national issues and, 48, 91, 141*f*, 144*f*
   tax incentives for, 57, 80, 111, 129
foundations, specific
   Amway Environmental Foundation, 142
   Battle Creek Community Foundation, 142
   Bay Area Community Foundation, 142
   Blue Cross and Blue Shield Foundation, *140*
   Community Foundation for Southeastern Michigan, 66, 129*f*, 142, 146
   Community Foundation of Monroe, 105
   Community Foundation of Northeastern Michigan, *102*
   Richard and Helen DeVos Foundation, *135*
   Domino's Foundation, 142
   Dow Corning Foundation, 142
   Herbert H. and Grace A. Dow Foundation, *101*, *101f*, 132
   Dyer-Ives Foundation, 132
   Family AIDS Foundation, *124*
   Fetzer Foundation. *See main entry*, Fetzer Institute
   Max and Marjorie Fisher Foundation, *124*
   Ford Foundation. *See main entry*
   Four County Foundation, 142
   Fremont Area Foundation, 134
   Fremont Foundation, 134
   Frey Foundation, *123*
   General Motors Foundation, *140*
   Gerber Companies Foundation, 105

Gordy Foundation, *119*
Grand Action Foundation, *123*
Grand Rapids Foundation. *See main entry*
Guggenheim Foundation, *128*
Hudson-Webber Foundation, 132
Kalamazoo Foundation. *See main entry*
Kellogg Foundation. *See main entry*,
    W.K. Kellogg Foundation
Kresge Foundation. *See main entry*
La-Z-Boy Foundation, 105
Leelanau Township Foundation, *98*
Lovelight Foundation, *124*
Edward Lowe Foundation, *139f*
Masco Corporate Foundation, 105
Metro Health Foundation, 140*f*
MichCon Foundation, 142
Michigan Native American Foundation, 142
Michigan Women's Foundation, *140*, 142
Miller Foundation, 132
Mott Foundation. *See main entry*, Charles
    Stewart Mott Foundation
Louis and Helen Padnos Foundation, 105
Elsa U. Pardee Foundation, 103
Points of Light Foundation, 133
Saginaw Community Foundation, 142
Skillman Foundation, *109*
Standard Products Company Charitable
    Foundation, 142
Steelcase Foundation, 105, 134*f*
Harry A. and Margaret D. Towsley Foundation,
    132
Turn 2 Foundation, *146*
United Jewish Foundation, 125*f*
Upjohn Company Foundation, 142
Jay and Betty Van Andel Foundation, *135*
Whirlpool Foundation, 105
Foundations Under Fire (Reeves), 122
Four Leaf Clover Club, 97*f*
4-H programs, Michigan, *98*, *104*, 136*f*
Fourierism, failure of, 18
Fowlerville, MI, tornado damage, 56*f*
France, impact on Michigan, 12, 14
François, Simeon. *See* St. Lusson, Sieur de
Franklin, Rabbi Leo, 59
Frederik Meijer Gardens, *135*
Fremont County, 105
French Moral and Benevolent Society of Detroit
    and its Vicinity, 12
Frey, Edward J., *123*
Frey, Frances (Mrs. Edward J.), *123*
fruit crops, 70, *76*
funding sources for public good, 34*f*, 95
    business, ix, *16*, *19*, 25, 88
    foundations, ix, 80, *145*
    government, 11, 14, *24*, 41, 55, *104*
    individuals, viii*f*, 25, 27, 34–35. (*See also*
        fundraising; *specific individuals*)
    industry, ix, 12*f*, 35*f*, 45*f*
    religious organizations, 15*f*, 59, 61*f*, 62
fundraising, 34–37, 87
    bond drives, *63*, 66*f*, 70
    item sales, 75*f*, 94*f*
    joint efforts, 82, 91*f*, 93*f*, 106, 115*f*
    joint efforts, as models, *59*, 66, 106–107
    publicity for, viii*f*, *36*, 82*f*, *146*
    social events, *36*, *92*, 116, *146*
    street solicitation, 61*f*, 86*f*, 106*f*
fur trade, 2–3, 3*f*, *16*
furniture industry, 65, 105

G

garbage collections, *52*
Garden, MI, lumbering near, *74*
gardens, 55–56, 69–70, *104*, *109*. (*See also* parks,
    botanical)
General Federation of Women's Clubs, *63*
General Foods Corporation, *92*
General Motors (GM), 96, 142, *145*
    officers, 73, 75, *84*
Gentile Co-operative Association, Chicago, 97
gifts. *See* donations
Girl Scouts of the USA, 103*f*, *140*
GM. *See* General Motors (GM)
Gnagey family, emigrants, 50*f*
Goddard, Robert, rocketeer, *128*
Gordy, Berry, *119*
Gordy, Esther. *See* Edwards, Esther Gordy
Gore, Albert, Sr., 129
Gospel of Wealth, 46, 48, *138*
governments
    actions by, 57, 87*f*, 89*f*, 120
    as beneficiaries, *102*, 107
    education of officials in, 141, 141*f*
    funding by, 6, 11, 87*f*, 89, 136, 141
    intervention of, debated, 86–87, 89–90
Grand Haven, MI, *16*, 88
Grand Rapids, MI, 22, 58, 58*f*, 65, 117
    benevolent societies, 25, 66
    donations collected, 38*f*, 86*f*, 94, 94*f*, 95*f*
    ethnic groups in, 117, 121*f*, 130*f*
    as foundation beneficiary, *123*, *135*
    Great Depression and, 87, 87*f*, 89, 89*f*
    relief work in, 37–38, 91*f*, 97*f*
    street sites, 23*f*, 58*f*, *60*, 73*f*, 86*f*
    wartime relief work in, 34*f*, 67, 69*f*
    women's clubs, 61, 99*f*
Grand Rapids Anti-Tuberculosis Society, 65*f*, 75*f*
Grand Rapids Charity Organization Society,
    40–41
Grand Rapids Foundation, 66
    activities funded by, 117, 118, 118*f*, 121*f*
    creation of, 80*f*, 81, 82*f*
Grand Rapids South High School, 95*f*
Grand Rapids Union Benevolent Association, 25*f*,
    25–26
Grand River, *16*
Grand Traverse County, 70, 111*f*
grantmakers, seminar, 136*f*
grantmaking, ix, 95, 98*f*, 134, 134*f*
    as foundation risk capital, 143–144
    legal definition, 129
Gratiot County, treasurers, *8*
Graves, S. George, 80*f*
Grayling, MI, parks, 88
Great Awakening, 19th century, 15, 17, 18
Great Depression, 56, 81, 86–87*f*, 89, 89*f*, 89–91
Great Lakes region, 2, 7*f*, 8–9, *59*, 88. (*See also*
    names of specific lakes, e.g., Lake Michigan
    region)
Great Seal of Michigan Territory, 18*f*
Great War. *See* World War I
Green Bay, shoreline park, 88
Green Pastures Camp, Jackson, 99*f*
Greenfield Village, Dearborn, *76*, 77, 77*f*
Gregg, Rosa, 63
Griffith, Roberta A., *60f*
Griffiths, Martha, 132
Guiding Star (club), 63

H

Habitat for Humanity, 142
Hackley, Charles, 48
Hall, Tolman W., *27*
Hall, Mrs. Tolman W., *27*
handicapped persons, *68*, 81, *128*, 141*f*
Hannah Schloss Settlement, Detroit, 58
Harbor Springs, MI, community foundation, *123*
Harold Upjohn School, 105*f*
Harper, Walter, *19*
Harrison, Basel, 8–9
Hartwick, Karen Michelson, 88
Hartwick Pines State Park, 88
Haserot, Francis H., *98*
Haserot Park, Northport, 98
Hastings, Eurotas P., 17
Haviland, Laura Smith, 6, *32f*
Haydon, Charles B., journal, 33
Hayes Body Corporation, 94*f*
health care, *10*, 82*f*, *83*, *124*
    for blacks, *32*, 51*f*, *63*
    for children, 85*f*, 103*f*, 105, 107*f*, 136*f*
    funding for, *59*, *68*, *128*
    for indigents, 6–7, 11, *52*, 107
    institutional, 28, 53*f*, 103*f*. (*See also* hospitals)
    regional, 73*f*, 111*f*, 117*f*
    standards for, 26, 44, 57
hearing-impaired persons, aid, 105*f*
Hebrew aid societies. *See* United Jewish Charities
Helping Hand Mission, Detroit, *68*
Henry Clay (steamship), *10*
Henry Ford Trade School, *76*
Hermansville, MI, logging, 45*f*
Highland Recreation Area, 88
Hill, Arthur, 48
Hill, Grant, *146*
Hillsdale County, health service, 85
Hispanic-American Council, Kalamazoo, 143*f*
Hispanic-Americans, 118, 120, 143*f*. (*See also*
    Latinos in Michigan)
historic preservation, *76*, *109*, *139*
HIV, prevention, *146*
Hoeft, Paul H., 88
Hoffman, Paul, 112
Holland, MI, foundations, 103, 105
Holland American Aid Society, Kalamazoo, 50*f*
homelessness. *See* housing, lack of
Honolulu House, Marshall, *109*
Hoover, Herbert, 69, 86, 89
hospitals
    as beneficiaries, 25*f*, 48, *63*, 99, *102*
    operation of, *10*, 19*f*, 35, *52*
hospitals, specific
    Butterworth Hospital, Grand Rapids, *135*
    Henry Ford Hospital, Detroit, 75*f*, 77, 112
    Harper Hospital, Detroit, *19*, 19*f*
    Lakeview General Hospital, Battle Creek, *92*
    Leelanau Memorial Hospital, Northport, *98*
    Mary Free Bed Hospital, Grand Rapids, *60*
    Oliver Mining Hospital, Ironwood, 73*f*
    Sinai Hospital, Detroit, 99
    Sparrow Hospital, Lansing, 65
    St. Vincent's Hospital, Detroit, *10*
housing
    discrimination in, *63*, 67*f*, 96–97, 115, 120
    lack of, *13*, 22, 38, 42, 50
    locations, 66*f*, 96, 118
    low-cost, 118, *124*

shortages, *8*, 96, 138

types, 7, 15*f*, 23, ***92***, ***123***

for women, *116*, 117*f*, *140*

Hoyt Library, Saginaw, 48

Hubbell, Dr. Julian B., *47*

Hudson (firm), 96

Hudson, Joseph L., 129*f*

Hull House, Chicago, 58

human immunodeficiency virus. *See* HIV

humanitarianism, 15, 17, 78

spirit of, ***43***, 57, ***76***

hunger, 7. (*See also* starvation)

alleviation of, viii*f*, *8*, 87*f*, 89*f*

causes, 38, 44

Hunting, David, Sr., 134*f*

Huron, Lake, *47*

Huron City, MI, fire, *47*

Huron County, fire, *47*

Huron County Women's Club, 69

Hussey, Erastus, 21*f*, 22

Hutchins, Lee M., 80*f*

I

ignorance, training ground, 26

immigrants to Michigan

from eastern Europe, 73*f*, 99

from western Europe, 3, 9*f*, 50*f*, 59, ***74***

immunization programs, 107*f*

improvement projects. *See* civic projects; sanitation, improvements; self-improvement

In As Much Circle of King's Daughters and Sons Club, 62, *63*

Indians, Michigan. *See* Native Americans *and specific tribal names*

indigents, ix, 6–7, 11–*13*, 42, 97*f*

caused by, 20, 38, 40, 48

health care for, ***52***, 107

help for, ***16***, 23, 41, 87, 91*f*

poorhouses for, *10*, 26, 28, **52**

as result, 22, 44, 57

industries. (*See also* specifics, *e.g.,* mining industry)

downsizing of, 138, 141–142

growth and development of, 57*f*, 72, ***135***

Ingham County, poorhouse, 26

injustice, 57, 62–*63*, 67*f*

insane asylums. *See* mentally ill, institutional care

insurance industry, ***123***

Interlochen Center for the Arts, ***119***

Internal Revenue Service (IRS), 129–130, 131

international impacts, 103, ***124***, 128*f*

Ironwood, MI, hospitals, 73*f*

IRS. *See* Internal Revenue Service

Isabella County, 30*f*, 70

J

J. W. Wells State Park, *88*

Jackson, Helen. *See* Claytor, Helen Jackson

Jackson, MI, 22, 61, 99*f*, 103, 105

Jackson, Roscoe B., memorial, 95

Jesuits, 2–3, ***16***

Jeter, Derek, *146*

Jewell, Marjorie C., *116*

Jewish Welfare Federation, ***124***

Jews in Michigan, 33, ***52***, ***124***

aid for, 37, 58–*59*, 99

job opportunities. *See* employment

John Ball Park, 38*f*, ***135***

John F. Kennedy Center for the Performing Arts, ***92***, ***124***

Johnson, Dorothy A., 133, 134*f*

Johnston, Alice, *116*

Jones, MI, preservation, ***139***

Journal of Political Economics, The, 56

Junior Achievement, Grand Rapids, ***123***

K

Kalamazoo, MI, 20*f*, *36*, 37, 50*f*, 65

as beneficiary, ***52***, 53, 90–91, 120*f*, 138*f*

clubs, 44*f*, 58, 61

health care institutions, 28, 103*f*

Kalamazoo Central High School, 94*f*, *146*

Kalamazoo County, 8–9, 18, 90–91, ***128***

Kalamazoo Foundation, 66, 94, 105*f*

creation of, *80*, 81, 90*f*, 132

support for cultural programs, 107, 120*f*, 138*f*, 143*f*

Kalamazoo Horse Association, *36*

Kalamazoo Institute of Arts, 107

Kalamazoo Sanitary Fair, 35–*36f*

Kansas settlements, ***39***

Kaufman, Louis G., ***84f***

Kaufman Fund, ***84***

Kearney brothers, dog, 95*f*

Kellogg, Dr. John Harvey, 53*f*, ***79***

Kellogg, Will Keith (W.K.), 79*f*, 85

as entrepreneur, ix, 53*f*, 78*f*

as philanthropist, ix, 75, 80, 100. (*See also* W.K. Kellogg Foundation)

Kellogg Biological Station, 81

Kellogg Company, 105, 131

as business, 53*f*, 65, ***79***, 90

Kellogg Experimental Farm and Forest, 78*f*

Kellogg Foundation. *See* W.K. Kellogg Foundation

Kent County, viii*f*, 26, ***123***

Kettunen Conference Center, Tustin, *104*

Kewinaquot, Chief, ***16***

King, Charles, 73

King, Rev. Martin Luther, Jr., 120

Kitty Litter, product, 100, ***139***

Kresge, Sebastian S., ix, 75, 80–81*f*, 100, 107–108

Kresge Eye Institute, 107, 107*f*

Kresge Foundation, 114, 132

beneficiaries of, 80–81*f*, 94–95, 107, 107*f*, 118

Kundig, Father Martin, *10*

L

labor

business and, *54*, ***76***

collaboration with employers, 106, 115*f*

conflict with employers, 57

conflicts with employers, 105–106

discrimination, *59*, 96–97

wages for, 85*f*, 90

women in, force, 57*f*, *63*, *116*, 117*f*

labor colonies, for indigents, 42

labor unions, ***52***, 106, 121

Ladies' Library and Literary Club, Lansing, 65

Ladies' Library Association, Kalamazoo, 44*f*

Ladies' Society, Detroit, 14

Ladies' Society for the Support of Hebrew Widows and Orphans in the State of Michigan, 37

Ladies Soldiers' Aid Society, Kalamazoo, 35–*36f*

Laframboise, Joseph, ***16***

Laframboise, Mdme. Madeline, ***16***

Lake Huron region, *47*, *88*

Lake Michigan region, parks, *88*

Lake Odessa, MI, women's club, 61–62

Lake Superior region, 41*f*, *88*

land, 78*f*

claims to, *3f*, 3–4, 7

donations of, ***16***, *19*, 28, *88*, 108–***109***

ownership, 15, 18

ownership restrictions, 3, *27*, *59*

Lansing, MI, 64*f*, 65, 106*f*, ***145***

Lansing Bureau of Charities, 58

Lapeer County, *47*, 142

Latinos in Michigan, 117, 117*f*, 118

migrant workers, 85*f*, 130*f*

philanthropic heritage of, ix, 59

leadership, personal

African-American, 21*f*, ***39***, 62, *66*, 99*f*

development programs, 118, 143*f*, 144*f*

Hispanic-American, 118, 130*f*, 143*f*

League of Women Voters, 61*f*

Leelanau County, MI, *98*

Leland, Henry, 64, 73

Lemmer, John A., ***74***

Lenawee County, *32*, 94*f*, *104*

libraries, 46, 48, ***68***, 112*f*, ***124***

Life (magazine), 95–96

Lincoln, Abraham, 31, 31*f*, 34, *36*

Lions Club, 91*f*

Lithuanian-American Mutual Aid Group, 73*f*

living conditions, 6–7, 85*f*, *140*

in Michigan cities, 7, 44, 64, 96–97

local impacts, viii*f*–ix, 66, 106, 115*f*

Logan Female Antislavery Society, 21, ***32***

logging. *See* lumber industry

London Charity Organization Society, 40

Lore, John S., 133*f*

Lowe, Edward, ***139f***

Lowell, Josephine Shaw, 42, 56

Ludington, MI, *88*

Ludington State Park, *88*

lumber industry, *47*, 72, ***74***, *88*

fueled Michigan's growth, 45, 45*f*, 46*f*

Lundy, Benjamin, 21

Lutherans in Michigan, 9*f*

Lydian Association of Detroit, *63*

M

Mackinac Island, ***16***, 91*f*

Macomb County, 142

Madison, James, 7

malaria, 8

Man Who Discovered the Golden Cat, The (Lowe), ***139***

Manistee, MI, shipping, 46*f*

Manley, Frank, 108, 118

manufacturing, ***139***. (*See also* specific industry, *e.g.,* automobile industry)

Mar-A-Lago, Palm Beach, ***92***

March of Dimes campaign, Lansing, 106*f*

Marquette, MI, 35*f*, 41*f*, 46*f*, ***84***

Marquette County Savings Bank, ***84***

Marquette Iron Range, 41*f*

Marshall, MI, ***109***

Martin, Nancy, *19*

Mawby, Russell G., *104*, 129*f*, 132, 133*f*, 141*f*
  work with Congress, 131, 144*f*
Mawby, Ruth (Mrs. Russell), *104*
McCarthy Era, 111, 115, 125
McCoy, Elijah, inventor, 62, *63*
McCoy, Mary (Mrs. Elijah), 62–*63*
McCusker, John J., 37
MCFYP (Michigan Community Foundations
    Youth Project), *98*, 129*f*, 142–143, 144*f*
McGregor, Katherine Whitney, *68f*
McGregor, Tracy, *68f*
McGregor Fund, *68*, 118
McGregor Institute, *68f*–69*f*
MCHP (Michigan Community Health Project),
    85, 95
Mears, Carrie, *88*
Mears, Charles, memorial, *88*
meatpacking industry, *52*, 57
Meijer, Frederik, memorial, *135*
men
    as beneficiaries, *68f*–69*f*
    as charity workers, 12, 14, 62, *68*, *140*
Menominee tribe, 2
mentally ill, institutional care, 28
Merrill Palmer Institute, *68*
Mesick County, 107*f*
metals industry, 94*f*, 105
Methodist Children's Home, Detroit, 80–81*f*,
    94–95
Methodists in Michigan, 9*f*
Metro Health Foundation, 140*f*
MichCon Foundation, 142
Michelson, Karen. *See* Hartwick, Karen
    Michelson
Michigan, Dept. of Public Health, *140*
Michigan, Legislature, *54*, *60*, 62, *88*, *139*
Michigan, State Park Commission, *88*
Michigan Antislavery Society, 22
Michigan Community Foundations Youth Project
    (MCFYP), *98*, 129*f*, 142–143, 144*f*
Michigan Community Health Project (MCHP),
    85, 95
Michigan Council for the Arts, 120
Michigan Emergency Cash Flow Loan Fund, 138
Michigan 4-H Foundation, *104*
Michigan history, *88*. (*See also specific ethnic and
    religious influences*)
    British occupation, 3–4
    emigrant settlements in, 6–8, 9, 9*f*, *16*
    French explorers, 2–3, 3*f*, 4*f*, 9*f*
    Indian settlements in, 2, *43*
    industries in. *See* specifics, *e.g.,* lumber industry
    maps in, 4*f*, 17*f*
    philanthropy in, continuous, 41*f*, 94, 144
    state reputations in, 6, 8, 95–96
    as U.S. territory, 6–17, 18*f*, 21–22
    water routes in, 17*f*, 47
Michigan History Magazine, 61
Michigan League for Human Services (MLHS),
    138, 141
Michigan Native American Foundation, rise
    of, 142
Michigan Nonprofit Association, 133*f*, 136*f*, 141
Michigan Nonprofit Forum, 133*f*, 141
Michigan Opera Theater, *124*
Michigan Scene, The (periodical), 133
Michigan Soldiers' Relief Association,
    Washington, D.C., 35
Michigan Soup House, Washington, D.C., 35

Michigan State University (MSU), 37*f*, 85, 132
    cooperative agreements, *104*, *135*, *139*
Michigan (steamship), 7*f*
Michigan United Health and Welfare Fund,
    106–107
Michigan Women's Committee of National
    Defense, *52*
Michigan Women's Foundation, *140f*, 142
Midland, MI, 35*f*, *101f*, 103
Milford, MI, parks, *88*
milk supplies, inspection, *52*
Milliken, Helen W., *140*
mining industry, 12*f*, 31*f*, 41*f*, 72
Minnesota Mining and Manufacturing Co. (3M),
    109
Miss United Fund, viii*f*
missionaries, 17, 23*f*, 30*f*
    Jesuit, in Michigan history, 2–3, 9*f*, *16*
MLHS. *See* Michigan League for Human Services
    (MLHS)
money, ix, 2, *16*, 28, *61*
Monroe County, 105
Monteith, Rev. John, *13*
Moral and Humane Society, Detroit, 12
moral deficiency
    overcoming, 20, 34–35, 40–42, 44
    overcoming, in indigents, 7–8, 11–12, 14
Moralez, Virginia, 130*f*
Mormon church. *See* Church of Jesus Christ of
    Latter-Day Saints
Moslems in Michigan, *52*
Motown Record Company, *119*
Mott, Charles Stewart, 133*f*, 143–144
    as philanthropist, ix, 73–73*f*, 75, 100, *145*. (*See
        also* Charles Stewart Mott Foundation)
    Senate tax reform testimony, 127, 127*f*
Mott Camp, 100*f*
Mount Pleasant, MI, *43*
MSU. *See* Michigan State University
Murphy, Frank, 86
Murphy, William, 73
museums, specific
    Jesse Besser Museum, *102*, 103
    Henry Ford Museum, *76*–77, 77*f*, 95
    Grand Rapids Art Museum, *135*
    Hitsville, USA, *119*
    Museum of Modern Art, New York, 95
    Van Andel Museum Center, *135*
music programs, *98*, *109*, 138*f*
    concert halls, 46, 56*f*
    operas, 56*f*, *124*
    symphony orchestras, *92*, 95, *135*
Muskegon, MI, 48
Muskegon County, *104*
My Life and Work (Ford), *76*, 77

N

NAACP, 120
Nash-Kelvinator Corporation, 96
National Academy of Science, *101f*
National Aeronautics and Space Administra-
    tion, *128*
National Association for the Advancement of
    Colored People (NAACP), 120
National Association of Colored Women, *63*
National Center for Voluntary Action, 133
National Cultural Center, *92*

National Historic Landmark District, Marshall, *109*
national impacts
    on Michigan, 15, 35. (*See also* wars)
    of Michigan groups, 22, 66, 106, 108
    of Michigan philanthropists, viii*f*–ix, *13*, 20,
        54, 56
National Organization of Women (NOW), 120
National Symphony Orchestra, *92*
National VOLUNTEER Center, 133
Native Americans. (*See also specific tribal names*)
    education of, *13*, *98*
    immigrants and, 2–3, 3*f*, 4, 9*f*, *43*
    living conditions of, 2*f*, 7, *16*, *43*, 120
    philanthropic tradition of, ix, 2–3, 9*f*, *43*
    tribal chiefs, 8–9, *16*, 23*f*, *43*
Neuman, Paul, 131*f*
New Deal, 89*f*, 89–90
New Detroit, Inc., 117*f*, 118, *124*
New England, North America, 9, 15, 18
New France, Michigan as, 3
New York City Charity Organization Society, 42
New York Yankees (team), *146*
Newaygo County, 105, 134
newspapers, specific
    Chicago Tribune, 111
    Detroit Free Press, 30
    Detroit Gazette, 12
    *Detroit Michigan Essay; or Impartial
        Observer,* *13*
    Flint Journal, 144
    Genius of Universal Emancipation, 21
    Grand Rapids Evening Press, 53
    Kalamazoo Gazette, *146*
Newton, Isaac, ix
nonprofit institutions
    cash flow loans by, 138, 141
    growth of, 57, 75, 141
    Michigan Nonprofit Association, 133*f*, 141
    tax reform and, 75, 112, 125–127, 129–134, 143
Noonday, Chief, 23*f*
Northeastern Michigan Development Bureau, 57*f*
Northport, MI, *98f*
NOW (National Organization of Women), 120
numismatics, *84f*
nurses
    education of, *60*, 75*f*, 108
    women as, *10*, *19*, *32*, 49*f*

O

Oakland County, foundation, 142
Ojibwa tribe. *See* Chippewa tribe
Okie, Frank, inventor, *109*
Old Fort Mackinac, honor guards, 91*f*
Olds, Ransom E., 64*f*, 64–65, 65, 73
Oneida community, utopian society, 18
Ontonagon County, 69–70
operating foundations, 129, 134
Ora et Labora settlement, 9*f*
orphanages, 22, 26*f*, *32*, *52*, *59*
orphans, 22, 26–*27*, 37, 67
Osborn, Chase S., *13*
Oshtemo Township, Kalamazoo County, *128*
Ottawa tribe, *16*
ownership. (*See also* land, ownership; stock
    ownership)
    private *vs.* public, 18, 57

P

P. H. Hoeft State Park, 88
Padnos, Helen (Mrs. Louis), 105
Padnos, Louis, 105
Panic of 1837, 15
Panic of 1893, 48, 50–51, 53f, 55–56, 88
paper industry, 65, **74**
Pardee, Elsa U., 103
parks, 38f, 46, 48, **88**, 98
    botanical, 38f, **101**, **135**. (See also gardens)
    zoological, **124**, **135**
Patman, Wright, 125–126
Patriotic Leagues, World War I, 63
pauperism. See indigents
Payton, Robert, 2
Penn, William, **43**
Penny Savings Societies, 58, 61
Pentwater, MI, parks, 88
personal improvement. See self-improvement
petroleum industry, **124**
pets and pet products, 95f, 100, **139**
pharmaceutical industry, 65, 80f
Pharmacia & Upjohn (firm), 65
philanthropy, viiif–ix, 28
    business influence on, 40–42, 66, **139**, 143–**145**
    cultural effect on women, 35, 37
    definition and scope, 2, **79**, 82, 107
    funding for. See funding sources
    Native Americans and, 2–3, 8–9, 9f
    organizations for. See benevolent societies;
        charitable associations; foundations
    religious influence on, 7, 9, 11–22, 40, 86f, **102**
    secular influence on, 15, 23, 28, 44, 78
    social conditions effect on, 37, 48, 94
    social conditions (post-1960) effect on, 114,
        117–118, 120–122, 134, 136
    social conditions (post-1980) effect on, 138,
        141–142
    as social responsibility, 58, 61, **124**
    tax laws and, 112, 114, 125–127, 129–132
    visions of, ix, 118, **128**
Pingree, Hazen S. ("Ping"), 53f, **54f**, 55, 56
pioneers, ix, 15f, 27, 45, 91
Plainwell, MI, book exchange, 112f
planetariums, **84**, **102**
Plymouth, MI, circuit rider, 17–18
police protection, 63, 117
politics, **52**, 54, 57, 61f
Pollack, Lana, 140
Pontiac, MI, 62, 88, **145**
poor people. See indigents
poorhouses, 10, 26, 28, **52**
population, Michigan, 2, 3, 72
    19th century, 4, 7, 15, 22–23, 64
Port Huron, MI, community foundation, 103, 105
Port Huron Relief Committee, 47
Porter, John, **145f**
Post, C. W., **79**, **92**
Post, Marjorie Merriweather, **92f**
Postum Cereal Company, 65, **92**
Potawatomi tribe, 2–3, 8–9, **16**
poverty. See indigents
Presbyterians in Michigan, 17, **102**
prisons, 42, **52**
professional sports, **128**, 146
Progressive Movement, 65, 78
    approaches to, 57, 61–62
    reformers in, **52**, 54

Prohibition laws, 18, 20f, **32**, 82, 85
Protestants in Michigan, 34. (See also specific
    denominational names)
Public Domain Commission, Michigan, 88
public education, 14, 24, 107, 118. (See also
    under schools, public)
public good, ix, 2, 17, **83**, 146
    sharing for, 41f, 46, 48, 144
public health, 11, 85, 95, 140. (See also diseases;
    sanitation)
public works projects, 46, 53, 55, 87–87f, 89–89f
Pullman railroad cars, 55, 57
Puritan influence, 9

Q

Quakers in Michigan, 21–22, **32**

R

racial discrimination, 99f
    in employment, 64, 85f
    in housing, 63, 67f, 115, 120
railroads, 54, 55, 69f, **74**
    figurative, 21f, 21–22, **32**
    in the Upper Peninsula, 41f, 50f
Raisin Institute, **32**
Raisin River, **32**
Ransom Fidelity Company, 65–66
Rare Coin Company of America, **84**
Reagan, Ronald, 141
recording industry, **119**
recreation facilities, 58. (See also parks; types,
    e.g., children's camps)
    for African-Americans, 62f, 67f, 70
    construction of, **74**, **123**, **135**
    for youth, **84**, 85, **92**, **109**
Red Cross (organization). See American Red
    Cross
Red Feather campaigns, 93f
reformers. (See also Great Awakening, 19th
    century)
    in charitable associations, 22–26, 28
    of charity itself, 40–42, 44
    part of the Progressive Movement, **52**, 53f,
        54, 57
refugees, **39**, 67, 121f
regional impacts, viiif–ix, 34
relief work, 97f
    during Civil War, 30–37
    during depressions (19th century), 15, 23,
        37–38, 50–51, 53
    during depressions (20th century), 86–87,
        89–91
    upon natural disasters, 47, 56f, 89f
    during World War I, **52**, 63, 67, 69–70, **76**
religions in Michigan. See specific denominations
renovation projects, **84**, 98f
Reo Motor Company, founder, 65
research, 80, 103, 118, **128**, **135**
    employment, 81, 90
    medical, 75f, 94, 103, 107, **135**
retail industry, ix
Returning Cloud (Ottawa chief). See Kewinaquot,
    Chief
Reuther, Walter, 106
Richard, Father Gabriel, ix, 10, 13f
Richardson, William C., ix, 136f
Richland, MI, 78f

Richland Township, Kalamazoo County, 90–91
Richmond, Sarah, 34f
rivers, 17f. (See also specific river names)
Rockefeller, John D., 78, 80, 100
Rogers City, MI, 88
Romney, George, 107, 132–133, 133f, 134f, 141
Romney, Lenore (Mrs. George), 136f
Roosevelt, Franklin Delano, 89f, 89–90
Roosevelt, Theodore, **52**
Roosevelt School, Flint, 97f
Roscoe B. Jackson Memorial Laboratory,
    Maine, 95
Rosie the Riveter, 57f
Royal Oak, MI, women's club, 62
Russell and Ruth Mawby Learning Center, 104

S

Saganing, MI, Chippewa settlement, **43**
Sagatoo, Mary Cabay, **43**
Sagatoo, Peter, **43**
Sage Library, Bay City, 48
Sag-e-maw, Chief, 8–9
Saginaw, MI, 45, 48, 62, 142, **145**
Saginaw River, 8f
Salvation Army, viiif, 61f, 91f–**92**, 105, **135**
Sanilac County, 47
Sanitary Commission. See U. S. Sanitary
    Commission
sanitation
    for disease prevention, 34–36, 45
    improvements, 7, **52**, 63
    lack of, 23, 44
Sawyer, MI, parks, 88
Schetterly, Dr. H. R., 18
Schloss, Hannah, memorial, 58
scholarships
    specialized, 85, 98, 105, **119**, 146
    tax reform and, 126, 129
Schoolcraft, MI, Underground Railroad, 22
schoolhouses, 24f, 25
schools, 73f
    for adults, **32**, **60**, 75f, **76**
    athletics at, **84**, **92**, **102**, 146
    for disabled students, 105f
    general funding for, 85, 107, **124**
    for indigent children, **13**, 14, 24
    inspections of, **52**, 134f
    public, 85f, 94f, **101f**, **145**, 146
    racial make-up, **32**, 121
    religious, **16**, **43**, 73f, **135**
Science Resources Center, Midland, **101f**
SCLC (Southern Christian Leadership
    Conference), 120
Scotch Settlement School, Dearborn, 24f
scrip, 87, 87f, 89
Second Great Awakening. See Great Awakening,
    19th century
self-improvement, 7, 9, 15, 140
self-sufficiency, 45, **59**, **83**
settlement houses, 58, 58f, 63
settlements, **39**
    of emigrants to Michigan, 6–9, 9f
    of Native Americans in Michigan, 2, **43**
Seventh-Day Adventists in Michigan, 18, 53f
sewage facilities, inadequate, 23, 44–45
sewers, **52**, 55
Shaw, Josephine. See Lowell, Josephine Shaw
shelters. See housing

Shiffman Clinic, Detroit, 99
shipping industry, 41*f*, 46*f*, 65, 88
Shiras, George, III, 35*f*
Shiras Institute, 35*f*
sightlessness, prevention of, *60*
Sigma Pi Phi (fraternity), 62
Silver Lake State Park, 88
Sisters of Charity, *10*
Skillman, Robert, *109*
Skillman, Rose (Mrs. Robert), *109*
slaughterhouses, sanitation in, *52*, 57
slavery, *32, 39*
　　anti-. *See* abolition movement
Sleeper, Mrs. Albert, 69
Sleeping Bear Dunes National Lakeshore, 88
smallpox vaccinations, 11
Smith, Laura. *See* Haviland, Laura Smith
Smithsonian Institution, 64*f*, *101f*
social conditions, 57, *60*, *146*
　　effects on. *See under* philanthropy
social Darwinism, 46, 48, 57
social welfare
　　government programs for, 86–87*f*, 89*f*, 141
　　philanthropic programs for, 106–107, *124,*
　　　　140, 141
socialism, 46, 56
soldiers
　　aid to, and their families, *63*, 70, 94
　　hospitals for, 19*f*, 35
　　killed by disease, 8, 38*f*
　　supplies for, *30*, 33–35
Soo Locks, park, 88
South Haven, MI, donated goods, 89*f*
Southern Christian Leadership Conference
　　(SCLC), 120
Southwest Michigan Tuberculosis Sanitorium,
　　103*f*
Spiritualists in Michigan, *52*
sports industry. *See* professional sports; recreation
　　facilities
St. Clair County, *47*, 59, 142
St. Louis, MI, 8
St. Lusson, Sieur de, 3*f*
St. Vincent Orphan Asylum, Detroit, 26*f*
Standard Products Company Charitable
　　Foundation, 142
Stansbury, Margaret, 57
Starr, Floyd, 90*f*
Starr Commonwealth School for Boys, Albion,
　　90*f*, *102*
starvation, 22, 26, 48
steamships, 7*f*, 8–9, *10*
stewardship, 46
stock ownership
　　Ford Foundation, 112, 130
　　foundation regulations about, 130–131, 144*f*
　　General Motors, 73, 75
　　Kellogg Foundation, 131
streets, 26
　　condition of, 44, *52, 63*
　　as donation collection sites, 61*f*, 86*f*
　　as public works projects, 55, 89*f*
Sts. Peter and Paul School, Grand Rapids, 73*f*
Studebaker (firm), 96, *109*
Success Clubs, 58
suffrage movements, 27, 37, *39, 52*, 62
Sunday School societies, 34
swampland, 6, 7–8, *74*
synagogues, 59

T
tax reform
　　1969 legislation, 112, 114, 126–127*f*, 129–134,
　　　　143
　　post-World War I, 75, 77
　　during Progressive Movement, *54, 57*
taxes
　　estate, 77, 80
　　excise, 126, 129, 131
　　income, 57, 75
Taylor, MI, corporate foundation, 105
TB. *See* tuberculosis
teachers, 24, *32, 60*
temperance movement, 20, 34, 82
temples. *See* synagogues
theism, influence of, 7, 9, 11–18
Third America, The (O'Neill), 75, 77
Thomas, Isiah, *146*
Thomas, Lynn (Mrs. Isiah), *146*
3M Company. *See* Minnesota Mining and
　　Manufacturing Co. (3M)
Three Oaks, MI, 88
Thumb (Michigan region), 9*f*, 47, 57*f*
Thursday Group, Detroit, *68*
Tiffin, Edward, 7
timbering. *See* lumber industry
time, as gift, 2, 7, *16*
Towsley, Harry A., 132
Towsley, Margaret (Mrs. Harry A.), 132
trading posts, 3*f*, *16*, 23*f*
Truth, Sojourner, 29*f*, *39f*
tuberculosis, 65*f*, 75*f*, 85*f*, 103*f*
Tuscola County, fire, 47
Tustin, MI, *104*
Twentieth Century Club, Detroit, *63*
typhoid, 57

U
U. S. Christian Commission, 35–36, 36*f*
U. S. Congress, 120, *139*
　　elected members, *13*, 35*f*
　　regulation of foundations, 57, 75, 111, 131, 143
U. S. Congress, House, 125, 126, 132, 144*f*
U. S. Congress, Senate, *83*, 111, 127, 127*f*, 129
U. S. Constitution, amendments, *52*, 57, 62, 75, 82
U. S. Dept. of Agriculture (USDA), *52, 104*, 136*f*
U. S. Dept. of War, 94*f*, 96
U. S. Postal Service, buildings, *109*
U. S. Sanitary Commission, 34, 36*f*
Ubly, MI, fire, 47
UEA (Urban Education Alliance, Inc.), *145*
UJA (United Jewish Appeal), *124*
Underground Railroad, 21*f*, 21–22, *32*
unemployment, 7, 25, 81
　　aid to ease, 86*f*, 87, 89*f*, 89–90
　　caused by economic depressions, 38, 48, 50, 56,
　　　　86–87
　　caused by urbanization, 22–23, 44
　　rates of, 85, 86, 141–142
　　workfare to alleviate, 53, 55, 89*f*, 91
Union Army, 34–35
Union Army, Michigan troops, 30–33, *36*
　　casualties, 33, 34*f*, 38*f*
　　2nd Michigan Infantry, 31*f*
　　3rd Michigan Infantry, 34*f*
　　25th Michigan Infantry, *30*
Union Station, Grand Rapids, 69*f*

Unitarians in Michigan, *52f*, 53
United Community Services, Detroit, *68*
United Fund movement, viii*f*, 106–107, 115*f*
United Jewish Appeal, *124*
United Jewish Charities, 59, 59*f*
United Way of America, 7, 118
　　Michigan predecessors of, viii*f*, 66, 106, *124*
　　Michigan units, 105, *135*
Upjohn, Harold, school, 105*f*
Upjohn, William Erastus (W.E.), 81, 90*f*, 90–91
Upjohn Company, The, 65, 81, 142
Upper Peninsula Development Bureau, 85*f*
Upper Peninsula (Michigan region), 3, 85*f*
　　as beneficiary, 12*f*, 35*f*, 73*f*, *84*
　　logging in, 45, 72, *74*
　　mining in, 12*f*, 31, *41*, 72
　　railroads in, 41*f*, 50*f*
Urban Education Alliance, Inc. (UEA), *145*
Urban League, Detroit, 51*f*, 62*f*, 99*f*, 126*f*
Urban League, Grand Rapids, 118
urbanization, 118
　　as cause of social problems, 22–23, 44–45, 138
　　downtown renewal in, *124*
USDA. *See* U. S. Dept. of Agriculture (USDA)
utilities, ownership, 57
utopian societies, 18, 18*f*

V
vagrancy. *See* housing, lack of
Van Andel, Betty (Mrs. Jay), *135*
Van Andel, Jay, *135f*
Van Andel Institute for Education and Medical
　　Research, *135*
Van Buren County, 33*f*, 70, 85
Van Wagenen, Isabella Baumfree. *See* Truth,
　　Sojourner
Vargas, Guadalupe, 130*f*
Vision Enrichment Services, Grand Rapids, *60*
visually-impaired persons, *60*, 105*f*
volunteerism
　　gender and, 31, *140*
　　for public good, ix, 2, 141
　　voluntary societies, 18, 133. (*See also*
　　　　benevolent societies)
volunteers
　　peacetime, 42*f*, 98, 143, 144*f*
　　wartime, Civil War, 31–37
　　wartime, World Wars, *52, 63*, 66*f*, 69–70, 94
　　wartime, World Wars youth, 70, 94*f*, 95*f*
voters, 27, *52*, 53*f*, 61*f*, 121
voyageurs. *See* Michigan history, French explorers.

W
W. E. Upjohn Institute for Employment Research,
　　81
W. E. Upjohn Unemployment Trustee
　　Corporation, 81, 90
W.K. Kellogg Foundation, ix, 21*f*, 131
　　CEOs, R.G. Mawby, 129*f*, 131–133*f*, 141*f*, 144*f*
　　CEOs, W.C. Richardson, ix, 136*f*
　　creation of, 53*f*, 78*f*, *79*–80, 85, 100*f*
　　educational interests of, 81, 108, 112*f*, 117
　　international interests of, 103, 107
　　national interests of, viii*f*, 118, 143*f*
　　organizational leadership of, *98*, 129*f*, 132, 141,
　　　　142–143
　　regional interests of, 81, 85, 95, *140*, 141*f*

Wallace, George, 121
Warren, Edward K, *88*
Warren, MI, tank production, 96
Warren Woods State Park, *88*
wars, specific, 30
   Civil War, *8,* 30–38*f,* **39**
   Revolutionary War, 7
   War of 1812, 7–8, 11
   World War I. *See main entry*
   World War II, 57*f,* 94–96, 100
   Vietnam War, 121, 121*f*
Washtenaw County, temperance, 20
water supply, 45, **52**, 57
Wayne County Home for Feeble Minded, **68**
wealth, *54,* 138
   attitudes toward, 11, 46, 48, *138*
   kinds of, ix, 2, 12*f,* **16**, 33
   sharing of, ix, 2–3, 7, 56
well-being. *See* health care
Wells, John Walter, memorial, *88*
Wells, Ralph, *88*
Welsh, George, 87, 89
Western Health Reform Institute, 53*f*
Western Michigan University, **139**
Wharton, Clifford, 132
White, Capt. Alpheus, *10*
White, Peter, 46*f*
White, William S., 143
white pine forests, 45, 48, **74**, 88
Whiting, James, 73
Whitney, Katherine. *See* McGregor, Katherine
   Whitney
widows, aid societies for, 37, 70
Williams, Fannie Barrier, *63*
Williamson, Kenneth, **79**
Willing Workers (club), *63*
Willow Run, MI, 96*f,* 96–97
Wilterdink, John Anthony, 33
Wisconsin Land and Lumber Company, 45*f*
WKKF. *See* W.K. Kellogg Foundation
women
   as beneficiaries, 25–25*f,* 28, **68**, *116, 140*
   education of, 35, 37, *140*
   employment of, 21, 49*f,* **52**, 57*f*
   housing for, *116,* 117*f*
   organizations for, **52**, 120
   organizations of, *10,* 14, 35. *(See also* women's
      clubs; *specific organizational names)*
   rights of, *27,* **32**, *39*
   roles of, expected, *27,* **32**, *63,* 75*f, 140*
   roles of, unexpected, 21
women's clubs, 41*f,* 44*f,* **52**, 61–65, 70
women's suffrage movement, *27, 37,* **52**, 62
Woodbridge, William, **13**
Woodward, Augustus, **13,** 24
workfare, **68**–69*f,* 87–87*f,* 89–89*f,* 91
Working Woman's Home, *116*
World War I
   bond drives during, *63,* 66*f,* 70
   conduct of, 49*f,* **76**
   poster promotions for, causes, 58*f,* 69–70
   women workers during, **52**, 57*f, 63,* 67, 69–70
Wyandot tribe, sharing among, 2

Y

YMCA (Young Men's Christian Association), 34,
   65, 70*f,* 105
YWCA (Young Women's Christian Association),
   65, 99*f, 140*
YWHA (Young Woman's Home Association),
   116f, 117*f*
Young, Coleman, *146*
Young Men's Benevolent Society, Detroit, 23, 25
Young Woman's Home Association (YWHA),
   Detroit, *116f,* 117*f*
youth, *140*
   development programs for, 90*f,* 129*f,* 142–
      143, 144*f*
   as foundation beneficiaries, 85, **102, 109**,
      129*f,* 142
   organizations for. *See* Camp Fire Girls;
      specifics, e.g., Boy Scouts of America
   rural, activities, 85, *104,* 112*f*
   scholarships, **119,** *146*
   as wartime volunteers, 70, 94*f,* 95*f*

Z

zoos. *See* parks, zoological